Hot Times

Hot Times

TRUE TALES
OF
HOLLYWOOD
AND
BROADWAY

By The Dean of
Show Business Columnists

EARL WILSON

Contemporary Books, Inc.
Chicago

Library of Congress Cataloging in Publication Data

Wilson, Earl, 1907–
    Hot times.

    Includes index.
    1. Entertainers—United States—Biography.
I. Title.
PN2285.W48   1984   790.2′092′2 [B]   84-5835
ISBN 0-8092-5427-1

Published by Contemporary Books, Inc.
180 North Michigan Avenue, Chicago, Illinois 60601
Manufactured in the United States of America
Library of Congress Catalog Card Number: 84-5835
International Standard Book Number: 0-8092-5427-1

Published simultaneously in Canada by Beaverbooks, Ltd.
195 Allstate Parkway, Valleywood Business Park
Markham, Ontario L3R 4T8 Canada

My wife Rosemary Wilson and son Earl Wilson, Jr. voted unanimously that this book be dedicated to my wife Rosemary Wilson and son Earl Wilson, Jr.

CONTENTS

ACKNOWLEDGMENTS

I thank those gentlemen of the world, Bob Hope and the late Groucho Marx, for helping me pursue the great laughs of Show Business. I also thank those mega-star merchants of mirth—Joey Adams, Milton Berle, George Jessel, Harry Hershfield, and Joe E. Lewis. I likewise boast of the encouragement of playwright Howard Teichmann, editor-author Paul Sann, newspaper friends, and the unsung and generally forgotten publicists and press agents who have helped keep these stories alive.

Hot Times

A CONFESSION

After living for more than 40 years with actors and actresses in that gigantic mental institution, Show Business, I am fond of my fellow inmates and willing to share my survival secrets.

They're all insane, they're *actoromaniacs* suffering from *actoromania*. They're followers of Thespis, The Greek poet who invented tragic drama, and are thus *Thespians* or *Thespomaniacs*.

It was professor-playwright-biographer Howard Teichmann of Barnard College, coauthor of *Solid Gold Cadillac* with George S. Kaufman, and Professor of Classical Languages, Charles W. Dunmore of New York University, who said the newly-minted "Thespomaniac" was a proper term for those maddened by a desire to be actors. Thespomaniacs thus join such well known maniacs as dipsomaniacs, kleptomaniacs, pyromaniacs, and nymphomaniacs.

As the wisest of the pack, actor-playwright-director-producer Elia Kazan said one night, giving an address at an Actors' Studio award ceremony, "You must think we're all cuckoo."

How could I a simple Ohio farm boy, with meager journalistic training around state fairs, state penitentiaries and state legislatures, get trapped into having bodily contact with Veronica Lake, Zsa Zsa Gabor, Elizabeth Taylor, Mae West, Joan Rivers, Fatty Arbuckle, Stan Martin, Jerry Lewis, Red Skelton, and the genius who invented video cassettes (or cassettes video)?

Yes, and how else could I have been talking to Libby Holman, the "Body and Soul" torch singer of the '30s and '40s, and hear her remark concerning an unpopular acquaintance, "Why don't we invite him up to my place and we'll kill him?"

Libby had a delicious sense of humor and said it with a merry laugh. But I was nervous. Libby had been indicted in the death of her husband, Smith Reynolds the playboy, but had not been tried, and was free, the family claiming it was suicide.

I was barely 30, still remembering the electric chair executions I had witnessed frequently at the Ohio State Penitentiary, when I was in the Broadway glamour world, writing a column, and endeavoring to be perfectly calm when one of the loveliest stage beauties invited me to go along with her and several guests into her bathroom while she performed bodily functions rather than halt or even slow a fascinating conversation about her dear friend Noel Coward.

Up to that time in New York my *metier* had been covering executions at Sing Sing (I knew my way around a death house) or interviewing guys in New Jersey who had an invention that would take the shine out of your pants.

Show business I knew only by rumor but I could describe it and its participants: rumpots, nymphomaniacs, prostitutes, fakes, liars, cheats, pimps, hopheads, forgers, sodomists, slobs, absconders—but halt. I understate it horribly.

Actually, they were as nice a bunch of innocent, wide-eyed confused, lost little children as you'd want to meet—suffering this *actoromania* because some proud parent had told them in a kindergarten stage play that they were wonderful. They had ruined their lives by believing it.

My first night as Saloon Editor for the *New York Post,* I brushed off my tux and wore it proudly, believing everybody went formal after sundown. I learned that to wear a dinner jacket ususally meant your were confused with the headwaiter.

As a nighttime boulevardier with free drinks and free dinners, I was pampered and petted (petted much less than I had hoped) and soon grew weary of hearing these actors with this incurable disease, *actoromania,* yowling, "I MUST ACT. I HAVE TO ACT OR I WILL DIE."

They never died. That was the trouble. They acted. Often they squandered their family's life savings awaiting for a walk-on part in a Broadway flop and were again waiting tables and again on unemployment.

"Have you ever reflected on the life of an actor?" Elia Kazan asked that night when he bared their souls for them.

"He or she has to win the favor of absolutely everyone in the wolf's circle of our theater starting with the director," to get and keep the job. The agent first, the director's secretary, the leading lady and leading man, the producer, the producer's wife, the critics, the critics' wives, the critics' girlfriends, and then, more finicky than the rest, the general public.

"They compete," Kazan proclaimed, "for untold awards . . ."

For Oscars, Tonys, Emmys, Grammys, Obies, Golden Globes, Silver Phalluses, and so on.

"Still here we are, apparently so avid for recognition that we call you together at a hundred and a half a plate to watch us give still another set of prizes—to ourselves!"

"Cuckoo" to him. But generally in Show Business, on Broadway and Hollywood, it is "temperament."

Or merely "self confidence." Never insanity or egomania. Napoleon was thought daft for confusing himself with the law and the state. Madame du Pompadour was adjudged balmy for allegedly saying "After us, the deluge."

On Broadway that conceit is accepted routinely along with "top billing" and "star's dressing room" and "best table in the house" and "six personal bodyguards."

Who said "I am the greatest"?

Not Julius Caesar, not General Douglas A. MacArthur, but Gorgeous George, the wrestler, then the pugilist Muhammad Ali, and finally, the fat comedian Jackie Gleason who probably wasn't joking and undoubtedly meant every syllable when he roared "I am the greatest."

And so it was glamour on the wing as a columnist, London to

Rome to Moscow, preserving my innocence against the scarlet women from Gloria Swanson to Mae West to Marilyn Monroe to Jayne Mansfield. And I foresaw the ruin of Show Business. The world would be over-entertained and finally collapse under the weight of its own hamminess.

But cable TV and home video spared it. We will be working a 20-minute week and seeing TV or its satellites 22 hours a day. There will be reruns, cyclings and recyclings of recyclings, and we won't even go to offices. We'll just "televise it in" by computer. Everybody will be his own Michael Jackson home video "Thriller" and we will have to be reminded that there is work to be done somewhere some part of the day.

And here's my confession.

I immensely enjoyed those long stretches of my insanity over four decades. Now nearly everybody not already in Show Business is trying to get into Show Business.

Presidents, dictators, generals, trophy-toting athletes, astronauts, would-be vice presidents, ex-secretaries of state, and suspected wife-poisoners all have an "act."

They have a hilarious monologue, at least 10 minutes of fast anecdotes for a Merv Griffin or Johnny Carson spot, or they can have it by tomorrow morning. They know about watching the red light on the TV camera and they have a witty get-off line. They might even have a song. So get with it, get in it, you'll eventually have to go a little crazy. Along with me.

1

40 YEARS
IN A
PHONE BOOTH

There are sex-minded savants who would doctor Shakespeare by changing "All the world's a stage" into "All the world's a bed."

They'd have Hamlet soliloquizing, "There's a little bit of bed in every good little girl."

I wouldn't. Covering Broadway for 40 years, I didn't long for lust but was after laughter. Shelley Winters and June Allyson recounted their bedtime stories in their "menoirs." I searched for the humor, comedy, pranks, gags, and gaffes that make Show Business such a wildly warm, wonderful world. Sometimes the star was not the most bedded wench but the producer, laughing up his bankruptcy as he shrugged off the million in IOUs that he left behind.

Hunting humor, I mingled with the great ones: Barbra Streisand, Goldie Hawn, Mae West, Katharine Hepburn, of course Marilyn Monroe, and Judy Garland. And the men, from Charlie Chaplin to Spencer Tracy to Burt Reynolds and John Travolta.

Too often the gag I sought had a sad punch line: death by drugs or a leap from a roof or a bullet in the brain.

Telling the readers as much of these bizarre tales as I could at that time—saving the rest for my secret archives—I became a bit of a freak myself as I fell asleep at my typewriter, pounding out a syndicated column read around the world.

When the lawyers for Howard Hughes's estate said sexy Terry Moore would be rich because she insisted Hughes married her on a ship and then destroyed the ship's log, I gloated.

Torrid Terry told me that story long ago. I wasn't convinced.

I printed some of it, cautiously. I had known shapely, beautifully bouncy Terry back to the opening of the Hilton Hotel in Istanbul, when the question was whether she had on underthings when she showed her legs for photographers.

Now 51 (somebody said 54), Terry told me she'd give her tithe—"10 percent off the top"—to the Mormon church. She might announce the title of her book, *Howard Be Thy Name*, and she might also marry "the right man."

I thought of all the frenzied hours I'd spent prying into celebrities' secrets: Johnny Carson's, Liz Taylor's, Jackie Onassis's, Liza Minelli's, Robert Wagner's.

And that famous actor whose girlfriend in his show had a baby, and his wife knew—and approved!

Once, to get into Brigitte Bardot's well-guarded suite at the Plaza, I wore a fake mustache, pretended to be a handyman come to test her lightbulbs, and even wore a handyman's uniform when I banged on her door.

I had hoped to find her in her most famous lack of costume, but she was having a small dinner in her suite with some friends. Most cordially she admitted me and permitted me to monkey around with the lightbulbs.

"Could I have your autograph for my little boy?" I begged her.

"Ah, oui, oui," she answered. "How old is your leetle boy?"

"Going on 30," I said. Dear B. B. would not autograph a towel as she then wouldn't have a thing to wear. I left with my toolbox without telling B. B. my real identity. Later, when my story was published with my picture as a handyman, B. B.

approved and met me for a drink. I was not in my uniform.

The response to this and other stunts encouraged me to look for more. I got my hair dyed red. I got a permanent wave. The red hair was damned hard to lose, and so was the wave. I impersonated a woman shopper trying on dresses at a 14th Street department store bargain stampede. It wasn't very sexy.

Tony Perkins appeared on the Broadway stage with his backside bare. I didn't need to ask how he felt. I already knew, having gone to several nudist camps wearing my favorite disguise: baseball cap and sneakers.

I learned by listening to things people said.

"Elizabeth Taylor is eating for two (—two regiments)," Joan Rivers said.

Marilyn Monroe spoke of panties. "Panties gag me," quoth Marilyn.

"Why do people object to nudity?" curvaceous Carol Lynley said. "It's only skin."

It was my wife's brilliant idea to dress up our hired girl, Mavis, who's from England and talks like a dockhand, in furs and finery and pass her off to Prince Philip at a charity affair as a New York socialite. She was warned to keep her mouth shut.

Prince Philip was charmed to be photographed with her (Ethel Merman was there, too) and didn't know the picture with Mavis wound up in a ladies' room in Plymouth where Mavis's mum was the matron.

Oh, the society balls! At a couple I was mistaken for a waiter.

The best party I ever got thrown out of was charmin' Sharman Douglas's black-tie reception for Princess Margaret at the Beverly Hills Bistro. Sharman gave me the finger personally because I had on a four-in-hand instead of a black tie.

"Damned fool," snapped Milton Berle. "Always carry a black tie in case you want to crash something formal."

Sharman, daughter of the late Ambassador Lewis Douglas, was truly charming.

"You may leave by the front door," she said, hastening me out.

I was just as nice. "No, I left my coat on a sack of potatoes in the kitchen," I said. She encouraged me to crash her next party in New York and recognized me presiding over the cold cuts in the kitchen and didn't squeal. In fact, she called me at 5:00 A.M. to congratulate me on my performance.

On a quite different occasion I met one of my favorite actors, and one of my favorite people, Van Johnson—recovering from cancer, healthy and ambitious, his limp gone. He was trying to learn a script from a tape recorder, which he listened to while he slept. Both Phyllis Diller and Marlene Dietrich told him just to attach the earphones to his ears when he went to bed.

"Did it work?" I asked.

"No. Both my ears were busy. I was married to Edie Wynn at the time."

I had other singular experiences. Joan Crawford required guests to take their shoes off at her apartment door to save a gem of a carpet.

I tiptoed through the carpet at Merle Oberon's vast villa at Acapulco, where you faced a line of empty shoes, usually white and spotlessly clean. Such VIPs as Senator Jacob Javits and Douglas Fairbanks, Jr., went about sockless on the white rugs.

"Feet that do not shed their shoes are not invited back," it was whispered.

FLASH, FLASH. I discovered falsies; I became every flat-chested girl's bosom pal.

Bust padding! "What God's forgotten, we stuff with cotton. We fix flats."

Girls had been cheating with "cheaters" for years. It remained for this intrepid columnist to hiss the news to the menfolk and warn them to look into it.

"Gay deceivers!"

Columnist Sidney Skolsky had been scandalizing Hollywood by asking, "What do you wear to bed?" Now, thanks to my bravery, an interviewer could ask the screen beauties, "What is your bust size? Do you wear falsies, or do you have realsies?"

Ann Sheridan, Jane Russell, Marie Wilson, Olivia de Havilland, and other ladies with formidable forefronts—how did I forget Lana Turner?—usually got flustered and stammered a little at the question, then said, "You wanna see?" and pretended they were going to open the blouse and show you.

The flatties didn't like it. But the girls with the realsies flaunted them. Then shapely Marie (The Body) McDonald gave me a famous interview.

"Brother, I'm loaded," she began. "I'm about the only girl out there on our lot that has her own figure.

"So many of them wear padding. On a hot day Joan Fontaine took out her bust pads and fanned herself with them."

Dorothy Lamour's sarongs, she suggested, were specially built. And she gave the impression that Miss Lamour's feet were false.

"Hollywood's False Front" was the theme of my interview.

Marie was no longer Hollywood's bosom buddy. They denounced her for telling the bare facts. Then Marie denied she'd said those things. She hadn't even seen me. But I had witnesses, who said she really had said it.

"And a lot more that he didn't print," added one witness, publicist Bernie Kamber.

Falsies went public. *Reader's Digest* accepted the word. It got into some dictionaries.

Curiously, fashions in bosoms changed. For a time big breasts were not popular. Designers began covering up what they'd been uncovering. A flat-chested look was desirable.

The story of the haves and the have-nots, the endoweds and the unendoweds, is a long and amusing one to which I must devote much more study. I want to concede that if I had not overheard my wife and two other women discussing falsies one day, if I had not continued to eavesdrop on this fascinating conversation, I would never have become the Christopher Columbus of the bust pad business.

Let me forecast also that bosom styles will change—there'll be big bosoms and there'll be small bosoms, but there will always be a Dolly Parton.

Although the Bible warns us against gossip and bearing false witness, and while I keep these admonitions before me, certain alleged facts push their way to the front, demanding the attention of this humble show business reporter who doesn't like to be called a rumormonger.

There was, for example:

Mike Todd, Elizabeth Taylor's third mate, the most charming "Con man," the most gifted hustler who ever made a sucker out of Broadway.

I speak no ill of him. Beautiful women tumbled before his colorful carnival-lot patter in which he said he was a con merchant. On a plane I saw stewardesses hasten to massage his feet. Rich ladies invested in his shows. He exploded at seeing this last mentioned, claiming that it made him sound like a procurer. I wrote an article for *Liberty* magazine reporting that stripper-actress-author Gypsy Rose Lee put money in their show *Star and Garter,* and then more money when it was needed. "The Great Ziegfeld" bought scores of copies of the magazine in Times Square, hoping it would not reach members of his family who would not look kindly on it. Gambling away thousands of dollars that he did not have was one of his eccentricities.

There was "Mammy"-singing Al Jolson, the King of Show Business, who was a millionaire love machine.

"You ain't heard nothin' yet," he would say at the Winter Garden when he sent the musicians home and took over the stage for himself. He could have referred to his stream of female visitors backstage before and after his performances. He was known for settling business arguments with associates by saying, "I've got $8 million. How much have you got?"

Jayne Mansfield—and this calls for delicacy, too—took a guest into a lavatory on a plane with her but justified it by saying, "What's wrong with it if it's your husband?"

A stickler for frankness, Jayne told me that she was posing as an art model when she married the first time, "and I had a baby nine months and 10 minutes later." Liked by men, she was less popular with women who thought she was a Marilyn Monroe imitator. Publicity-mad, Jayne considered a failure every day when she did not conceive an idea to get her picture in the paper, even when it meant going to some show besides her own just to get in "the crowd shots." She died, decapitated in a crash. She was not a star, but she was a big name, and her big bosom was very big in the picture papers and magazines.

Beautiful Ava Gardner, in my presence at a divorce-getting hideaway in the Nevada mountains, told a Spanish bullfighter guest, "Get me a piece of ice."

Ava carefully explained to the bullfighter, who was trying to learn English, "A piece of ice is not the same as a piece of ass."

Princess Grace's father, Jack Kelly, was rumored to have come to New York from Philadelphia to hunt down would-be wooers of his beautiful young daughter, just starting a career. Big Jack Kelly was reported to be in a violent mood.

Grace and Prince Rainier never learned how I got the first news of her first pregnancy when there was speculation about whether they could be parents. My "source" and I plotted how to get the story a year ahead.

Poor Marilyn Monroe revealed to my wife (the B. W.) what she was doing all those hours she was keeping reporters waiting "while she got dressed."

My wife burst into her bedroom and found her sitting at the mirror at her dressing table, fully dressed, looking at herself, Marilyn Monroe enjoying Marilyn Monroe.

Dear, befuddled Marilyn was so mixed up, so confused, "fantasizing" so much her last months, that her intimates don't know which of her stories to believe. However, those whom I know well credit her account of her meetings with President John F. Kennedy, because she discussed it with her trusted columnist friend, Sidney Skolsky. Marilyn told Skolsky and others, "It was Jack. . . ." and laughingly added, "I think I made his back feel better." Skolsky died recently without adding anything to the story, too ill to write more about it. But we do know that Marilyn told close friend Henry Rosenfeld that he must take her to Washington to see Mr. President at the show *Mr. President* opening in September. Marilyn didn't make it. She was found dead a month earlier, under circumstances still in dispute, after telling Peter Lawford to say goodbye to his wife and himself "and the President."

It was a zany world where events didn't always make sense. Tragedy shifted suddenly to comedy without warning. You were seldom prepared for it. "Ribbing" and "roasting" became an art.

Jimmy Dean was quoted about some of his young followers who were speed demons with hot cars and cycles. How much did they pay for a gallon of gas?

"I don't know. I never bought a whole gallon."

Some meetings I remember with sadness. One-time dear friend of John Travolta, Diana Hyland, who died of cancer, came from Cleveland, and I liked her immediately.

She came from TV. "I met you at Warners in Hollywood at a cocktail party," I said.

"No, I've never been at Warners," she said.

"Of course you have. I'm infallible at remembering people from Ohio, my native state," I said. "You'll think of it."

"The only other columnist I ever met was Hedda Hopper," she said.

"We have a striking resemblance," I said. "What picture are you doing?"

"Lady Peale."

"Oh, the Beatrice Lillie life story."

"No, Norman Vincent Peale's wife, Lady Peale."

"Are you sure?"

"I'm positive."

"Oh, positive thinker; I get it."

"No, I'm a negative thinker. I'm in favor of slow planes. They give you more time to get out alive. I'm not antinudity. If a girl is shown getting out of a shower into bed with a man, she shouldn't be wearing a riding habit."

"How right you are. Have you remembered when we met at Warners?"

"I told you I've never been at Warners."

"I'm going to look it up in my card file at the office, and I'll call you with the date and the details," I said.

And sure enough, there it was in the files: Summer of 1961. Warners. Hollywood. Met beautiful blonde actress from Cleveland—Diane McBain.

Great personalities—really "characters," like Bob Mitchum— make life bearable. I always felt Mitchum wanted to be like Humphrey Bogart. Mitchum was the first hippie back when marijuana was still called "grass." When he was arrested for possession he knew he was finished. A judge asked him his profession.

"Ex-actor."

Sometimes he said, "Ex-actress."

He said he was similar to Tallulah Bankhead, who claimed she'd been smoking pot for 25 years every day but hadn't found it habit-forming.

I visited him in Ireland where he was not only smoking it but growing it—so he said, anyway. "What do you think of legalizing it?"

"I don't know. I don't know."

Back in New York, I wrote a piece about our conversation, but since it was a sensitive subject, I sent him a copy for his approval.

"You've got me awful vague," he said when I phoned. "You got me saying, 'I don't know.' "

"Would you like to be more specific?" I asked.

"I sure would."

"OK," I said. "The pencil's poised, waiting for your answer. What do you think?"

"I don't know," said Mitchum.

I started this chapter meaning to tell of all the years I've spent in phone booths turning in my stories.

I mustn't forget a switch, when a reporter from Brooklyn phoned in a story to me.

I was a rewrite man on the *New York Post* with a headset on, taking a story from one of the famous Feeney brothers in Brooklyn who spoke pure Brooklynese.

"It's a big erl explosion," Feeney said. "Biggest erl disaster I ever saw. Blazing erl is flowing in the streets. Loss in erl will be in the thousands. You ought to come over here and see this erl on fire!"

Then he said, "Well, goodbye, Oil," and hung up.

2
JUST
STUTTERIN'
ALONG

Where could I go for laughs when Broadway was still young and so was I?

To the Great Groucho, of course: he who refused to join any club that would have him as a member; he who went on a famous hunting trip ("I shot a bear in my pajamas. How he got in my pajamas, I'll never know.").

To Ed Wynn, the punny, funny lithpin' Fire Chief; to Eddie Cantor and his banjo eyes and "If You Knew Susie;" to cheapskate Jack Benny, to Fred Allen's Alley; to young Milton Berle, who introduced a singer "who is very well reared, looks good in front, too; to Dwight Fiske and "Mrs. Otis Regrets;" and to plainspoken B. S. Pully and his "venereal material."

I started covering Broadway in the early '40s just in time to hear Stutterin' Joe Frisco, thought by many to be the funniest man alive.

They called him a "horse degenerate" whose life was betting on the races. He could barely read and write. He made $3,000 a week with his "racetrack routine," but all he wanted was a winner.

Rival comics said he faked the stutter. It gave him time to think of a bright snapper. His impediment did not impede.

J-J-Joe F-F-F-Frisco reigned as king at the Club 18 on 52nd Street when Mark Hellinger and Tommy Manville brought in their ladies.

When a woman started for the powder room, Jackie Gleason would yell, "Mention my name and get a good seat." Frankie Hyers would bellow, "Get a load of that hat. How does she expect *us* to get laughs?"

Frisco's real name was said to be Louis Wilson Josephs, and he was believed to be descended from Emperor Franz Josef. He had eternal bad luck at the track, and his act reflected his anger. An entire library of his jokes (in stutterese) was compiled by comedian and lecturer Peter Lind Hayes.

He was constantly wiped out at the track and borrowing. Bing Crosby, already a rich man, had lent Joe $50 at the track, and Joe had come through with a winner.

Frisco became an instant millionaire. He swaggered about the bar, flaunting his money, shaking the ash from a Havana, buying drinks. He encountered his benefactor, Bing Crosby, said, "H-h-hey, kid," handed him a five-dollar bill, and commanded, "S-s-sing two choruses of 'Melancholy Baby.' "

One of those vaudeville survivors who would not lower his price, Frisco once remained in his hotel room for weeks, living on room service, declining to talk to agents or potential employers about working for $200 a week less.

"Come down and talk it over," an agent pleaded.

"What?" replied Frisco. "And g-g-get locked out of my r-r-r-room?"

His fortunes and misfortunes varied. He tried to bet 50¢ in a blackjack game. The dealer scoffed, "We don't bet that kind of money here."

"T-t-t-take any part of it," snapped Joe.

He had a running battle with other comics who were jealous of his stuttering gimmick. Once, at Charlie Foy's club in San Fernando Valley, comic Ben Blue was trying out new jokes. He missed a couple and said, "I'm forgetting my material."

"But you're remembering everybody else's," said Joe.

Joe thought Irving Berlin's voice was good but not powerful. "You have to h-h-h-hug him to hear him," Frisco said. One day little comedian Jerry Bergen, less than 4½ feet tall, came to a table at Lindy's. He came just up to the top of the table. Frisco looked at little Jerry with his head alongside the plate and the silverware and said, "Who ord-ord-ordered John the Baptist?"

Bob Hope knew his ability and invited him to his big Los Angeles home. "What a big h-h-house," cracked Joe, "for such a sm-small talent."

Frisco suffered cancer in his 60s and was confined to a wheelchair. The Masquers raised money to bury him. In his last speech to his old friends he said he had "the big Casino."

"I've been in Show Business 50 years," he said. "This is the first time anybody ever g-gave me a dinner and I c-c-c-can't eat it."

Comedians still quote his words of warning to the illustrious Enrico Caruso at a prestigious benefit. "Don't do 'Darktown Strutters Ball,' " he told the Great One. "I use that for m-m-m-my f-f-f-finish."

Although I came in a little late on the Joe Frisco era, I was a bit early on the sex joke period. The naughty word *pregnant* was just being allowed in movies after censors had been blasted for barring it. They were even allowing men and women to be seen in bed together. Somebody said the most beautiful curves in the world were a woman's breast and a horse's rump.

Alberto Vargas's blonde, beautiful, busty Vargas girls were breathtakingly nubile and were shown on calendars.

I dared print a joke from the *Cincinnati Enquirer*.

Trying to find a man named Sexauer working in a large plant, a man asked the phone operator, "Do you have a Sexauer?"

"Sexauer! Sex hour! We don't even have a coffee break!"

Just as intrepidly, I printed that bosomy Blanche Thebom of the opera sang at a Community Chest fundraiser in Louisville where everybody stared at her low-cut gown.

When the chairman announced, "The chest went over the top," the Episcopalian minister who'd been staring at Blanche's bodice said, "I've been expecting it all evening."

It was the Betty Grable and Rita Hayworth pinup period.

A pinup girl didn't pin up anything.

Carole Landis, the busty beauty, one of the USO entertainers, was dancing with a Britisher who couldn't keep his eyes off the V of her dress.

"Is the V for victory?" he asked.

"Yes," replied Miss Landis, "but the bundles are not for Britain."

A Washington machine shop posted this:

"GIRLS: If your sweater is too large for you, look out for the machines. If you are too large for your sweater, look out for the machinists."

Photographers of girls had a new slogan and battle cry: "Don't shoot till you see the whites of their thighs."

Miss Gypsy Rose Lee, the stripper, was much quoted. She was restrained in her stripping. She didn't really take off much. She just rolled down her stockings and chattered. Denying she was an intellectual (she was an author), she said, "Men don't like me for my mind but for what I don't mind."

Popular storyteller Harry Hershfield told of a preacher who denounced gambling so vociferously that a member of the congregation shouted, "Dat's preachin'!"

He screamed against drinking, and the member of the congregation shouted, "Dat's preachin'!"

He orated against sneaking out in the woods and making love, and the same voice shouted, "Dat's meddlin'!"

Fred Allen wrote an introduction for a book by columnist-humorist H. Allen Smith. So Arthur Godfrey wrote one for a book I put together.

"Earl Wilson is easily recognized. He has a strange growth on his neck. It's his head. When clothiers picked their Best Dressed List, Wilson typed it. If he weren't a columnist, he wouldn't attract any more attention than a burp in a brewery."

Playboy tried to decide whether it could go any further in exposing its naked beauties.

It decided it could, should, and would—and did.

One of the falsie companies belatedly boasted that it was now "making mountains out of molehills."

Comedian George Burns, a success by marriage (to Gracie

Allen), told a very clean story beloved by his best audience, Jack Benny.

Burns was reminiscing with Fanny Brice, the comedienne, about playing the Chicago Theater. For some reason, Miss Brice denied ever playing there. Burns insisted. She still wouldn't admit it.

"Yes, you did," argued Burns. "For three weeks. I'll even tell you who was on the bill with you. And your salary was . . . "

Fanny again said, "No."

"Five thousand a week," said Burns.

Fanny didn't say "No" that time. "Sixty-five hundred," she said.

Mrs. Robert A. Taft, wife of the U. S. Senator from Ohio who had his eye on the White House, also got a laugh with some nonsexy material.

She made the Republicans jump up and down with glee when she said, "To err is Truman."

And anyway, what was I doing there?

I was born in a farmhouse near Rockford, Ohio, to Arthur Earl Wilson, 18, and Chloe Huffman Wilson, also 18, who had lived on neighboring farms. At 15 I was getting a dollar a day driving a water wagon for a threshing ring on summer vacations. Because my father became a real estate broker and had a typewriter, I went into journalism.

The weekly *Rockford Press* printed everything I wrote, including news of our kids' baseball team, with all my bylines, from Chesty Wilson to H. Earl Wilson. I had cards printed "Scoop Wilson, The World's Greatest Sports Writer. It must be true—he admits it."

Upon being graduated from Rockford High at 18, with a typewriter all my own, I became sports editor and also sports staff of the Piqua, Ohio, *Daily Call*—for $15 a week. When my salary went to $30 in less than a year, I decided there was lots of money in the newspaper business.

I jumped to the Tiffin, Ohio, *Tribune* and Heidelberg College, making all those calls from phone booths to get sports news part-time; then to Ohio State; International News Service, covering the Ohio State legislature; the Ohio Prison, where I saw numerous electrocutions. I worked in Springfield, Akron,

Sandusky, and woke one day in Washington on the *Washington Post* copydesk writing headlines.

I didn't want to be a copyreader. I wanted to be a writer.

They had a writer, several of them, including the later famous and acclaimed Raymond Clapper.

Very cleverly, I devised a way to show them how good an interviewer and writer I was. I set up an appointment to interview Gertrude Stein, who happened to be visiting Washington. I didn't tell the *Washington Post* about it. I'd just turn in my article and show them what talent was rotting away on the copydesk.

But the butler at Gertrude Stein's host's house was suspicious.

He asked for my credentials, which I lacked; he phoned the *Washington Post*, which was not really aware of me just yet. To make it more embarrassing, Gertrude Stein was the guest of Eugene Meyer, publisher of the*Washington Post,* who had promised her she wouldn't be pestered by interviewers.

And she was being pestered by some of Eugene Meyer's own idiot would-be interviewers.

"Fire Wilson" seemed to be the solution.

Because I wasn't a drunk or a gypsy, the boss of the copydesk pleaded for me and saved my job.

"He's just a kid trying to get ahead," he said.

"And evidently needs one," everybody agreed.

Discouraged, I was about to go back to Akron and be an editorial writer, but Walter Lister, city editor of the *New York Post,* offered me $45 to join his rewrite crew. *A writer!*

"I advise you to go back to Akron and be happy," Lister said in a telegram. I wired back, "I don't want to be happy. I want to work for you."

Arriving in New York in May 1935, when FDR was still in his first term as President, I took a stroll in the city I intended to capture. I came out of the hotel and hesitated. Which way did I go? I turned right. It was early, but the Great White Way seemed dark. And it got darker.

"Akron is jazzier than this town," I thought.

I'd gone downtown instead of uptown; I'd headed into the very-closed-up-at-night Garment District instead of into Times Square. Wrong Way Wilson!

Anxious for my first interview, I met notorious-four-letter-word author Jim Tully (who came from my neck of the woods in Ohio). He was drinking whiskey from a bottle in the Algonquin lobby.

"Jim Tully, the four-letter-word man, gave an interview about and mostly in four-letter words," I wrote. It consisted mostly of dashes, blanks, stars, and exclamation points: ***!!***.

I liked it. Tully didn't. He demanded that I be fired. This was getting monotonous.

Then I met Dorothy Parker. She was fascinated by the fact I'd gone to Heidelberg College, which was partially supported by the Reformed Church.

"What do they call the church that isn't reformed?" she wanted to know. "The Hog Wild Church?"

Suddenly I was thrown into the world of celebrities. I went to a reception for the Duke and Duchess of Windsor, where a girl reporter who'd lost her invitation moaned, "I'm going to cut my throat."

"I'm going to cut the Duchess's throat," smiled cynical, sharp-tongued, Café Society expert Dixie Tighe. She did—in her column.

"Make contacts," they advised me. I made friends with Hollywood producer and malapropist Joe Pasternak, who told me in fractured Hungarian and English that when he arrived here, an immigrant, he found 10-dollar greenbacks on the streets on the Lower East Side.

He put his foot on one of those greenbacks so nobody'd steal it, then took it into a doorway to appreciate it.

It was very green, and it looked authentic, and it said, "Walk upstairs to Greenberg's Clothes and save $10."

It proved there was no such thing as a free lunch in New York, though for pretty and cooperative girls there were probably free suppers and breakfasts, Joe said, adding, "Take that home and maul it over."

Handsome, swashbuckling movie star Errol Flynn was suing *Confidential*, the scandal magazine, for $1 million for publishing that he took a yachtful of prostitutes on his honeymoon.

I managed to be with Flynn at the zebra-striped El Morocco

nightclub when he sat next table to *Confidential* publisher Bob Harrison and twitted him about the $1 million lawsuit.

"Will you settle my $1 million suit for $500,000?" Flynn heckled Harrison, who said, "No, you've no case."

"Would you give me $250,000?" said Flynn, enjoying it.

"No, no, nothing," said Harrison.

"$100,000? $50,000?" bargained Flynn, laughing. "You won't give me any money at all? Well, in that case, how about a two-year subscription?"

Howard Hughes was around in tennis sneakers and the one shirt he claimed he washed out himself, stashing beautiful girls away in apartments or hideaways, trying to fly me to San Diego personally, because he thought that while I was interviewing Ingrid Bergman there I would share her with him.

With himself as pilot, Hughes flew Hollywood stars to New York to set speed records in his Constellations and waited for a tail wind to try for another record on the return. Hughes's good friend, ex-newspaperman and publicist Curly Harris, had gotten everything the stars desired—nylons, cigarettes, theater tickets.

"Curly Harris can get you a tail wind," exclaimed pretty Bonita Granville (now Mrs. Jack Wrather, friend of the Ronald Reagans).

Hughes liked to go out with Curly Harris. Curly never let him pay for anything; Hughes called him "Big Spender."

"Say, Curly," Hughes said one day. "Are you on somebody's expense account?"

"Yes," said Curly.

"Whose?" said Hughes.

"Yours," said Curly.

Once, when Hughes was twitted about being thrifty, he paid the tips in advance for everybody served, brushed, or toweled in the men's room. "Mr. Hughes has taken care of it," the attendants told their men's room customers. The son of the Old Curmudgeon, Secretary of the Interior Harold Ickes, objected and insisted on taking care of his own "gratuity."

There was money around. Tobacco heir Dick Reynolds,

tipping headwaiter Joe Lopez at the Copacabana, asked what was the biggest tip he had ever received.

"One hundred dollars, sir," said Lopez.

"Next time anybody asks that, you can say $200," said Reynolds, handing over two hundred-dollar bills. Turning away happily, Reynolds asked, "Who gave you that hundred-dollar tip?"

"You did, sir," replied Señor Lopez.

In searching for laughs, I at first overlooked comedian Joe E. Lewis, "the Aristotle of the Bottle," whom I didn't care for. He had a scar on his cheek, left by Chicago mobsters who thought they'd killed him.

To me, really a beginner as saloon editor, he was "too inside." He opened his act by saying or singing, "Voom, voom, voom. It is now post time. I can hardly wait to hear what I'm going to say.

"You're my kind of people—drunks," he continued.

But he grew on me. I soon liked him very much; in fact, I adored him and loved the boozers he talked about and emulated.

His fans learned and memorized his lines:

"I was doing very well in the hospital; then I took a turn for the nurse."

"A man is not drunk as long as he can lie on the floor without holding on."

"What do you mean, was I ever sober? I was sober four times today."

Joe E. also had a song, "The Groom Couldn't Get In," and another one, "Sam, You Made the Pants Too Long." Joe E. had an amazing following, including big gamblers and horse players.

At his ringside one night, who should be dozing but elder statesman Bernard Baruch, advisor of Presidents and Winston Churchill?

"Bernie," said Joe E. to Baruch from the mike, "I didn't mind you falling asleep during my act, but it kinda hurt me when you didn't say 'Good night.' "

Joe E. Lewis, I finally decided, was to many drinking Americans what Oscar Wilde was to British barflies. Joe E. became one of the flowers of Saloon Society. My wife and I once stayed at a not-so-well-known hotel in Miami Beach, which had a publicity-conscious doorman.

Joe E. invited my wife and me to the track. I had to work. He took my wife and delivered her back to the hotel. When I returned from leaving my column copy at Western Union, the doorman said, "Mr. Wilson, I told you we get a lot of celebrities at this hotel."

I waited for the name of the Big Celebrity.

"Joe E. Lewis dropped his tomato off here this evening."

Groucho Marx was the one I wanted to meet. I found he liked my wife.

He liked anybody's wife.

They were talking about food. "I made a stew one night for my dinner," my wife said.

Groucho: "Anybody we know?"

The fresh young columnist and his fresh young wife met Groucho in Hollywood where he played a familiar gag. "I would like to invite you to dinner. Do you like fried chicken? What do you like to drink? Could you make it Thursday night?"

"Yes, yes, yes," we said to everything. "What's the address?"

"Wouldn't you like to know?" asked Groucho.

It was a delightful and delicious dinner, with Groucho having warned us, "I don't care how late you get there as long as you leave early."

We loved him over the years and saw him often wearing his beret, sometimes a little cranky and testy, almost always making jokes—"always on," as the other Hollywood comedians said.

Groucho recounted to us his talk with a priest who said, "I want to thank you for all the joy you've given the world." Groucho said he replied, "And I want to thank you for all the joy you've taken out of the world."

The holy man, Groucho said, asked, "Do you mind if I use that in my sermon?"

I pursued young Hoosier comedian Herb Shriner, from Fort Wayne, who said, "I was born in Ohio but moved to Indiana as soon as I heard about it." He had a drawly Will Rogers manner and said, "We had a pretty lively bunch back home. Saturday night' wasn't nuthin' for us to come into town and watch a few haircuts."

Sam Levenson was the only comedian I could think of except Red Skelton who laughed at his jokes before he told them. "I know what's comin'," he said.

Sam the bar mitzvah favorite made up the line familiar to all the Jewish boys, "Today I am a fountain pen."

I made up a poem at about that time—a jingle—and decided when it started coming back to me from press agents who attributed it to others that it was OK to admit paternity.

> Girls who wear slacks
> Please by all means
> Make sure your end
> Justifies your jeans.

In Brooklyn a high school kid was writing jokes and mailing them to me on postcards, and I was printing some of them. Press Agent Dave Alber asked me, "Who is that writing those gags?" Dave Alber met the kid and hired him to write 50 gags a week. The kid was Woody Allen, who is very appreciative to this day. "You always got me the big-money jobs," he says.

Yes, Woody Allen, who said he couldn't make the chess team because of his height.

J-J-J-Joe Frisco came to mind again recently when Raymond Massey, noted for his portrayal of Abraham Lincoln, died of pneumonia at 86. Frisco, the stutterer, had said several decades ago that Massey dressed like Lincoln and tried to look like Lincoln: "He w-w-won't be s-s-s-satisfied till he's assassinated."

The trend to deflate, to let the air out of someone's ego, to downplay, to rib, to roast has been around a long time. I was "honored" at a March of Dimes dinner where the biggest stars on Broadway praised me.

The great names, from Charles Laughton to George Jessel to Johnny Carson, applauded as comedian Jackie Kannon (from the Rat Fink Room) said, "Wilson never made an enemy.

"To sum up his career," continued Kannon, "no guts."

Putting down the columnists is a prevailing sport. Joey Adams, the AGVA (American Guild of Variety Artists) president, was toastmaster, and he recalled Arthur Brisbane's once being asked whether columnists are newspapermen.

"Would you call a barnacle a ship?" Brisbane answered.

It was an appropriate story to end the discussion. Joey Adams had since become a columnist and his wife Cindy had become another one, and they ought to know.

Broadway had an undefined, uncharted Gagland, a comedians' refilling station, where they swapped, bought, sold, and stole jokes—colorful hangouts like Kellog's Cafeteria, where you met Petey Wells, the World's Worst Comedian; the Automat; Lindy's; the Lambs Club; the Friars; and Hansens Drug Store, where you could listen all day and all night for the price of a couple of cokes and you could probably charge that.

Thievery was approved; Milton Berle, a child actor who became a millionaire before he left his teens, called himself "The Thief of Bad Gags." Fred Allen called him worse.

I went to Newark to see Berle's comedy act. "I loved Jack Benny's show," Berle said. "I laughed so much I dropped my paper and pencil."

Benny was respected for getting the supposedly longest laugh. It was the classic "Your money or your life?" Benny repeated the challenge: "Your money or your life . . . [very long pause] . . . I'm thinking it over."

Berle kidded himself about his new nose. "I'm going to make some nosereels. I have a lot of fun on my own hook."

Young writers started selling gags for $5 and became comedy consultants in Hollywood. One of them, Coleman Jacoby, spurned Hollywood's offers to stay in New York. He deplored the thievery. "Some comedians have very witty ears," he said.

He had a mustache. "Women don't like mustaches. They don't look good in them. . . . I have the most wonderful wife in the country. I hope she stays there."

Jacoby's clever sense of comedy helped steer Jackie Gleason along the rocky road to riches. Jacoby and partner Arnie Rosen enjoyed the usual success story with their talented discovery: they broke up.

There was an attractive, intelligent publicist, Seaman Jacobs, who married beautiful stripteaser Margie Hart. He was always getting off funny lines. My wife suggested he write jokes. He became a top comedy supplier for radio and TV in Hollywood, one of his best customers being Bob Hope.

I admired these writers, quaint people sometimes, occasionally very cynical and sad, generally not properly paid, and with a different outlook on life than most of us.

Solly Violinsky's real name was Ginsberg, and he was born in Russia. Because he played the violin in vaudeville, he named himself Violinsky. He was a gifted songwriter and member of ASCAP (American Society of Composers, Authors, and Publishers). That organization asked members to wear membership buttons on their coats.

"Am very enthused about wearing membership button on my coat but at present do not have a coat," he wired. "Please advise."

Solly took an ad in *Variety:* "Wish to borrow $1,000, but party must be reliable."

Solly liked the terseness of a man like Wilson Mizner, who once ran an art gallery. A customer bored him asking about prices and inquired about the price of a copy of *The Last Supper.*

"Three dollars a plate," replied Mizner.

There were comedy writers who suffered from the stinginess of comedians. There were zanies like Eddie Davis the cabdriver, not to be confused with comedian and singer Eddie Davis of Leon & Eddie's. One comic who almost never changed his act but got a million laughs was Gene Baylos, famous for his frugality.

Rival clowns said Gene gave his wife one subway fare a day and after that she was on her own. He had a piece of business that was surefire with me.

"I got a toothache," he would say. "But the boss here just fixed me up with a cheap dentist." As Gene Baylos said this, little white particles of Life Savers or another candy mint, looking very much like pieces of teeth, would trickle from his lips, supposedly the dentist's handiwork.

I must have laughed helplessly a hundred times seeing him do this.

Gene would boast that he was doing very well, but as he said this he would surreptitiously stick a roll from the table in his pocket and pinch out a burning cigarette and put that in his pocket.

Of course there are a few very clever ones like Joey Adams, who became the leading MC, the "Toastmaster General" successor to George Jessel, who became a walking encyclopedia of humor and author of many books on humor.

I remember when Joey hadn't written one book yet—he was just starting.

Would I write the "forward"—that's how he misspelled it— for the first one? I told him I believed the word he meant was not *forward* as in "forward pass" but *foreword*.

Joey may not have been able to spell, but he knew what he was doing.

"You're so damn smart," he retorted. "Just for that you also have to write the precipice."

Joey Adams found that he could be in your thoughts every day. He sold a publisher on the idea of printing his jokes on calender pads. Here's one:

"Sign in a maternity shop: 'Way-out dresses. You should have danced all night.' "

All that was at least 30 Joey Adams books ago. President Reagan is a Joey Adams devotee. At a New York tribute to the President the tables were turned and Reagan introduced Joey!

Joey Adams is a great gag machine, but one of our best satirists is Mark Russell, who is brilliant in commenting on Washington.

Describing a drunk at the National Press Club bar who had a lot of spillage, Mark said, "He didn't send his suits out to be cleaned. He sent them out to be distilled."

3

THE THURBER STORIES

The James Thurber tales about Ohio have one simple character-
istic that sets them apart: James Thurber probably never heard
of them, until one day when somebody asked him, "Did you
ever hear this Thurber story about Ohio?" By this time he was
already a legend himself, and stories were labeled Thurber
stories to make them seem funny before they were told.

They were recounted largely at cocktail parties which
Ohioans especially have forever attended in herds (and hordes).
And one favorite "Thurber story" concerns just such a cocktail
party.

"There was this cocktail party" in New York, and the
Ohioans of the guest list seemed to have gathered in one corner
and were talking vociferously about their favorite subject—
Ohio. This concentration of Buckeyes discussing Ohio made a
Texan jealous or envious, and he boldly accosted Thurber and
said, "What is it about you Ohioans? You always go to a cocktail
party in New York and brag about what a great state Ohio is. If

it's such a great state, why didn't you stay in Ohio instead of coming to New York?"

And Thurber drily replied, "You see, out there, competition was too tough."

An artist as well as one of the most gifted of American humorists, Thurber at 65 had been blind for 10 years but was the happiest man I knew. He found amusement in his blindness.

I took advantage of an opportunity to be around him and went back to Columbus and Ohio State University, Thurber country, when he dedicated new Denny Hall in 1960.

Surgeons insisted he undergo five operations to save one eye so he could continue to draw, he said.

"Draw!" he said he shouted at them. "I only draw when I'm sick of the story I'm writing. Besides, I've got enough drawings to reach from here to Seattle."

He offered his eye to research, and one surgeon, he claimed, "twittered with anticipation, saying, 'I can hardly wait to get my hands on it.' "

He joked about his blindness. He went to the Columbus mayor's office to be photographed with a plaque.

The photographer, who didn't know he was blind, asked, "Can we get a picture of you reading the plaque?"

"Certainly, and as an old newspaperman I'll give you the headline," said Thurber. " 'Thurber Regains Sight in Mayor's Office.' "

Thurber was a good drinker at times; at other times, not so good. His friends related that he once thought he had lost the use of his legs and couldn't walk anymore. He discovered he had his right foot in his left shoe and vice versa. He also had a hobby of throwing furniture.

Thurber confessed at a cocktail party that when he was a reporter for the *Columbus Dispatch,* the *New York Post,* and the *New Yorker,* he used the name James Grover Thurber. He and Elwyn Brooks White were writing short pieces for the *New Yorker,* so short that Editor Harold Ross said, "Look, you guys, your signatures are longer than your stories." So it became James Thurber.

During his blindness Thurber learned to write stories in his head. He would memorize an article in his head and then correct it in his mind and go back and fix it—then dictate it to his secretary. A lot of people tried it and couldn't do it. It was a trick Thurber learned when he was a reporter required to phone in stories without writing them beforehand.

Thurber, in his reminiscing, said that, while a reporter for the *New York Post*, he sent 25 stories to the *New Yorker*—all of which were rejected.

"I was all packed, ready to go back to Columbus," he said. "One day I picked up the F.P.A. (Franklin P. Adams) column in the *Herald-Tribune* (which printed promising contributions) and found that a piece I'd sent him was going to occupy his whole column the next day.

"I unpacked."

In Columbus Thurber was a friend of reporter and humorist John McNulty, about whom many drinking stories were told.

Sent to a distant city on a big story, McNulty was not heard from for three days. When morgues and hospitals were being checked for his body, came a telegram:

"Please wire $50 and middle initial. Want to join the Elks."

Fired for drinking on another occasion, McNulty walked into the office of Editor Bob Ryder of the *Ohio State Journal* and said, "Now that I have been fired I suppose there is a vacancy on the staff."

"True," said Ryder. "I would like to apply for the job," said McNulty.

He got it.

According to one legend, Thurber took McNulty to *New Yorker* editor Harold Ross and proposed he be hired as a reporter—and Ross snapped, "Reporter, hell. He'll start out as managing editor like everybody else."

Thurber was beloved by the Ohio State faculty folk. The student paper, the *Ohio State Lantern*, got notorious for its sloppy proofreading. Professor Billy Graves gave an interview on how bad it was and said *Lantern* proofreading was abominable.

"LANTERN PROOFREADING ABDOMINAL, SAYS BILLY GRAVES," ran the *Lantern* headline on that story.

Professor James E. Pollard was Ohio State University information officer and publicity chief. As a student in journalism, I covered his office for the *Lantern*. One day I asked him for news, and Pollard, who was trying to cover up a faculty battle over academic freedom, said, "Young man, my job is not to get news in the paper but to keep news out of the paper."

Thurber still had much to say in his last few years. He remembered when he was a reporter on the *New York Post* (then the *Evening Post*), going to New Jersey to interview Thomas Alva Edison, who supposedly never slept but just took naps—with his head on a dictionary.

"They told me when I got there, 'Mr. Edison is asleep.' I said 'I thought he never slept.' The great sleepless wonder who never slept was asleep at three o'clock in the afternoon!"

Edison had boasted he'd never see another newspaperman and certainly would never talk to one. Thurber waited 'til Edison awoke and the nontalker talked his head off.

As for sleeping late, Thurber himself occasionally saw friends, still in his bathrobe and pajamas at three in the afternoon. He stayed up late "watching" TV though he couldn't see it. He could picture the gun battles in the westerns. "I can hear the bang-bangs clearly," he said.

With the success of *The Thurber Carnival,* the artist-humorist-philosopher also became enshrined as a prophet. Did he have another play? He quoted Marc Connelly, who said, "Yes, I've finished one, but not on paper."

He claimed to be upset over the failure of today's young people to learn history. Girls didn't care for history, he said. "Ask them to name nine Presidents and they'd say Roosevelt five times and have a hell of a time getting four more."

But it was always thus, Thurber granted, going through the business of wiping his glasses, though he couldn't see through them.

"I remember the last day of history class at Ohio State in 1914," he said. "The last bell had rung. Professor Arthur Schlesinger, Sr.—the old man—said to one student, 'Mr. Spencer, who is the President of the United States?'

"Mr. Spencer replied, 'Woodrow Wilson.'

"Professor Schlesinger said, 'Thank you very much. I was determined that you get one question right this year.' "

The Thurber legends will continue to grow—and expand—because each story finds an enthusiast who says it's been related incorrectly and needs to be told properly. The Algonquin Hotel, where Thurber and his wife Helen resided, is proud that several of his drawings of "The Match Game" are on the wall showing what went on at the Artists and Writers Restaurant and Costello's bar. Thurber was known as a fairly quiet drinker there. An Algonquin executive asked the barman for some Thurber anecdotes.

"Thurber was an important figure," the hotel man said.

"Figure?" said the barman. "The only figure I can remember in connection with Thurber was seven. He always ordered Seagram's 7. He'd say, 'Give me some of that cheap whiskey.' "

Helen reacted strongly to this tale. "The story's wrong," she said. "He always ordered Seagram's VO. He never drank cheap whiskey in his life."

Mrs. Thurber, who had gone through "that dreadful night" at the Noel Coward party, said, "Jim liked to tell stories and sing while drinking, and then he could get mean. Yes, mean. Especially to women."

"What did he get mean about?"

"He'd think of something."

The story about Thurber's getting his shoes on the wrong feet is not quite true, Mrs. Thurber maintained.

"Jim was with Bob Benchley and tried to get Benchley's shoes on instead of his own. Benchley's shoes were much too small for Jim's feet, and it looked strange."

The Thurber circle of intimates who knew him from the Algonquin were somewhat startled by the disclosure that he could draw and do cartoons cleverly. But Thurber didn't permit this to change the even tenor of his ways. He said his blindness probably helped him as an artist.

"If I'd been able to see clearly what I'd done, I might not have let it out of the house," he said.

It all came to pass because his brother William shot him in the left eye with a bow and arrow when he was six. Later he lost the sight in his right eye also.

I was still a student at Ohio State University when Thurber came home to Columbus and told us in journalism class and in the Sigma Delta Chi journalism fraternity how he and E. B.

White, his collaborator on *Is Sex Necessary?*, had broken the news to an editor that he was now an illustrator too.

They took sheaves of drawings to the book editor, who said, "I suppose this is a rough idea of drawings for the book."

Thurber was amused, but White took that as a slur and declared, "These are not a rough idea—these are *for the book!*"

After the book and nondrawings took off, there were those who said the *New Yorker* had discovered the new genius.

As though arguing for him, *The New York Times*, in publishing his obituary, also reprinted one of his best-known cartoons. It shows a man and woman in bed. The man, bald and middle-aged, looks very worried.

"All right, all right, have it your way—you heard a seal bark," the woman in bed is saying in the caption.

Leaning across the top of the headboard of the bed is what Thurber contended was a seal. It is one of those seals which, from the expression on its face and its stance, could have been barking.

Thurber, from boyhood to his death, lived in another world, his friends said, and *The Secret Life of Walter Mitty*, about an unimportant man who dreamed dreams of being a hero (in the daytime), they cited as a certain example. Mrs. Walter Mitty sat beside her lover, knowing he was dreaming and scared that they were going into the ditch.

Thurber's writing seems to be better and funnier every year. He never found time to write one special book concerning his blindness. He had found a title for it, though: *Long Time No See*.

Thurber accepted his fame as an artist self-deprecatingly.

If he hadn't been blind, he said, he could have seen his work and might not have let it out of the house.

"How nice that would be, if an artist could draw and paint and didn't have to look at what he has done. The possibilities are boundless," he said.

Thurber was very big on dogs. People who claimed to know something about art spoke feelingly of his "economy of line." That was an expression to cover cartoonists who were anxious to get to the ball park or racetrack and disposed of the chore with a minimum of slashes.

Like Lincoln writing Gettysburg addresses, Thurber sketched

on the backs of envelopes, menus, napkins, and tablecloths. He drew huge-eared dogs that were as unlike other dogs as Thurber was unlike other cartoonists.

Thurber left a trail of drawings behind him, many at Costello's bar, some at the Artists and Writers Restaurant on 40th Street near the *Times* and the *Herald-Tribune* and the Algonquin. The drawings were popular, although somebody dared ask Harold Ross, "How can you keep on your staff a fifth-rate artist?"

"He is not a fifth-rate artist," Ross answered. "He is a third-rate artist."

Thurber created beasts that were not identifiable to some students of the animal kingdom. His women were not contest winners. But they were interesting. And they reflected some of the testiness he felt when he got into arguments with women friends in bars and at parties.

There was no' doubt that Thurber liked to show off his memory. He recalled phone numbers, addresses, birthdays and didn't write them down. He would phone some acquaintance and astonish the person by wishing him a happy birthday, which had just popped up in his memory although he hadn't thought about it for eight years.

"He could have got some of that from his mother," Mrs. Thurber said. Thurber told me himself that his mother once told him that I'd published an incorrect birthday for a friend of hers. I was wrong by one day.

It was a close family. Thurber's mother was always looking out for him. "One year when I paid $80,000 in taxes my mother tried to get Mr. Truman on the phone. She was going to tell him, 'My son is not very strong and can't see and can't pay all that. I wish you'd do something about it.' The only reason she didn't tell him was the circuits were always busy."

A neighbor lady subscribed for several years to the *New Yorker* but didn't read it. Her explanation touched Thurber. "I just take the magazine to help Jim," she said. It was that kind of loyalty and neighborliness that led Jim to say that someday he'd like to settle down in Ohio and operate the Columbus Buggy Whip Company.

Thurber enjoyed a Broadway hit, *The Thurber Carnival*, in

his last years, although he could not see it. My last recollection of him is sad. A Noel Coward show, *Sail Away,* was having an opening night party at Sardi's East.

When I arrived I found Thurber asking for me.

"Coward won't talk to me," he announced. "He's mad at me about something."

Coward was surrounded by his fans all wishing him well with the show, but I managed to speak to him and tell him what Thurber had said.

"What's wrong with him? I've already talked to him twice," Coward said.

"He says you and he are the only guys still writing after 20 years," I said.

Coward shrugged. "So what?"

People moved around to talk to each other. James Thurber talked to various friends. Finally I noticed that Thurber, who was not part of that night's show, was trying to make a speech. He stood up to speak.

But he faced a wall and addressed it.

In his blindness and the evening's confusion, with no arrangement for seating, Thurber did not seem to know that he was addressing the wall and not the party guests, who weren't attentive. Those of us who knew what was happening were shaken by the tragedy. And we felt worse later, when Thurber was taken to a hospital and operated on for a blood clot on the brain. He died of pneumonia about three weeks later at age 66.

At his death Thurber was acclaimed by William Shawn, then editor of the *New Yorker,* as "one of the great comic artists . . . and one of the great American writers of our time."

4
FOR
THE LOVE
OF KATE

Remembering always to "keep it amusing" and forever searching for laughs, I turned my attention to one of America's great comedy figures who couldn't pronounce the word *really* but enunciated it as "rally"—"rally" she did—Katharine Hepburn.

"I love you, rally I do." You could hear Miss Hepburn being impersonated by impressionists and imitators on the air and in nightclubs constantly.

Freckled, red-haired, angular, tallish, seemingly bosomless, Miss Hepburn was already the Hollywood veteran with at least 15 movies under her skinny belt by the time I got to meet her. She'd won an Oscar for *Morning Glory,* and Dorothy Parker had commented, upon seeing her on the stage in *The Lake,* that she "runs the gamut [of emotions] from A to B."

She was in her late 20s, and yet she still had that Bryn Mawrish debutante affectation in her strange voice. She'd been married to a Philadelphia society boy, Ludlow Ogden Smith. This was supposed to have been a secret, and when asked whether she was married, she sometimes answered, "I don't remember." Her voice was lofty and expensive-sounding when the press asked whether she had children.

"Yes, six," she laughed. "Three white and three colored."

There was comedy in her married name. She was now Katharine Smith, or, if she wished, and she never did wish that, she could shorten it to Kate Smith. The singing Kate Smith was plump, and the acting Kate Smith was, in the words of some of her family, a bag of bones.

She was a tall, spare, aloof, proud Connecticut Yankee who was remarkably independent of spirit. You could go to hell for all she gave a damn. And people liked that. They still do.

Kate Hepburn was at war with the press, and I was one of *those*. There was a delightful MGM publicist, Jack Donnelly. He liked people and admired talent, and he liked Miss Hepburn. He wanted people to understand her. He must have been persuasive in telling her about me because we rode up to Hartford on the New Haven one autumn afternoon and she was nice. She rally was. Rally she was. She saw us at her parents' pleasant home with a well-tended lawn and big front porch.

Although she did not have the curves of Jane Russell or Carole Landis, there was sex appeal in her stride and her height. She was a golfer and tennis player, and you could not forget the trousers she wore. There was something about them and her legs encased therein.

Rally there was.

Sitting before a burning fireplace, she laughed that high-styled laugh and apprised us of how she had scandalized the town. I listened carefully for the Hepburn sound.

"Muhthuh" (mother) had been surprised at the reaction.

"Yah, yah, yah [yeah]."

"Shaw [Sure]."

It appeared to the townsfolk that she was riding a bicycle bare-bottomed.

"I got this English-style racing bike, and I get my hands way down on the bars and my bottom way up on the seat. I wear old white shorts. They get a little dirty, and they don't look white any longer. They look flesh-colored. I go like mad. People see my bottom way up there, and I guess they think it's my bare bottom they're seeing. Anyway, that's what Muhthuh heard. That I was riding bare-bottomed.

"Now rally. . . ."

We agreed, riding back to New York, that Kate was "a wonderful dame" but misunderstood, and I said I was going to write about her that way in the future. She was dating Howard Hughes and Leland Hayward, both pilots, and she learned to fly herself. After one of his record-breaking trips, Hughes got a ticker tape parade, and we wrote that Hughes and Kate were seeing each other that night. They had to go through back entrances to avoid the crowds. Katie liked that. It gave her another opportunity to thumb her nose at the press.

Her great love affair with Spencer Tracy was starting, but we couldn't see it at first for Tracy's wild drinking. He was the kind of tippler who would roam through a hotel lobby naked, looking for some means of getting a drink late at night. I heard that he did that in the Sherry-Netherland Hotel in New York.

Tracy called Kate "Her Highness" when they starred together in *Woman of the Year* and *Keeper of the Flame* and later in *The Sea of Grass*.

"I'm just a supporting player; she's the star," Tracy told me when I saw them on the MGM lot in 1946. I had seen him at the Beverly Hills Hotel, and he was cordial and said, "You want to come out and watch Her Highness? It'll be very educational."

Tracy was already known for a remark attributed to him, that to be an actor, "just learn your lines and don't bump into the furniture." Supposedly, Kate, at their first meeting, pointed out that she was taller than he was and he said—or somebody else said—he "will cut her down to his size." This got mixed up in the retelling of the retelling. Kate was very pleasant to me, and I decided she had remembered me from the visit to Hartford, or maybe it was because Tracy was being hospitable and had invited me to the filming.

She was in pants—"slacks"—sitting in one of those director's chairs with a towel around her head, but she was called to get into a white lace dress suitable for the 1890 story. When she returned in that costume she said, "Oh, are you still here?"

I grunted that I still was.

"I thought we'd be able to avoid you," she added.

"I thought that's what you wanted, so I stayed longer," I mumbled, not knowing quite how to take her.

"Should I put that in my column?" she asked.

"Do you intend to write one?" I asked.

"I don't intend to sink that low," she said.

I thought it was all in jest, but the more I thought about it, the more I wondered if it was serious. Her "rally" seemed to have vanished, but her "Yah, yah" was still there.

Tracy was the most delightful host and most self-deprecating.

"I did a scene yesterday that will revolutionize the industry," he said, talking to Elia Kazan, the director, and Melvyn Douglas. "I walked over to a wagon and put a basket in it, and then I walked down the road. I did that whole gigantic scene without forgetting one thing. Of course I didn't have any lines. You do a scene like that 15 times and you get silly. Now you know why actors go nuts."

Tracy grinned and said that's why he wanted to get out of the movies and go back to the stage. He said that there he would probably run into things he'd already done.

"Instead of Old Vic's, they now call it Old Tricks," he said.

Hepburn's *The Philadelphia Story* with Cary Grant, and *Keeper of the Flame* with Tracy, plus *The Woman of the Year* with Tracy made her The Woman of Those Years in Hollywood, and her romance with Tracy was openly discussed for the first time.

Known as a lovely man when he was sober, and a gifted actor, he was tolerated and forgiven many, many times. He was getting to be in his mid-40s, which he felt meant he was getting to be a bit old for a leading man. Miss Hepburn had no lush young curves to waste, either, and her reputation for being "difficult" still clung to her. Hollywood in the beginning tried to force her to give up trousers, and she threatened if it stole her britches, she would walk through the lot in her underpants. She says it did and she did.

The Beverly Hills Hotel pool was the prestigious gathering place, and often you could hear the crack of racquet against tennis balls on the tennis court just to the rear.

Frequently one of the racquet-wielders was Miss Hepburn. She did not go into the pool, however; at least not while others were using it. She added a slight touch of mystery to the neighborhood—she and Spencer Tracy.

Although it was the Bosom Era, Miss Hepburn did not compete, and she was never accused of taking up falsies or bust sculpture. Some people wished she had. It wasn't until the early 1950s, when Kate and Tracy were filming *Pat and Mike,* that Garson Kanin came up with a true and devastating line, which he gave to Tracy to utter. Kate's biographer, Gary Carey, says Kanin's line, which Spencer Tracy delivered in Brooklynese, was "There's not much meat on her, but what there is is cherce."

Everybody agreed with that answer to the bosom deficiency problem, even Kate, who had gone through a lot in her day, first having her trousers stolen from her by Hollywood skirt fanatics. Then came the monstrous charge that she was "box office poison" when several of her films failed to draw a large audience. Next came the publicizing of the affair with Tracy, which started some magazine stories about a subject not mentioned before. One columnist wrote that it was "the greatest love story never told"—but it was told now, and soon everybody knew a little or a lot about it.

For Tracy to call her "Her Highness" was a good-humored admission that she was queenly, the royalist, the boss. Biographer Gary Carey called it arrogance. He also said she won four Best Actress Oscars and never picked them up. He said further that George Cukor slapped her, and that she slapped Peter O'Toole, and that she expectorated (oh, all right, spit, spat) at Sam Spiegel and Joseph Mankiewicz, but implied that they all loved each other and this was just high-spirited.

Tracy was a man you could just not call "Spencer." It got to be Spence very early.

I interviewed him once during his arid period, the latter part of his life, when he very much resented that he had to drink what he called "sasparilla."

He marveled at that.

"A girl came here to interview me, and she'd never heard of sasparilla," he said. It was "sarsaparilla," defined as a drink from roots, maybe something in the neighborhood of root beer.

"It's pop!" he said scornfully. "Something you get in drugstores. I think you can take it with castor oil. They put it up in fancy bottles, and charge you half a buck."

He was a man's man but a woman's, too. He had surprisingly massive shoulders and reddish sun-tanned hair with a little splash of light right over the middle of his forehead. He had heavy, hard-looking hands.

Though tremendously successful in pictures, he was suffering a depression, and it was because he was successful—in pictures.

"Frankly, I don't give a damn what you write about me in your column," he said. "I've got to go back to Hollywood and knock off an epic, then I'm coming back to Broadway and see if I can still act.

"It's your goddamn movie name that causes you trouble," he went on, having another slug of the "sasparilla" in a demitasse cup. "You make so much money, your economic problem ceases to exist. No options to worry about. The dough rolls in. You forget how to act because you don't have to act anymore.

"I heard of a guy got a 15-year contract at MGM.

"If I had a 15-year contract, I could think of nothing but get a .45 and blow my brains out. To *think*," he exclaimed, "of coming in that gate at MGM or, for that matter, any gate *for 15 years!*

"A Broadway show would give me a chance to see if I can still act. I used to be able to act.

"Broadway doesn't care about your goddamn movie name.

"And you," he growled. "Why aren't you interviewing somebody important? Some surgeon or scientist instead of a lousy movie actor who drinks pop?"

When he told me this he was worrying about getting old.

"I'll be 45 tomorrow," he said.

As for "Her Highness," of course she encouraged him and helped him try to find contentment on the stage, and she tended him and nursed him when he was dying. He was not happy with his results on the stage. Miss Hepburn did not stay out of the public eye.

When she decided to do *Coco* on the stage—a musical about the Paris coutourier Coco Chanel—she was determined to speak the word "shit" just as lyricist Alan Jay Lerner and she had planned it. Frederick Brisson, the producer, may have had doubts, but Kate never did, and when she looked at the wreckage of a fashion showing, and then at the audience, and said "shit," the theater-goers roared.

Some cynics said the show was a lot of that four-letter word she used, what with Kate trying to sing, but that word was enough, and Kate got standing ovations, which rather amazed her, or so she said.

The backstage area at the Mark Hellinger Theatre was nevertheless a battleground between Kate and the actors and musicians, who claimed they were freezing because cold-blooded Kate wanted the room temperature kept at about 60 degrees.

And "Her Highness" battled with the musicians and stagehands about their cigars.

Her tangles with the press continued. She was self-conscious now about her profile and objected to pictures. I figured in one of these skirmishes.

A pretty little blonde actress, Alpha Blair, had turned photographer. She was the girlfriend of an assistant of mine. I had noticed that a car and chauffeur (not a limousine, more like a station wagon) waited at the stage door for Kate. I translated that scene of Miss Hepburn's running to the car each night into a picture idea for the *New York Post.* I mentioned the possibility to Alpha Blair. After all, it was like she was a member of the family.

Alpha waited for Kate and tried, but the dialogue she got was more memorable than the pictures.

Alpha was such an innocent, slight-looking little girl, and Hepburn's words as Alpha remembered them were so harsh.

"Get away from me, you little brat, or I'll punch you in the nose" is what she said as Alpha recalls it.

I had a personal experience with Miss Hepburn that was additionally revealing. Paul Sann, then executive editor of the *New York Post,* was bringing out a book on the fads and fancies of America and wanted to use a photograph of Katharine Hepburn on a skateboard.

The photographer was Katharine Hepburn's nephew. A simple letter of authorization from him was needed. But New York couldn't seem to find him, so New York called Beverly Hills.

Paul Sann phoned me at the Beverly Hills Hotel and asked if I could run down Miss Hepburn and maybe find out if she might know how we could reach her nephew.

She was on a picture. I phoned public relations.

"It'll take a while," I reported back. "It'll be hell to get through to her, and she's not cooperative, so it might take a week. We'll give it a try."

My wife and I started out for lunch. In the corridor a door opened, and a woman looked out. "Isn't that Katharine Hepburn?" I said.

"Miss Hepburn," I addressed her, and begging her pardon, I stated my problem.

Reaching into a bag, she brought out a pocket phone book and said, "I think I have it right here, but if I don't, I can easily get it for you. No, here it is, his number in Florida."

We were surprised that it took 10 minutes instead of 10 days.

5

THE
FUNNIEST
FEMALES

Jane Fonda discovered Physical Fitness, and Joan Rivers discovered Physical Fatness—on Elizabeth Taylor.

Joanie Rivers just happened to notice that Elizabeth Taylor heard that "life is a banquet" and was taking it literally. If Liz was eating for two (herself and a baby elephant), Joan wickedly called it to the attention of the world. Joan was rewarded with a promotion to Johnny Carson's vacation replacement. Joan became the most talked-about TV spieler in the country. You are going to hear about her for a long time, which just shows what TV audiences want nowadays from their comediennes. They want murder.

When Joan explodes before you on "The Tonight Show," laughing a little hysterically at what she has in mind for your entertainment, applauds you and herself for being there, and says, "Can we talk?" you probably do not stop and say, "She's a Brooklyn girl who went to Barnard and got a Phi Beta Kappa key (if they still give keys). What the hell is that dame doing here?"

You find out soon enough that she's been perfecting this role of female insulter for 15 or 20 years. She didn't become a bitch overnight. She's got experience as a bitch.

Joan gasps; she seems to get out of breath; she acts a little scared at what she's going to say.

She has been called a Don Rickles in panty hose, but it may be that she is even more shocking than Rickles or his contemporary, Buddy Hackett, who stunned crowds at the Palace Theater by saying "ass." Before Joan discovered that Elizabeth Taylor appeared to have a tapeworm, I interviewed her and took some notes on her descriptions of people she liked a whole lot.

Nancy Reagan, she said, "has bullet-proof hair."

Rod Stewart has "a road-map complexion."

Mick Jagger is "Ugly Lips."

Barry Manilow: "Could you believe that nose?"

Roman Polanski "now travels in a school bus."

A certain lady of royalty "has seen more ceilings than Michelangelo."

America has had funny ladies who didn't always mean to be funny, like Carry Nation. Martha Raye could practically put a billiard ball in her mouth. Beatrice Lillie could see a pigeon and twitter to it, "Any messages?" Dorothy Parker, finding office life dull and sexless, hung a MEN sign on her office door and found things picking up. Bette Midler is a huge comic talent, besides being sexually alluring. Bette had a routine about a "Sophie" and her boyfriend discussing each other's sexual inadequacies and adequacies.

When some of Sophie Tucker's fans said they didn't think Sophie Tucker ever went that far, Bette said, "Who said it was Sophie Tucker?" So there!

Sophie Whoever-it-was was a good chunk of material, and I give Bette credit.

Joan Rivers does not have the scope, the stage, to commit laughter as Bette does. However, Joan has problems of bad taste to consider. Sometimes she skirts bad taste, and she doesn't always skirt it. She possesses daring, and you can see from the spark in her eyes what she's going through and she isn't going to spare herself.

She claims, for example, that her mother, wife of a doctor, tried to get her to marry a transvestite.

"Marry him and you'll double your wardrobe," her mother said, says Joan.

Joan Molinsky had been dirtying up or cleaning up her comedy material in the Catskill Mountains clubs, waiting for Johnny Carson to discover her, and he did, and people were soon saying she was so good that she should have her own show.

I told her I'd heard she was becoming a successful dirty comedienne.

"Oh, you thrill me when you call me a dirty comedienne," she said. "If I could be dirty like Buddy Hackett or Redd Foxx, I'd be a sellout."

Joan's family was not in full accord with her choice of profession. "My mother is to blame for me not being dirtier. She told me a bed is only for two things: for sleeping and for putting things on. For putting coats on at parties. Like a checkroom."

When Joan sold out Carnegie Hall, she was still honing her machete. She said Jackie Onassis, for example, "looked like E.T. without makeup."

Some lovers of laughs contend that Phyllis Diller, the lady of the facelifts, a Bob Hope favorite, should be listed as Funny Lady No. 1. She still refers to a one-time husband and partner as Fang.

There's a Chicago product calling herself Pudgy who lets the people in the audience answer questions about themselves and provide the comedy.

When you've watched Joan Rivers interview a movie star you've had an experience. It resembles a prizefight with two boxers squaring off in the ring with their fists up.

Joan's up clapping her hands, applauding the audience, the guests, and the interviewee. Let's hope the target is TV star Victoria Principal. Joan hurls questions at her and practically calls her a liar about her "engagement" to Andy Gibb. Joan reminds her that she had shown her an "engagement" ring and

Joan has commented that the diamond is disappointingly small.

These cats are snarling at each other at the climax, and Joan can't wait to have her return to the show so she can pounce on her again.

It's another Dempsey-Tunney match, a grudge battle. And Joan will have rough questions for her.

It may be because she was a fat kid with a more attractive sister that Joan makes so much of the alleged piggishness of Liz Taylor.

Joan got rid of the fat. Later, living on her earnings as a comedienne in Greenwich Village, she came to her present skinny look.

It takes enormous ego to be a comic—to be confident you can make people not only listen but laugh. Though Joan sometimes looks fragile and nervous, she actually has guts. If you object to her material, it may be that you're not smart enough to appreciate it. She says her best audiences are college people or college-educated folk with more than average sophistication.

The New York women go daft about her contention that Elizabeth Taylor is eating her way into oblivion.

"New York women," she has said, "are beasts. Hollywood women are prettier but slower. New York women know what to do with an ugly face."

"My God, she should know," a New York woman could retort. "Joan has had everything lifted."

Fifteen years ago, when she was much less well known and reshaping her image, clowning at the Copacabana, she said "Number 13 is unlucky for me—it's my bust size."

Joan is confident that with all the tricks she's become very attractive and seductive, although the gentlemen who like curves are a bit disappointed.

When cohosting the show, she asks women about their affairs, giving the impression that practically everybody is having one.

Well, Joan got mixed up once with a college professor. In fact, they were engaged. The engagement was broken by the professor's wife—she got pregnant.

Joan dismisses her husband No. 2, Edgar Rosenberg, a producer from England, as probably having opened a door for her once. "That was a mistake. He thought it was somebody else." They produced a picture about a pregnant man, *Rabbit Test.*

Joan's husband warned her that their movie would be a bomb, offering her statistics that showed that her favorites such as the Marx Brothers got bad reviews.

We used to see her trying to get laughs at Upstairs at the Downstairs, and we knew that someday somebody would discover her.

It was Johnny Carson who told her she would be a star and helped make it happen.

She lacked stature—physical stature, being only a little over five feet tall. Her voice is a little strident at times, but it has authority.

And she attains stature by picking on big people.

Joan doesn't insult nobodies.

There are no laughs in that.

But if she reads from a newspaper column a line—"What important actor refers behind her back to his wife as 'The Cow'?"—that would get a laugh, and no name is used.

In magazine interviews she has pictured herself as tacky. She claims to take all the Kleenex and soap with her when she leaves a hotel because she remembers when she lived on ketchup. She nominated Dudley Moore and Susan Anton as the tackiest.

"She [Susan] has hickies on her knees. You should have a sexual relationship, but don't flaunt it when it's that grotesque.

"Edgar is a little strange, too. He's so English he wears vests with his pajamas, but he once mooned David Brenner from a limousine he was riding in."

Even those of us who liked her a dozen or more years ago didn't foresee her having the popularity she now gloats over.

She handles the sexy remarks more adroitly now than she did. In '71 she came out for midiskirts rather than minis. "If you're in a hurry, you don't have to shave your legs as far up."

That, of course, was before Physical Fatness.

And Elizabeth Taylor.

Joan got paid back by Liz and Friends when the Friars Club turned on her at their annual dinner honoring Liz, May 1983. Liz had made sure Joan wasn't attending the dinner. Dinah

Shore, the mistress of ceremonies, started the cannonading, saying, "If you can't afford a $5,000 table to see Liz, you might as well go over to Lexington Avenue and see Joan. She's got a formica table." The knowing people understood that to indicate that Joan was being served at a cheap lunch counter while Liz was in the midst of all the champagne and luxury.

"We are not here to praise Joan Rivers," Roger Moore said, "But to bury her." Buddy Hackett said, "A Peeping Tom threw up on Joan's window last night." Liz couldn't restrain herself and at one point called out, "Joan Rivers, if you're here, eat your heart out." Joan Rivers was working in Las Vegas and, characteristically, she interpreted all the insults as a compliment.

"All I can say is I've arrived," Joan told columnist Cindy Adams. "I'm thrilled. You know how wonderful that is for me? I'm made.

"Look, I've stopped knocking Taylor. I took her out of my act. Nobody cares anymore. She's old; nobody cares how fat she gets. I'm into more current people. Anyway, three nights before the event I called to wish her luck. She was out having dinner. The way she eats, no wonder she hasn't got around to calling me back."

Phyllis Diller came from one of my home towns, Lima, Ohio, and we sometimes got together and talked about how she went to Bluffton College (and I went to Heidelberg), and here we were sitting together at the Russian Tea Room and wishing we could order a bottle of Dom Perignon 1973 at $100—and whose name could we sign on the check?

Phyllis was just finishing her fifth appearance in Atlantic City, the new Las Vegas. She was hustling a book, *The Joys of Aging and How to Avoid Them*. She was going on 66 now and still kidding about the facelifts, which were true.

"I don't get dressed in the morning. I'm assembled; I'm just a bunch of spare parts. How many operations have I had?" She stopped to count them. "Four: two on the face, two on the body. I don't want anything, including me, to get old-fashioned."

Phyllis is really an attractive lady when she gets rid of the wig and ugly makeup and getup. She wanted an outfit nobody would recognize her in. A designer fixed her up with a nun's habit, which she wore without makeup. She went to the Waldorf Towers, and they wouldn't believe her when she said she was Phyllis Diller. She found one employee who knew her and was taken in.

There was one very pleasant thing about Phyllis's act. Two things! It was funny. And there was no mention of Liz Taylor.

What she didn't talk about much was her family, her real family. Five Dillers, two boys and three daughters, from her 25-year marriage to Sherwood Diller. She was real proud of them all, and she says she still has romance in her blood. She meets interesting men in her travels and says, "I love 'em and I dump 'em."

Phyllis proved in October 1983 that she was one of the boys as well as one of the girls when she dressed in drag—having had a tailor make her a man's suit—and crashed the Friars Club stag luncheon for Sid Caesar at the Sheraton Centre Hotel. Phyllis went all the way—all the way into the men's room, where she eavesdropped.

Wearing a small blonde fake mustache and with her hair combed sweepingly over her skull, Phyllis carried credentials showing she was "Phillip Downey." Her neat suit included a vest. The X-rated jokes pouring from the lips of toastmaster Buddy Hackett, Jack Carter, Jackie Vernon, and others and the badinage in the men's room amused Phyllis, who confessed, "I always wanted to hear what they say, and it was the dirtiest, funniest thing I ever heard."

Phyllis's disguise was so effective that the dais comedians, all friends of hers, never suspected the boyish listener was a girl who would blab. Phyllis posed for a picture at the door of the men's room ("Gentlemen") so nobody would doubt her claims that she was there. She denied the language shocked her, however, explaining that she once got involved in an auto collision with a truck driver.

Oh, the beauty secrets and secrets about beauties that I picked up along the wicked road I traveled.

Marilyn Monroe, the blond of blonds, had "mousey," darkish hair in the first "glamour" pictures remembered of her. Bob Mitchum knew from her husband, a coworker in a defense plant, and from Marilyn herself, who worked with him in a picture, that she had unusually difficult menstrual periods. He clinically discussed the peculiar construction of her vaginal area.

Her intimate friend, columnist Sidney Skolsky, remembered that she once had a driver stop a car she was riding in, allowing her to get out and claw the side of the road while she tried to get relief from pain.

When I was photographing Jayne Mansfield's internationally famous bosom once, she warned me, "Now don't photograph that left one." I think it was the left. It seemed to have some kind of a mark—not necessarily a bite.

Mae West, for whom her Canadian friends named their life belts "Mae Wests" in honor of her superstructure, was proud of that.

"My grandmother," she laughed, "had three." Breasts, she meant.

"But," she added, "I should have told that to 'Believe It or Not' Bob Ripley," referring to the artist who collected oddities.

Gifted actress Tallulah Bankhead, the Wham from Alabam' who called everybody "Dolling," kept little of her prodigious activity secret. She had tried everything, including cocaine, girls, and total abstinence. Bitterly angry once at *Time* magazine, she said to her frank friend, columnist Irving Hoffman, "I don't look 40, do I?"

"Not anymore," he replied.

Her interviews frequently included a reference to an ad lib she purportedly pulled off on a radio show with me. I said, "Tallulah, with your deep mannish voice, are you ever mistaken for a man?" She replied, "No, are you?"

Bursting with Southern hospitality, Tallulah took men and women guests to the bathroom with her, performing bodily functions rather than interrupt an interesting conversation. Tallulah also had an aversion to pants or panties and sat around without either. Her friend Tennessee Williams commented on this habit in his memoirs.

Alfred Hitchcock suffered through that eccentricity while

filming *Lifeboat*. Ernest Lehman quoted Hitchcock in *Screening Sickness and Other Tales of Tinseltown"* (Perigee Books):

> This actress came up to me . . . and said, Mr. Hitchcock, is there nothing you can do about Tallulah? She refuses to wear panties beneath her skirt, and every time she climbs up into the set. . . ." "Young woman," I replied, "That is not my department." "Then whose department is it?" she cried. "I suggest," I explained to her, "that you take it up with either makeup or hairdressing."

6

"EARL," COOED MISS O'BRIEN, "ARE YOU DOUBLE-JOINTED?"*

I'm the guy who was Margaret O'Brien's date last night. I failed to fascinate her with my ready wit, and she concentrated on drawing pictures on the back of a Stork Club menu. Imagine dining with a dame who looks up at you and says, "Excuse me, may I have the eraser?"

Then she says, "Are you double-jointed?" and you confess you are only double-meaninged, and she shows you she is double-jointed and can bend her thumb down along her wrist.

"Would you draw my picture?" you say to her, and then she tries and says, "I can't make a man out of your picture; I'll make a woman."

So then I see me on the back of the menu and notice I am wearing a dress and a veil and look very ravishing.

But Margaret, who is going to be eight on Monday, turned out to be the most popular gal I'd ever dated, for when we went into the Cub Room, George Jean Nathan, one of her discoverers,

---

*This chapter originally appeared as a column in the *New York Post* on January 10, 1945.

gave her a gardenia, and Moss Hart sent me a message saying, "Dear Earl, would it be possible for an aging playwright to meet his Dream Girl, Miss O'Brien?" I gave him an introduction.

"Would you want me to draw you a glamour girl or a Mexican?" asked my date.

I thought a glamour girl, and she said, "With pompadour?" and I replied I felt very stongly against girls without pompadours. "Do you want her to be a princess?" Oh, absolutely, at least. Sherman Billingsley sent her a gift in red crackly paper, and the little girl in pigtails, blue-and-white middy suit, and white boots seemed more enamored of the red crackly paper than of the contents. When our wild, wild fling was over at 10:00, she was still carrying the torn red crackly paper lovingly.

"No doubt, Margaret reads and loves my column?" I said self-effacingly to her mother.

"She doesn't read," her mother said. California requires school attendance at eight; Margaret starts tutoring this month. She memorized 11 pages of radio script for the Kate Smith program. When we left to go to the *Salute to the Wounded* show at Madison Square Garden, everybody looked at her admiringly. She walked on the stage before the many thousands of people and said, "I'm happy to be here."

When Milton Berle, the MC, asked her, "Where do you live—in Manhattan?" she answered, "No—at the Waldorf."

"I live at the Waldorf myself—the Waldorf Cafeteria," Berle said.

Later Jimmy Walker bent over her and took the small hand and said, "It's too late for both of us to be out; you because you're too young, me because I'm too old."

I felt a little antique myself after seeing this amazing child. She saw her movie, *Meet Me in St. Louis,* for the first time yesterday, and as she was already up two hours past her bedtime, we galloped home by special limousine.

She recites the Gettysburg Address glibly but has something she likes to recite better.

"The Uhtivity," she said.

"Nativity," corrected her mother.

"Nativity," said Margaret who, turning to her date, said, "What else would you like me to draw?"

7

BURT REYNOLDS
AS A BOY

You think it's easy being Burt Reynolds?

The press is on your back every day: "When are you going to marry Dinah, or Sally, or Lori? Are you looking for somebody younger? Isn't it a fact that you and Sally were secretly married in Boston last December?" That's the way it goes.

"I haven't even been in Boston," Burt says. "Where'd you get that story?"

"From a 'good source' in Aspen. I think when there's no snow there they sit around and make up phony gossip items."

I can't brag of knowing Burt Reynolds well, but all the time I've known him he's been unpretentious, the least flamboyant guy in the crowd. You're standing on the sidelines talking to some quiet stranger watching them film a picture, and you suddenly realize the guy you're talking to is the star, Burt Reynolds.

The first time I saw him I introduced him at a Broadway party, and I didn't know enough about him to make it interesting. That was before he ungirded his loins for *Cosmopolitan* magazine.

"Surprised you didn't think I was Marlon Brando," he said.

"Get that all the time," he explained.

"I got in fights over it." He laughed at one recollection: "I went to a party in Dallas with Don Meredith of the Cowboys. Somebody had already thought I was Brando. When I was out of the room Don told them I *was* Brando.

"When I came back into the room they started bugging me about being Brando, and I got mean and rude. The ruder I got, the more they believed it.

"Another time at an airport a little old lady said she knew I was Brando. I said, 'Lady, I'm not.' She walked away and came back and said she'd talked it over with her husband and they knew I was Brando.

"I got mad, lost my temper, and yelled, 'Damn it to hell, lady, I am not Brando!'

"She said, 'Ah, now we know for sure, you *are* Brando!' "

He was once in jail. Not a movie jail. He's been in lots of those, including Leavenworth. A real hoosegow.

"Yes, when I was 15. I felt stagnated. I ran away from home. My dad was police chief in West Palm Beach, Florida.

"I got arrested in Allendale, South Carolina, for vagrancy.

"The Allendale police found out who I was, and out of courtesy they called my dad and said, they had this kid here, is he your son?

"My dad said, 'Nope.'

"My old man could be tough.

"I figured since my dad didn't remember me, maybe I better go home and remind him.

"There wasn't any welcoming committee when I got off the Greyhound bus. I had a cardboard box with my stuff in it, and I must have looked like a vagrant going to the back door. I stuck my head in and tried to make a joke. I said, 'Do I still live here?'

"My mother cried and kissed me. My dad was sitting there eating breakfast. He didn't speak. He didn't even look up. He went to work without ever noticing me.

"Yeah, my dad could be tough. He didn't even talk to me that night and not for about three weeks.

"And, you know, that was the greatest thing that ever happened to me. My dad's attitude when I let him down. That straightened me out.

"Well," Burt Reynolds said, "after that I got interested in athletics—football, baseball . . . and . . ."

"Yes?" I said.

"I think we called it," Burt said, " 'chasing girls.' "

8

JUST
FOOLISHNESS

There's a lot of foolishness that goes on in the world that you wouldn't know about if some fool like me didn't tell you.

The night that Diane Keaton opened in a Broadway show, *Play It Again, Sam,* with a little mole wearing dirty tennis shoes, calling himself Woody Allen, she was "demolished with fear," she says, because Woody Allen and Tony Roberts came into her dressing room a few minutes before the curtain and said, reassuringly, "You'll be all right, Diane; don't worry about your hands."

"My hands! What about my hands?" she said. "Nobody has said anything about my hands. What is it now about my hands?"

"Just don't think about it," Woody said. "Don't even give it a thought."

"I'm sure nobody'll even notice," Tony Roberts said, and the two left her in a state of alarm about her hands and probably enjoyed their joke. Woody at times is like that. One time after a rehearsal he gave notes to the others in the cast and said, "I had one sheet of notes for Diane, too. What did I do with it?" He left her worrying about what might be in the notes.

Diane grew accustomed to Woody's eccentricities as the years went on and now regards the phony alarm about her hands as a minor incident, although she did wonder about her hands for half an act before she saw the supposed humor of it. You could expect almost anything from Woody Allen. But from Mrs. Robert Redford—well, she's different, isn't she, from the mole?

With her husband's approval, Mrs. Redford phoned their agent one morning and said, "I hate to tell you this, but I just felt I had to, but you know what a temper Bob has. . . ."

"Yes?" replied the agent. Redford was getting his first big break in *Barefoot in the Park*. Hollywood was offering deals. "What happened?"

"Well, Bob's in jail."

"In jail? My God, what did he do?"

"Well, this heckler down in front kept needling him with remarks, and Bob just left the stage and ran down after him. And you know he's got a powerful—"

"Did you call his lawyer?"

"Yes, and right now he's trying to raise bail. And the charge may be—well, there's the religious angle. . . . Just a minute. Somebody at the door. Oh, God, the police again."

And Mrs. Redford hung up just at the most suspenseful moment.

And the agent went frantic trying to get her back, but she made sure her phone was giving a busy signal for about half an hour, when she phoned the agent and said, "After all, it is April Fool's Day."

9
CREEPS AND CRUMBUMS

When Toots Shor's magnificent new saloon opened at 33 West 52nd Street in the Sexy '60s, a writer from the business page estimated that it cost $7 million, a largish bundle for a gin mill operated by a former Philadelphia bouncer and Wilkes-Barre BVD peddler.

Fat comedian Jackie Gleason, a close friend of Shor's, who boasted that he owed his excellent health to not eating there, said the lackadaisical cooks forgot to stir the soups, which were so thick and hard they had to be sliced and were suitable for throwing. Accepting the rumor that the financing was by the rich labor leaders of the Teamsters Union, Gleason sent Care packages of food to the opening and a floral piece reminiscent of a gangster's funeral offering. Gleason also sent a "poem":

> Good luck, Dear Toots,
> With your new domain
> Where joy will reign
> as well as tomain (sic).

It was a major event journalistically, and Bob Considine, the

Hearst columnist who was Toots's Boswell, summed up the world's greatest saloon keeper:

"It's quieter without the proprietor."

How to attain Toots's affection to the point where he acknowledged you to be a slimy, creepy, crummy bum was not always clear to some of his customers who seemed to plead for that honor. For some reason, I became "Early Curly" to Toots without the "slimy" handle. However, one New Year's Eve we were sitting in his bar at home, and he woke and scowled at me. I was wearing a crew cut similar to George Gobel's hairdo at the moment.

"You Gobel-headed creep," Toots snarled at me and returned to his dreams.

"Jiminy Crickets" was Toots's strongest epithet, but he was not above calling some of the lady customers "you old bag." The women mostly did not object and, in fact, I believe Ella Logan, Gypsy Rose Lee, and Sophie Tucker would have been complimented to be called an old bag.

Toots called himself "Tootsie the Pretty Jew," and when he was younger and thinner he was a handsome if slightly rotund citizen with fists that had persuaded more than one drunk to behave.

Possibly because I was a newcomer, also a *goy*, a Christian, in this crowd that was predominantly Jewish, he helped me and maneuvered and manipulated some news items so they came to me. I showed up at his "store," as he thought of it, at late lunchtime, around 1:00 P.M., when he would be at the front booth on the right side, raucously in command of the daily event, lunch. Toots loved lunch. Some proprietors didn't enjoy it, but Toots did, the drinking part especially.

"Sit down, you slimy, crummy bum! Whattayuh drinkin'?" You couldn't turn down a drink, or you shouldn't. It was an insult to "Blub." He knew you were there to pay your respects. To be called to his table and offered a drink was an honor, but it wasn't unusual to be summoned. At times Toots was offended to have nondrinkers around. My fellow columnist on the *New York Post*, Leonard Lyons, who didn't drink liquor but who swilled black coffee all day, was looked upon by Toots as a little snobbish.

Gleason was a special guest, more special than Frank Costello, the reputed mob boss who didn't come as often as he would have liked; he was afraid he would not help Toots's reputation. Comedian Red Skelton, a nondrinker, explained one day that he pretended to be staggering when he left, fearing that people seeing a customer emerging sober would start bad reports about Toots's booze not having the usual intoxicating strength.

Gleason was such a fixture at Toots's that he received mail there. I got mail there also.

One noontime Gleason was ripping open envelopes handed to him by Joe the maitre d', functioning from a rostrum at the dining room entrance from the bar.

"Get a load of this," shouted Gleason to me. "This Rosemary Williamson broad is writing me inviting me to a party." He handed the invitation to me to inspect.

Rosemary Williamson was a pretty girl in the newspapers. But the invitation was from my wife, Rosemary Wilson, inviting him to a surprise birthday party for me.

Jackie was confident, cocky, and in robust health and was taking on the world. He propounded a remarkable explanation for his riotous drinking.

"I drink to get rid of warts," he said.

Warts? He had warts?

"Not my warts," Jackie said. "Your warts. When I'm drinkin'," he smiled, and his plump round cheeks shook with happiness, "your warts and blemishes and wrinkles disappear. Everybody and everything is just beautiful. Just perfect. Everything that's ugly fades away. Every living thing is lovely and floating on a beautiful cloud, and there are no scars and no warts. Especially no warts!"

Jackie was overjoyed as he made this little speech—it was the first time I'd heard it, and I had to believe it was original. He told it in the hearing of his secretary Sydelle, who was always ready for the next line.

"Sydelle," he would say, "a little more wart medicine," and she would trot off to bring him a refill.

A drinking contest, sort of a World's Series, between Gleason and Toots, is still discussed by a few of the hardy survivors who cheered or groaned from the sidelines.

The event was not programmed but was strictly ad lib. Toots, a brandy devotee, had absorbed a bottle while observing the forenoon and noontime amenities and saw in Gleason a possible matinee challenger.

In fairness to Gleason, he did not know it was a drinking contest until he'd already consumed most of a bottle of Scotch.

As they sat at front tables on opposite sides of the dining room, Toots began roaring to him to drink up "like a man."

Taking this as personal, Gleason stood up to go to the men's room and wobbled, then fell onto the floor in a messy heap. The sound of his tonnage hitting the floor stunned the customers there for the oncoming cocktail hour.

Bob Considine and I reported the Major Event with the professional attention it deserved.

"Gleason lay there on his back, his ample proportions blocking the entrance to the dining room like a scuttled tanker immobilizing Suez," wrote Considine.

"Leave the bum there! He made his load, so now let him get up himself," bellowed Toots, ordering the waiters and captains to give him no help making his way to the john.

Patrons arriving for dinner had to detour around one of the best-known stomachs in America, still on display while Toots enjoyed the rest of his bottle of brandy.

Columnist-producer Mark Hellinger, who, besides making movies, liked to invite friends to his Hollywood home and get them blotto on martinis, was the type of literary lion that Toots preferred. Quentin Reynolds ("Big Quent") was almost as popular with him, but, after all, Mark was in there sponsoring the pretty Jew when he was a flat-pocket bum. Toots could also throw a big arm around Ernest Hemingway, Robert Sherwood, Damon Runyon, Grantland Rice, Bill Corum, Jimmy Cannon, Red Smith, and other sportswriters or mere authors and Pulitzer Prize winners. Ernest Hemingway once asked me in a letter from Cuba to say hello to Toots; "I wouldn't write to him during the baseball season." Another type of writer Toots liked was Gypsy Rose Lee, who was a great friend of Toots's longtime chum Rags Ragland. Rags complained that "Hollywood is trying to make a star out of me." He wouldn't permit it.

Toots could outroar most of them (it was his own place), but one he couldn't silence was his wife "Baby," whom he called

"Husk," short for Husky. A little blonde of Irish and Dutch descent, Catholic, she wasn't much over five feet and appeared to be 90 pounds to his 225 or 250. Toots's friends warned him against getting into arguments with Baby because she would destroy him with a word.

Though Toots's saloon was a man's joint, especially at noon, you did not hear any vulgar language spoken. His "Jiminy Crickets" expletive seemed especially tame coming from this hulk of manhood whose bouncer days were frequently recalled by patrons who put him in the same echelon or weight class as Detective Johnny Broderick. Johnny was a silent type in a business suit, with horn-rim glasses, seeming to be 50 and harmless, who was known to pick up the most feared hoodlum and deposit him in a garbage can.

Toots and I had a reason for special camaraderie. He hated Sherman Billingsley, the owner of the Stork Club. I didn't like him either.

"Sherm" was an ignoramus bootlegger from Oklahoma who, with the help of columnist Walter Winchell, became a leading speakeasy proprietor. Toots Shor had been one of his employees in one of the clubs, and Billingsley had elected to fire him. When Toots eventually got his own club, he naturally cast himself as Billingsley's competitor.

Billingsley's Stork Club Cub Room was already sacred to the Saloon Set when I began covering Broadway. I felt I had made it when I was admitted to the Cub Room and served food and drink I didn't have to pay for.

I arranged to run some caricatures of nightclub figures in my column, and the first caricature was of Sherman Billingsley.

I thought he would be flattered at being first to be caricatured. He didn't see that part of it. He hated the drawing. He looked bald!

He forgot that, but not completely. Winchell allowed me to sit at his special Table 50 a few times. Winchell was nice.

"You're doing a good job," he said. "You're not giving the racket a bad name like some of them." He probably referred to Ed Sullivan, columnist for the *Daily News,* a more dangerous competitor.

When I went on a book-promoting trip I told my assistant and legman, young Blair Chotzinoff, to "cover the Stork" for me. He was a good-looking, personable youth, son of music critic Sam Chotzinoff.

There were anguished cries when I returned. Blair Chotzinoff had been "barred" from the Stork Club. Billingsley "didn't want any assistants" in his famous club. Chotzinoff had "rolled up a house check." Actually young Chotzinoff was too bashful to roll up a house check; Billingsley had the whole "assistants" battle confused. The assistant he objected to was another assistant for another columnist.

Billingsley tried to make peace by sending me perfume and champagne (which I returned) but would not correct the misunderstanding with Chotzinoff. After another trifling incident I decided to bar the Stork Club from my column rather than having the Stork Club bar me. Champagne and perfume again were sent back to the Stork Club, and we never did make up (although Billingsley made efforts to do so).

By now Billingsley had a TV show from the Stork Club, interviewing authors and others. One night he had a famous book writer, to whom he said, "I hear you writ a book."

On the program Billingsley shuffled around the pictures of celebrities he had seen in his club. One night he was interviewing Carl Brisson, the singer, "the older girls' Sinatra," father of Fred Brisson, the husband of Roz Russell.

Billingsley held out a photograph of Toots Shor.

"Good-looking man," commented Brisson.

"I wish I had all the money he owes around town," Billingsley said.

The Shors happened to be watching the program. They phoned attorney Arnold Grant, who immediately prepared a lawsuit, one of the first alleging damages by television. The Toots Shor–Sherman Billingsley feud was out in the open.

Billingsley, despite all his gift-giving to celebrities, couldn't support his remarks about Toots, who sued him for $1.1 million. Billingsley took on other battles, with labor unions and business rivals, and even had some tiffs with his old reliable ally, Walter Winchell.

Lawyers battled and conferred and delayed and postponed.

Billingsley had put his foot in his mouth much too deeply. He finally agreed to give Toots $50,000.

They never made up, and Toots and his wife Baby celebrated.

They had an Abie's Irish Rose relationship. Toots sometimes went to Mass with Baby's family. One Sunday the bulk of Baby's family sat with Matty Tracy, a big gambler and track operator, who was feeling flush and put $100 in the collection basket.

Baby's mother witnessed this generosity and signaled, then whispered to all the rest of them to hold back.

"Matty paid for all of us," she said.

Toots's joint was the site of many stunts and displays. Toots, during one meat shortage, saw Charlie Chaplin in line for a steak and told him, "Be funny for the people." He knew Charlie wasn't a regular visitor; let him wait.

Famous Maxim's in Paris withstood a visit by Toots. When Maxim's proprietor came to New York we had him visit Toots.

Monsieur Louis Vaudable, who had been warned to expect the worst, excelled in hand-kissing, and Toots pretended to think that since he ran Maxim's, his name was Max. Or Maxie. "I saw your joint in the movie *Gigi*," Toots told him. "You should sue 'em."

"Where's your cellar?" Vaudable said to change the subject.

"In the basement. Where else would it be, you moron," Toots said.

"At the Waldorf, it's on the 18th floor," Vaudable said. "Could I see a wine card?"

"A what?" Toots acted flustered.

"A list of your best wines."

"Oh yeah, I think we got one around here. Hey, Ziggy, in that slop back of the bar, we got an old card with kinds of Dago red we serve. We don't have the year on our wine card, just the prices."

Ziggy came up with something bent and dirty, a candidate for the garbage. "Somebody stepped on it," Toots groaned.

Toots later brought him a real wine card that was quite respectable. Toots told him he served quite a lot of Vichyssoise.

"Yeah, well, that's really an American dish," the Frenchman said.

They got friendly, and Toots showed Monsieur around the kitchen. Each told the other that it was obvious he didn't know a thing about the restaurant business.

Toots once argued his dear friend Leo Durocher into a delicate trap that looked like it would disrupt their palship. Toots, who considered himself a master baseball strategist, had informed Durocher that he had made a colossal blunder, and Durocher told Toots he was insane.

"You're a slimy, creepy, crummy crumbum and also a piece of raisin cake," Toots snarled at Leo, who had thought up to that time that they were buddies. "You're a baseball imbecile."

"Why, you walrus," screamed Durocher, "when we beat Cleveland in the series you said I was a genius—thanks to your help."

"You bald-headed slob," roared Toots. "Why, if I was to name the 10 best baseball managers—"

"Name them; go ahead and name them!" shouted Leo. He was furious in this moment of truth. "Who's first?" he callenged Toots. "Stengel?"

"Casey Stengel?" bawled Toots. "Why, you baseball imbecile! The No. 1 baseball manager is Leo Durocher!"

There was an incredible turnout of prominent mourners at the January 25, 1977, funeral for Toots at Campbell's Funeral Parlor just a month after most of us learned the big man wasn't going to make it.

Across the closed top of the coffin was a ribbon on a blanket of red roses sent by Jackie Gleason.

On the ribbon were the words "Dear Toots. Hold a table for us. Jackie."

If Toots didn't invent the gospel "I don't want to be a millionaire; I just want to live like one," he was its first Apostle. He wanted to be a classy bum if "classy" meant "going first cabin."

"Tootsie, the pretty Jew," treasured friendship like few other inhabitants of his saloon world. They tried to be like him and return his "I love you" vows to men and women. They gave him—gave him, literally—many thousands of dollars to keep his restaurants from ruin. He gave himself an enormous birthday party, which he charged them for, and he loved it and so did the ticket-purchasers. He did make people happy, and if they got a little drunk in the process of getting happy—well, there was always Toots's remarkable philosophy, which he may have believed. "Whiskey never hurt anybody," he liked to say.

I covered his openings and his closings and hold him to have been "the nonpareil," as Jack Dempsey was, "the peerless," having no equal."

Bob Considine and I were in his last great saloon its final night when it was foundering. There was an obstreperous customer at the bar, which was almost empty. Toots was as annoyed at the loud-mouthed pestiferous slob as he was at the general business situation, which would see him go out of business next day.

Toots directed that the slob be ejected.

He would go out of business with a classy bar even if it was virtually empty.

And when the ejected patron came around the next day to complain of his treatment, he would find the place padlocked.

To the last, Toots, the classy bum, was a saloon keeper's saloon keeper.

10
MARILYN
AND HER MEN

Marilyn Monroe once kept me waiting an hour and a half beyond the time of our appointment and explained with actress logic, "I rinsed my hair in the shower and it came out purple stripes, so I had to go back in the shower and do it over."

The Sex Symbol of her time was unexpectedly frivolous in acknowledging lovemaking with the President of the United States, John F. Kennedy, telling two friends, "I think I made his back feel better."

Marilyn autographed a famous nude calendar picture to me, "I hope you like my hairdo."

She called her deep-browed, libraryish-looking husband, Arthur Miller, "Pappy."

When her friend, the late Wally Cox, was driving very slowly because she was in the car and feeling ill, she said, "I'm afraid you're going to be arrested for illegal parking."

Marilyn later suggested changing the nude calendar autograph to "I hope you didn't mind me not wearing earrings."

That was the Marilyn Monroe I knew from July 1949, when we did one of her first major interviews in New York, until her mysterious death in August 1962.

Marilyn was a couple of people. One was a scared child afraid she'd turn mad like her mother. The other could be described with an expression I don't care for. She was a "fun girl."

She laughed; she giggled; she did crazy, naughty, sexy things she probably shouldn't have; she danced; she sang; she got married and divorced; she moved in with guys and moved out; she was so freewheeling, so accommodating to movie producers and their friends that even Lee Strasberg, the great drama teacher, her most vociferous booster, said that Hollywood often thought she was a prostitute.

In the beginning Marilyn had a body that seemed to be made for love or at least sex, but her face was wooden.

Apologizing for the lack of animation in this blonde he was touting as a new sex bomb in his Groucho Marx film, *Love Happy,* producer Lester Cowan said, "It doesn't matter about her face. Every man who sees her wants to jump her."

She was such a noncelebrity then that I interviewed her only because I needed a going-away column.

But I noted that her "bountiful chest overflowed the five-column picture.

"She was lying back . . . hair down to her bare shoulders. . . . Her bust was creamy-looking against the black top of her negligee. . . ."

She was supposed to be 21 then, and Lester Cowan and his publicists were using a slightly different version of a press agent cliche: Marilyn was the "MMmmmm girl."

"MMmmmm . . . Marilyn Monroe, MMmm. . . ."

"Do you like men?"

"MMmmmm."

"Do men like you?"

"MMmmmm."

"Who's your favorite actor?"

"MMmmmm, Montgomery Clift."

"Why?"

"MMmmmm."

"Do men whistle at you?"

"Yes, but they also go 'MMmmmm.' "

"What do they want?"

"MMmmmm."

"Where did you get that walk, Miss Monroe?"

At first the girl with the creamy bust that overflowed everything had a smile that seemed to be frozen on. She may have
been shy. But the more she talked to men who appreciated her
creamy bust, the more she melted.

"Where did I get that walk? You don't like my walk?"

"Oh, no. It's splendid. Beautiful. Like a wiggle."

"I never took a lesson in my life. Groucho Marx said to me,
'Walk like this,' and I did." Groucho had demonstrated how she
should toss her buttocks, and she was a good student. Marilyn
gave a demonstration of her sexiest wiggling and waggling.

"MMmmmm."

Then Marilyn Monroe unbent; she ended her big freeze; she
thawed. And that's the "MMmmmm" I'm really interested in
now. But for her death, she would have gone on to become one
of our great comediennes, noted for her wit as well as her acting.

Marilyn was kidding us all the time.

She seemed so bashful and innocent when she first bounced
into the picture, but she had been married at 16 to a man who
was a watchman and a cop. She claimed that when she did that
famous nude calendar picture she was hungry and needed the
money ($50 from photographer Tom Kelly) for food and for
rent.

For one so wooden, she suddenly became glib.

I heard Marilyn using a routine for radio interviews.

"What do you wear to bed?"

"Just some Chanel No. 5."

"Is that all you have on?"

"Oh, no."

"What else do you have on?"

"The radio."

How clever of Marilyn, I thought, until readers told me I
could find those jokes in old vaudeville joke books.

And she was collecting prominent friends.

She had a drama coach, Natasha Lytess, who asked why her
face was so red.

"Howard hasn't shaved for four days," she said.

Howard Hughes, the indefatigable actress collector.

Marilyn Monroe was suddenly the biggest name in Show Business, leaving Elizabeth Taylor, Jane Russell, Ingrid Bergman, Ava Gardner, Shirley MacLaine behind. Agents and producers were fighting for her. Marilyn was appreciative of the help given her along the rocky way up.

One afternoon in Hollywood, at an apartment near the Hamburger Hamlet, the suddenly successful Marilyn showed me a scrapbook of press clippings. The first interview she did with me had first position in the book.

The legends about Marilyn were just starting. Joe DiMaggio was reported to have added her to his collection of scalps in New York and vice versa.

"Marilyn is supposed to have been raped when she was five or six—or eight or nine or eleven," they said, probably by a foster parent, and it left her a stammerer for quite a time, and the one thing she knew about all men ever afterward was they wanted to take her to bed and wanted her to stay with them all night.

When she was seven, a woman operating an orphanage told Marilyn to desist from calling her Mother.

"I'm not your 'Mama.' " the woman rebuked her. "You just board here!"

That could have been the reason for Marilyn's reticence at first, but when she finally made it in pictures she had the experience of being summoned by producers to be nice to a friend, and she knew what life was about.

Marilyn had to have a sense of humor. She was two hours late for her first date with Joe DiMaggio. She claimed not to know who Babe Ruth was and didn't invite Joe in. He invited her up to see his baseball trophies—a new one to Marilyn. She declined.

"He didn't score," Marilyn reported. The champion batsman struck out. He called her again, and again, and again for dates, and she refused. And then, just to be different, and feminine, she called and asked him to take her to dinner.

Joe got over his batting slump with Marilyn, and they had a beautiful little romance with quiet drives in Central Park at night (followed by reporters). Despite the fame of the affair, their marriage lasted less than a year.

One day a tipster electrified me with the word that "Playwright Arthur Miller has left his wife over Marilyn Monroe!"

The eggheaded, double-domed genius had dumped the Missus over the Sex Symbol with the big buzooms?

"Marilyn came home at 4:00 A.M.," reported Natasha Lytess, her drama coach and roommate, "and wanted to talk. I'd seldom seen her so contented. She took off her left shoe and wiggled her big toe."

" 'I met a man, Natasha,' she said. 'It was BAM. You see my toe? This toe? He sat and held my toe. I mean I sat on the davenport, and he sat on it, too, and he held my toe. We just sat looking at each other and talked and he held my toe. I guess we talked about something while he held my toe. Yes, I remember him talking about his next play while he held my toe.' "

They planned a honeymoon in a pretty little farmhouse "by the sea" near East Hampton: Miller's two children joining them, riding over the beach in their jeep; Marilyn trying to have a baby, having a miscarriage due to the tied-up tubes.

She was so proud of him. Would he write a Broadway play for her? Defensively, she answered, "He's not that type of writer."

"I wish I could," Arthur said. "Shaw used to do it. I never could."

Completely won over by the aura of his genius, she said that his dedicating a collection of his plays "To Marilyn" was "just the best thing that ever happened to me. . . . No, the best thing was when he married me."

It was the sleeping pills and the vodka and the wavering fidelity that brought her ruin when she was doing *The Misfits* for John Huston with Clark Gable. Miller had not encountered this type before. The story was that Miller, leaving their bungalow at the Beverly Hills for an appointment, had returned tor some pipe tobacco and found Mrs. Miller with Yves Montand.

She'd brought 500 pills with her to Reno. The Yves Montand incident was only one of the things that caused MMmmmm and A.M. to quit speaking.

Picture production stopped. Marilyn went to a hospital.

It could be a big story. I got the story from John Huston of how he'd tapered her off the sleeping pills, the uppers and downers, morning and night, by substituting tranquilizers.

"M.M. OFF PILLS" could be the headline. As I wrote it, I remembered my ethics, to get Marilyn's side of it. Terrified of any mention of pills, she dispatched press agents begging me not to print it—promising me a "good story" later.

"It's a deal!" She was divorcing Miller, that had to be it.

Marilyn kept me on the hook for weeks, but she kept her word. I got the exclusive, and I didn't know then that she didn't want pills mentioned because she was still dependent on them.

There were several mysteries besides the mystery of her death. Marilyn pretended to be an intellectual, a voracious reader, with a couple hundred books she had to have room for in her living quarters and a few attempts at poetry lying about.

Yet, "Marilyn had no information," confided one intimate, recalling hearing her ask, "How do you spell *were?*"

Falling into the world of psychiatry, finding herself in Payne-Whitney, and suspecting what she had long feared, that she had gone insane, Marilyn read up on the subject.

Reading from a lexicon, she asked Bob Mitchum, "What's eroticism?"

Mitchum told her.

"What's anal eroticism?"

He told her that, too.

Mitchum talked learnedly of her vagina. Making a movie with him, Marilyn had explained how the peculiar structure of her sexual machinery made her menstrual periods especially difficult.

It was prestigious just to be seen with her as her fame was increasing. My wife and I met her at the Beverly Hills Polo Lounge, where we drank champagne and toasted her success.

I was on a picture-taking kick and made a date to photograph her at the hotel. Quite surprisingly, she kept the date. She brought a camera of her own—given to her, she said, by Joe DiMaggio.

"Do you and Joe take pictures of yourself on dates?" l asked.

"Joe and I have better things to do at night than take pictures," Marilyn said.

It occurred to her, not to me, that Marilyn Monroe should photograph me, stretched out on a bed, showing my bare leg.

She took it, posing me properly first, and it came out good, for what it was.

We became friendlier, and the publicity about the naked calendar helped her—especially when she decided to tell the truth and admit that she was The Body in the picture.

"She fibbed a little about needing the money for rent," confided a close friend.

"She needed it to pay her overdue installment on a convertible."

Marilyn invited us one Sunday afternoon to her bungalow at the Beverly Hills. Her press agent, Patricia Newcomb, was there ordering us drinks, but Marilyn was in her bedroom getting dressed. We waited and waited and drank and drank, waiting for Marilyn.

Unaccustomed to these hours of waiting that the rest of us had been subjected to, my wife called out, "Marilyn, what's happening?" and walked into her room.

Marilyn was fully dressed and indulging herself in the narcissistic pleasure of looking at Marilyn Monroe.

That's what she had been doing all these hours she kept us waiting.

Looking at herself.

The girls did talk momentarily about brassieres. Though Marilyn claimed not to wear any, she did wear bras to bed, and being a size 37, she wore size 36, which made her, of course, look size 38 or 40.

Marilyn's appreciation of amusing things made many wonder how she became enamored of Bobby Kennedy, about whom many never could find anything very amusing. He was grim and deep and not as jubilant as his brother, The President. Her own manner, though, was wide open.

When she met the photographer Milton H. Greene, who later became president of her production corporation, she exclaimed, "You're just a boy!"

He replied, "You're just a girl!"

Marilyn met the brothers Kennedy with the help, no doubt, of Patricia Kennedy Lawford and her husband Peter Lawford. Meeting a Kennedy in those days was not difficult.

Columnist Sidney Skolsky was her confessor in all things, and one day she blurted out to Sidney, "It's not Bobby, you know.

"No," she said, "it's Jack." It was one of the few times she used that familiar term. Usually it was "the President."

"Are you surprised?"

"Nothing you ever do surprises me," he said.

Skolsky laughed. To the victor go the spoils. To the President goes the attorney general's girlfriend.

Skolsky's little protégé surely could maneuver. With the help of a new book, *Norma Jean*, by Fred Lawrence Guiles, everybody knew that she was having an affair with a married easterner. Those brothers Kennedy were unbelievable. It was just like in the Bible. They were trifling with Marilyn at their sister Patricia Kennedy Lawford's beach house at Malibu, and her husband, movie actor Peter Lawford, couldn't be blind to the whole thing, could he?

How did they split her up? Did they split her up?

Talk about White House leaks! There was a "beard" who delivered Marilyn to JFK's trysting grounds. The "beard" didn't blab, but some White House secretaries did, telling about nude swimming parties and the President's sexual appetite.

Marilyn's secrets poured out, too. How she went from brown brunette to bleached blonde, how she had some cosmetic surgery around her chin and nose, and how her teeth got capped.

She'd been in love with orchestra leader Freddy Karger, who was in love with somebody else, and Johnny Hyde, vice-president of a talent agency, was in love with her and told her to get her tubes tied because she was going to have to go to bed with a lot of men if she was going to be a big star.

In her final weeks there were rumors that she had lost her mind. I was fortunate in that I usually saw her when she was a happy girl.

She was in a giddy whirl of trying to get back to work after being fired. She was trying to change her will. She was posing nude for the first time since the calendar shots.

Joe DiMaggio, even as late as this, was trying to help her, pouring out his grief to my wife and me, sitting in Toots Shor's, asking where he had gone wrong. How could he get her back?

"What can I do" he asked us like a little boy.

In some manner, Marilyn in this very restaurant had once gotten a splinter in her celebrated rump. My wife had hurried with her to the ladies' room to extract it. When my wife explained it, several men had protested that they would have been happy to assist (one of her pantsless days).

I don't want to think of her that last night of her life, telling Peter Lawford on the phone that she wouldn't be over to have dinner.

"Say goodbye to Pat, say goodbye to the President; say goodbye to yourself because you're a nice guy," she said. She said nothing about Bobby, at least not as Lawford remembered it.

"She said goodbye—that's terminal!" Lawford cried when he repeated it to Milt Ebbins, his manager, and they set about warning her doctors and lawyer.

"I should have gone over there," Lawford has said all the years since.

Possibly she was unbalanced at this time—wearing black wig disguises as she ran to board that private plane of the Kennedys'; found in a naked heap once outside a hotel door; she was said to have been heard muttering suicide threats.

Yet she was so professional and Show Businessy when AWOL from Hollywood that she sang "Happy Birthday" before 20,000 to President Kennedy at Madison Square Garden.

She stole the show. Peter Lawford introduced her; she didn't come out; he introduced her a second time, she didn't come out. There were groans. She wasn't there! He introduced her a third time. Finally, oozing, inching, slithering, undulating, came "the late Marilyn Monroe."

"I can retire from politics after having had 'Happy Birthday' sung to me by a sweet wholesome girl like Marilyn Monroe," the President said.

The cheering for Marilyn drowned out the President's emphasis on the word *wholesome.*

"Marilyn was fantasizing so much," declares one from her circle, "you didn't know what to believe." Some did truly believe she should be confined.

She had soaring hopes for more sessions with JFK. She was determined to dazzle the Washington, DC, opening of Irving Berlin's show, *Mr. President,* and chose close friend Henry Rosenfeld to take her. She commanded him.

But that was to be in the fall. This was still summer.

I think of the laughs she laughed and the laughs she provided for others. I remember the famous skirt-blowing picture that all of us took (yes, even I took one) the night they were shooting *The Seven-Year Itch,* and Joe DiMaggio was around the corner, glowering.

Once she'd allowed me to go along with my camera to a famous photographer's studio for her to pose for a magazine cover.

In the dressing room I hopped up on a chair to shoot down on her famous cleavage, which she knew was her best, most photogenic feature.

"There he is, up on his little perch," Marilyn laughed.

The famous photographer suddenly said, "Could I borrow your camera? Something went wrong with mine." Marilyn and I laughed later at his device for getting me the hell out of his way.

Marilyn promised solemnly she wouldn't be late for another appointment with me (and she wasn't—only 15 minutes) because I was giving my wife a surprise party.

Not only had she kept her tardiness down to 15 minutes, but Marilyn sent a note: "Thank you, Rosemary, for sharing Earl with me today." And she sent along an autographed photograph by an illustrious portrait photographer whose subjects were kings and queens and statesmen and millionaires.

"It's very precious," she wrote. "I had only two left. I was saving them to show to my grandchildren to prove to them that once I was pretty."

Thus wrote Marilyn, who never became Grandma Monroe.

As though revealing a vital secret, Marilyn explained with almost childlike naiveté how she managed to be only 15 minutes late.

"I decided it was either my hair or being on time for you and your wife," she told me. "I decided that Rosemary was more important than my hair being right."

She nodded with pride as she said it.

Marilyn Monroe, the American chest champion, met Gina Lollobrigida, the Italian chest champion, in New York on the night of the great Skirt Blowing, September 14, 1954, and I confess that, accidentally, my wife and I were responsible.

We had a dinner date that night with Gina and her husband, Dr. Milko Skofic.

"What are we going to do with Gina afterward?" I asked.

"Take her over to meet Marilyn," my wife said.

A capital idea! Marilyn and Tom Ewell were scheduled to shoot a scene for *The Seven-Year Itch* at the Trans-Lux Theater, at 52nd Street and Lexington Avenue, about the time darkness descended. It would be a night scene.

These two bosom champions, Marilyn and Gina, had never met. We first had to convince Gina that it would be good publicity for her to meet Marilyn, then the hottest film star in the world.

Marilyn, concerned about the scene awaiting her, and in no need of publicity, was not eager to participate in a stunt when she had a tremendous evening ahead anyway with just that Skirt Blowing.

Popular magazine photographer Sam Shaw (later a producer) saw Gina, her husband, and the Wilsons arriving and quickly outlined the idea to director Billy Wilder, who later said that working with Marilyn was equivalent to being kicked in the crotch.

"The picture will break around the world," Sam Shaw said.

Marilyn was icy about it. She had no real dressing room in this movie theater. She was using a ladies' room to get made up.

"Have Gina slip in the side door and wish Marilyn luck," Billy Wilder suggested.

"It is a little extreme asking a star to entertain a competitor on the night of her greatest scene," Wilder said sharply.

But Gina brightly carried out her part. She had told us at dinner that, coming to New York on a plane, she had rehearsed answers to six questions she anticipated from American reporters.

"Instead they all asked me one question, 'What do you think of Marilyn Monroe?' "

The cheesecake darlings of two continents met on the stairway going down to the ladies' room.

Sam Shaw leaped in with his camera and shot them bosom to bosom, facing each other, each looking a little tense.

"Get in the picture, Earl," Sam Shaw ordered. "You brought them together. What a foursome! I'm speaking of the ladies."

It seemed to me that each girl tried not to be obvious about eyeing the other's low-cut V-neck.

Bust pushed forward, for the camera, Gina made her speech about the American reporter's questions.

"You know I have been called the Gina Lollobrigida of American films," Marilyn said to Gina.

Gina smile, and Marilyn remembered to wish her good luck for the opening of her film, *Bread, Love and Dreams,* in a few days.

It was all done inside the theater, out of the view of the fans and many, many photographers already gathering for the Skirt Blowing.

Thawed out by then, Marilyn returned to the ladies' room makeup task, pausing to say, "She's beautiful!" With a cheery " 'Rivederci," Gina left with her husband, not staying to witness the film history later made on the sidewalk. Nobody invited her.

Our pictures of the two bosom buddies meeting did indeed go around the world, as Sam Shaw had predicted, and the wire services began calling me for the photographs just taken.

But as a camera nut myself, I became one of the almost 100 photographers who stayed there most of the night, shooting Marilyn with her skirts blowing up around her thighs and panties.

"Joe DiMaggio's out there in that crowd, scowling," a photographer told me.

"Walter Winchell's with him, and he looks sore," another said.

Surely they took more pictures than would ever be needed of Marilyn with her skirts up around her neck. They shot her from back, side, and front, probably the sexiest pose ever conceived up to that time.

The *New York Post* published four of my pictures of Marilyn with her skirts blowing and a credit line so dear to me, *"Post* Photo by Earl Wilson."

Toward morning Marilyn began sharing the enthusiasm of the photographers, all of whom were shooting roughly the same picture for scores of outlets.

Those skirt-blowing pictures you saw—they could have been

from the wire services, they could have been Sam Shaw's, some of them could even have been mine.

Somebody phoned in a false fire alarm.

"Marilyn Monroe's set the town on fire," a voice said.

Marilyn looked down at the subway grate in the sidewalk.

"I wonder who's down there doing that," she said on the night that will be remembered for the meeting of the movies' Big Four.

The last lingering comment about the photographing of the two beauties was that "it had to be done with a wide-angle lens, of course."

11

MARILYN MONROE
WINS A
PRESS CONFERENCE

The producers thought that bringing Marilyn Monroe back alive, to the Broadway stage, would be simple. Well, they found out.

They needed, first, a spunky, funny, witty, naughty, flirty sex baby who could turn on King Tut. They also needed a mature, articulate woman capable of handling herself better in a meet-the-press type of confrontation than some senators.

As you know, so many who have never met her have written books about her. Having done the first New York interview with her and been her newspaperman friend during her busiest years, I feel like I should put in a few words of truth.

I can still see Marilyn clashing with the sharpshooters of London's Fleet Street when the rough-riding British press sniped at her while she filmed *The Prince and the Showgirl* with Laurence Olivier. At first they tried to put her down as a dumb blonde. They found out, too.

As her friend, I managed to be in London in July 1956, when

she arrived with her new husband, playwright Arthur Miller.

For two weeks the snobbish, defensive English journalists tried to get under her creamy skin. She received the greatest press coverage accorded any visiting actress.

In her own seductive way Marilyn was adored as much as Danny Kaye was when he was Princess Margaret's favorite star.

Marilyn was Page One for days. "She thinks she's Eisenhower," one press man said.

It was a strange spectacle for Marilyn, accustomed to the informality of Hollywood, with slacks, sports shirts, and sweaters. There were some bowlers and umbrellas, and there would have been more had it not been July.

Unlike the rowdy American reporters, they came with quiet dignity, but as the pack seemed to grow to a hundred, they relaxed and covertly waved to each other. But it was all-English. You would have thought there must be a monocle somewhere. My word!

In an anteroom Marilyn was amazed that she was almost on time. Arthur Miller was comforting her. He was supposed to "warm up" the audience as is done on television shows. Marilyn's press agents, hairdresser, drama coach, and secretary scurried about, checking with her in the anteroom. Because it was a remarkable press conference, I kept records of it.

One Oxonian had just said he was going to get an interpreter to translate Marilyn's American into English when Marilyn stepped into the room and onto the little stage.

"Marilyn!" somebody up front shouted.

They roared a welcome. It seemed strong enough to knock her over. Everybody got to his or her feet, standing up to try to see the Queen of Hollywood. It was a stampede. It was called a standing ovation, and Marilyn looked out at the crowd, startled, and waited for a moment of quiet.

Demurely, softly, she said, "Thank you for coming."

Another roar, the scrambling of shoes, the scraping of chairs. Somebody was introducing Marilyn Monroe, quite needlessly.

I couldn't catch the first few minutes, but I saw Marilyn clearly, standing there realizing she had won them already. "Early on," as they have always said, a voice said, "Has anything inspired you to study acting more?"

"Yes," she said, with her little-girl breathiness, "seeing my pictures has inspired me to study more."

The vicious British press was tamed instantly by her soft answer. The reporters actually applauded her reply.

It was such a perfect question for the moment, I suspected it was planted by her press agents.

Off and running now, Marilyn began her performance. She was cooing and crooning her words, flirting, laughing, inviting more questions. She knew she had them.

In the back a female voice asked: "When you're an old lady, is there any part you'd like to look back on as having played?"

It was an ideal spot for a commercial about *The Prince and the Showgirl.*

Marilyn rose above the opportunity.

She giggled. "When I'm an old lady I'd like to look forward to the parts I'm going to play."

"Well done. Smart gel," a man with a bowler in his lap said to me.

Just ahead lay the Diana Dors problem.

Shapely, blonde Miss Dors, "the Marilyn Monroe of England," had been quoted that Marilyn Monroe hadn't made a good film.

"Has not the name of Diana Dors become a bit tedious for you?" a man with a pipe and a tweed jacket inquired.

Marilyn magnificently turned the other cheek.

"No, I've been looking forward to meeting her," Marilyn smiled brightly. "There's a place for everyone, and there's enough of the two of us for everybody."

There was another patter of hand clapping. Marilyn, laughing, blew a kiss to the room. But "the heavies" were still to be heard from. A man who was said to be from *Punch* had the floor.

"Can you give us your tastes in music?"

"I love Beethoven very much." She hesitated. "At the same time I'm very fond of Louis Armstrong and Benny Goodman— American jazz."

"What Beethoven numbers in particular, Miss Monroe?" asked the executioner from *Punch,* quietly.

There was hardly a man or woman in the room who didn't feel sorry for her, who didn't feel she was trapped.

"Well," she laughed guiltily, "I have a terrible time with numbers. But I know it when I hear it."

The crowd laughed with her. The man from *Punch* sat down uncomfortably.

Another serious inquisitor asked, "How would you define the American way of life?" to which she answered, "How would you define the English way of life?" Inasmuch as much had been made of Arthur Miller being an intellectual, somebody asked:

"What is your definition of an intellectual?"

"Well, I guess you could look that up," Marilyn grinned.

I especially appreciated that answer. It was the one Casey Stengel gave to heckling sportswriters when he managed the New York Yankees: "You could look it up." Could Joe DiMaggio have given her that, based on his days with the Yankees?

But the press conference invitees liked it, too, or the way Marilyn tossed it off. Again they were on their feet (another standing ovation?). With perfect timing, Marilyn waved and blew kisses. Laurence Olivier once said, "Nobody ever won an interview."

Marilyn Monroe had certainly won a press conference.

Seized by Arthur Miller and her entourage, she was hustled away, calling, "Thanks, everybody." Some of her interrogators remained, saying such things as "She didn't say anything, but wasn't she great saying it?"

I remember these press sessions—there were conferences in other cities, too—because after one of them Marilyn whispered to me, "Come up to the room."

Arthur stopped me. Not Arthur Miller. Press Agent Arthur Jacobs, who reminded me that Marilyn was there defending her Hollywood image. "If you're seen going up in an elevator with her, the British boys will think she's favoring the American journalists."

"OK," I said, "but it looks to me like Marilyn is favoring the British. Like that party Dame Edith Sitwell gave her at the Sesame and Pioneer Club, just for Marilyn. Dame Sitwell said she had T. S. Eliot and Henry Moore for lunch and nobody cared, but everybody, including the manager, was insanely eager to meet Marilyn Monroe, and she's really quite remarkable."

So not only did Marilyn Monroe win the press conference, but I believe she and Arthur Miller were the only Americans ever to have a poem about them appear on the front page of a London newspaper.

It wasn't precisely a poem:

> They are here, the happy couple,
> He looks shy, she just giggles,
> Feminine beyond compare,
> Even standing still, she WIGGLES!

Yes, I'll always remember that London went quite bonkers over Marilyn Monroe.

FIRST
INTERMISSION

Right here I think we should take a short break—a breather, a seventh-inning stretch, an intermission, as we have in the theater. If stage shows have rest periods, why not books?

I pass along a few awakeners that may become fat paragraphs someday. I don't know the authorship of all of these. Some might even be mine.

There'll be a couple more intermissions later.

Anyway, some of Earl's pearls:

"I wonder if a doctor, treating himself for a persistent illness, ever says, 'I wonder if I should change doctors.' "

"A reporter must have a good nose for booze."

"Thank you, Rudyard Kipling, for permitting me to fool around."

"A woman is only a woman, but a good cigar is about two bucks."

"A historical novel has a lovely girl on the jacket but no jacket on the lovely girl."

"As James Russell Lowell didn't quite say it in the 1840s: 'And what is so bare as a dame in June. . . .' "

"Nowadays many a girl works her way to the top from her bottom."

"There's one thing to be said for a diet. It certainly does improve your appetite."

"Advice: Never give advice. Get an agent and *sell* it!"

"I didn't mean to take such a long leave of absence, but I discovered I have an incurable disease. I'm lazy."

"I dedicate this book to the Internal Revenue Service to whom I will always owe a great deal."

"Only out-of-towners appreciate New York. The native, receiving the city as a gift at birth, remains forever a little spoiled." (From *Earl Wilson's New York*)

"Buddy Hackett had charisma as a boy, but it cleared up."

"Why was Elizabeth Taylor so disappointed when she didn't get a Tony? Why did she want a Tony? Because she'd never had a Tony. She'd had a Nicky, a Michael, a Mike, an Eddie, two Richards, and a John, but she'd never had a Tony."

"I've just been in Peking and found where the best Chinese food is. It's in New York City."

"Sweater Girl Lana Turner is shaped like a chiffonier with the top drawer pulled out."

"I call it my dinner jacket because it always seems to have some of my dinner on it."

Gossip columnist Lee Mortimer was slugged in the men's room of a nightclub. . . . "The list of suspects has been narrowed down to 10,000."

"Busty Pia Zadora got the Golden Globe Award for her movie *Butterfly*. The truth was, of course, that she got the Golden Globe for her golden globes."

Sexy Actress Marlene Willoughby visited Hollywood.
"That stuff they call smog," she said. "That's not smog. That's cocaine."

My B.W. (Beautiful Wife) read about the Pope's being criticized by the clergy for politicking. It was denied but, said she, "Where there's white smoke, there's fire."

RULES FOR WRITIN'

Here's how to escape stress
And still write for the press
Banish words like fornicate
You've become quite celibate
You swap that great word *copulate*
For something innocent, *osculate,*
And when they say, 'We know you kissed her'
You answer, blushing, 'Certainly, mister
That was no lady, that was my sister.'

"I never give autographs. I just sign my name. It's quicker."

"Some people can't find things on their desk. I can't find my desk."

"A sexy Hollywood beauty said, 'I owe my success to being in the right place at the right time.'
'Right,' said another lady star. 'In the producer's bedroom when he is there.' "

"Celeste Holm is busier than Liberace's evening clothes."

"There must be a better way of starting each day than getting out of bed."

"Critic John Simon panned a Broadway show by saying the costume designer was asleep at the swatch."

INTERRUPTED PHONE CALL

"Better Business Bureau? Would you send us some better business?"

The B.W. said:
  "My husband is Taurus and he has the bull to prove it."

"Dean Martin goes in for antiques: Old Crow, Old Overholt, and Old Granddad.

"Phil Foster claims that before Shecky Greene reformed he was arrested for drunken driving. A guard said he was allowed one phone call. He phoned a liquor store."

Fashion note from Moe Popkin, the Oscar Wilde of Scranton, Pennsylvania: "Jeans are just a passing fanny."

"Show Business is that wonderful profession where one day you're a nobody and the next day you're waiting on tables."

"The coldest winter I ever spent was a summer in San Francisco. . . ."(Mark Twain)

PRESIDENT REAGAN often played straight for comedian Joey Adams:
  Reagan: "You're a comedian. Tell me a joke."
  Joey: "You're a politician. Tell me a lie."

When a horseburger stand opened next door, New York State Off-Track Betting put up a sign, "If you can't beat 'em, eat 'em."

"When I lay me down to sleep
  I can't because the rent's too steep." (Dr. George Kovacs)

Gifted public lecturer Goodman Ace, the critic and former comedian, didn't believe in free speech.
  "I believe they should be paid."

"Dear Social Security: 'Please send me my Old Age Pension now and I'll go to work when I'm 65.' " (Nipsey Russell)

"My wallet's full of big bills. I wish some of them were paid." (Woody Allen)

"Humorist: A comedy writer out of work." (Coleman Jacoby)

12
HOW TO
CRASH GATES

The king of the gate crashers, Morris Lieberman, is tall and broad-shouldered and looks authentic in a black tie. Seeing him crash a dinner, you would swear he looked like the chairman of the event. He recently thanked me for the good time he said he had crashing the gate at the Friars banquet for Elizabeth Taylor.

"Why thank me?" I asked. Sensing something, I said, "Where did you sit?"

"In your seat," laughed the 72-year-old retired Queens furniture salesman who's attended hundreds of New York charity dinners without invitations. He's been pursuing celebrities since July 4, 1928, when he went to Tammany Hall to hear Governor Alfred E. Smith accept the nomination for President.

"Do you mean that when I didn't go, you stole my ticket or place?" I asked Lieberman.

"No, no," he answered with a booming voice. "I got in the same way I've been getting in for 50 years. When I get in I get a seating list. It may say, 'Earl Wilson and Guest.' Maybe you didn't come. So I go to the table and say, 'Is Earl Wilson here?

I expected to meet him here.' I sit in your seat. The waiter says, 'You're Earl Wilson's guest and you're in his seat, so you might as well have his dinner.' He brings me your dinner and also champagne, and we have a good time."

"How was my dinner the night of Elizabeth's party?" I asked.

"Very good. It was Elizabeth's table. Of course she was on the dais.

"I don't go there to eat, though. That could get you in trouble. The waiter may ask for your dinner ticket."

Morris, having convinced the VIPs that he is one of them, maneuvers himself into one of the photographs. He sent me one showing him with Charlie Chaplin when Chaplin was honored in New York. When somebody asks, "Who is that guy in the picture with the President?" it may well be Morris Lieberman.

"You have helped me sometimes," he said, "by letting me walk in with you. I act like I belong there. Sometimes you might have an extra ticket, which you pass to me. Once you passed me a ticket to a Kim Novak picture.

"Do you remember the Marilyn Monroe opening of *The Prince and the Showgirl?*" he asked. I didn't. "She was with Arthur Miller and was very late and we all went in together. Marilyn was in pink—pink dress, pink hair, pink shoes. Even her skin was pink. She said to Arthur Miller, 'How do I look, Pappy?' "

The king has a secret. The Waldorf Grand Ballroom is on the third floor. "I take an elevator to the fourth floor," he says. "There's a back stairway down to the kitchen. I go through the kitchen into the ballroom and avoid all that security looking for us on the second and third floor. So there I am, in without having met any security."

But fate is funny.

He lost his wallet the night of the Elizabeth Taylor dinner.

Thinking it over, remembering all the events he had crashed—"seven Presidents, maybe eight," he thinks; the famous people he has joined and never been thrown out, so he says; he considers he has a special talent and should write his autobiography—this was the first time that he ever lost his wallet.

Did he lose it or was he hustled—was he pickpocketed? Could

the king of the crashers have been robbed by the king of the dips?

"Anyway, I had to borrow from one of the security men to get home." It didn't seem the right ending for a story about the gate crashers' gate crasher.

Morris Lieberman was right about the premiere, June 1957, when Marilyn was so late and so pink. Arthur Miller was thrilled; he kissed Marilyn on the dance floor at a champagne party afterward. Bernard Baruch was there with his ear trumpet turned up. Marilyn had several people helping her through the mob. Comedian Jack Carter looked at her leaning forward and bending over and remarked, "That's a wonderful pair of girl."

But there's more to Morris's story. He will send you a bale of material about himself, including a magazine article calling him the "Great Pretender." He is undeterrable. He says he is the No. 1 gate crasher in the *Guinness Book of World Records* and encloses a copy of a letter from Guinness saying Guinness doesn't record that "category" because there hasn't been "sufficient interest."

Newspapers have found that Morris had an advantage over other crashers. He was for a time acting as a publicist for the Waldorf and also in the catering department, helping in the dining room if needed.

"What I really enjoy," he confesses, "is getting in the pictures."

On the walls of the Palm Beach house are pictures of Morris kissing Barbra Streisand on the mouth, of Morris with his arms around Judy Garland, of Morris seated on a speakers' platform with the Richard Nixons and Nelson Rockefeller, of Morris at the John F. Kennedy inaugural (an autographed picture), of Morris with Bobby Kennedy, Jackie Onassis, Loretta Young, Shelley Winters, Liza Minnelli, of Morris with Mae West, seeming to be escorting her to the opening of *Myra Breckinridge*.

Mae West may have wondered, just as the other celebrities did, who was the big fellow rushing out to greet her, with arms and mouth open? She had no idea. Morris's technique is to persuade them he knows them and they know him. He exclaims, "We meet again!" They can hardly reject that salutation.

Fearless Morris says that once, when Aly Khan was dancing with Princess Margaret, he cut in.

He conversed with the Duke of Windsor, telling him they were married "the exact same day"—not quite true by a couple of weeks.

He chatted down to earth with Harry Truman, about both having a grandson named Clifford. He apprised King Simeon of Bulgaria that he had an autographed picture of his father King Boris taken with Morris and says he sent him a copy.

Mrs. Lieberman (his wife Fay) doesn't go on these crashings and has said that he doesn't belong there. Morris thinks he definitely does. He has a thousand pictures demonstrating that he is one of them, that he belongs.

The last time I talked to the Great Crasher he said, "I'll see you."

"Oh?" I said.

"At your dinner." He was confident that he would be coming in the usual way.

13

"DON'T PRINT THAT!"

It is a famous story among the gossip writers of the world, who are unusual people to begin with.

The Moslem prince Aly Khan had wooed and won the sexy American film beauty, Rita Hayworth, in a spectacular international courtship that gladdened the hearts of some newspaper readers (and bored hell out of others).

Now the communist mayor of the village of Vallauris on the French Riviera had agreed to marry them. What a pretty ending for the love story. The mob was gathering.

A French scandal paper intruded rudely. It published a headlined story that Rita Hayworth was expecting a baby.

Aly Khan was righteously outraged. Had there ever been anything so boorish? The author of the shocking article, a flip, witty, irreverent French journalist, followed through by arriving brazenly to cover the wedding.

The irate prince naturally learned he was there.

Confronting the journalist personally (so the legend goes),

Aly Khan stormed at the fellow, "Are you the reporter who published that my fiancé is pregnant and we are not married yet?"

The French reporter did not shrink. Yes, he was, he nodded.

"Don't you realize," shouted the prince, in a very fine fury, as good a fury as he had ever had, "what a monstrous thing you have done to me?" He drew a long breath to start over. "And what you have done to my father, the Aga Khan, the head of millions of Moslems. As I myself will one day be the head of millions of Moslems. Do you understand what you have done to me?"

"But, sir," replied the journalist quietly, "I have done nothing to you."

"Done nothing to me, to *me?*" thundered the prince. "I, who someday will be the head of millions of Moslems!"

"I never said you were the father," softly said the scandalmonger.

The tales of Aly Khan's lovemaking—how he and a dinner companion might disappear for a stroll in the garden between courses—were many and colorful, but the prince was not as warm and cordial as Humphrey Bogart, who was always a more fascinating interviewee.

That was because Prince Aly Khan was not a drinking man.

Bogart, who gave me several stories, including the exclusive news that he was going to marry Lauren Bacall, usually greeted me with the attitude "Who are we going to louse up today?"

Once Bogie confided to me that something must be wrong with Mayo Methot's pitching arm (Mayo was his wife at the time) because she had been missing him with the martini glasses she threw at him.

I tried to help him with interviews by getting around to certain interesting questions. Sitting in the 21 Club one afternoon, we got to the subject of the 3 Bs (Boose, Busts, and Behinds). I mentioned that Lana Turner, who had been in the news lately, was very callypygian.

"Callypygian?" He rolled it around.

"It means having a beautiful behind," I said.

"You're lying!" he said.

"I'll bet you," I said. We argued about the spelling. I decided it was *Callipygian*.

"I'm going to call *The New York Times*," Bogie said, ordering another drink. He called for a phone, he called *The Times* library, told them it was Humphrey Bogart and he had a problem. He wished to know the meaning of *callipygian*. *The New York Times* person in charge of people like Humphrey Bogart trotted off to a dictionary and returned.

"What does it mean?" Bogie said into the phone. "I'm a son of a bitch! 'Having well-shaped buttocks.' Lana Turner has a pretty ass. How did you know that, you bastard?"

"I looked it up yesterday," I confessed.

14

LEO
THE LIP
AND GARBO

It was back when Leo Durocher was managing the New York Giants, sassing umpires, operating on the interesting theory that nice guys finish last, and never shutting his mouth. Leo the lip talked to everybody—himself if he couldn't find anybody else to listen.

Leo boarded a plane from L.A. to New York and discovered he was sitting beside Greta Garbo, who not only talks to nobody but "vants to be alone."

Garbo—she was probably using her Harriet Brown phony name and the airline didn't know it had placed the Silent One beside Big Mouth.

And so, because Leo's got to talk, got to say something, he opened up and told me about it the next time I saw him in a popular saloon.

"I went to my usual seat next to the exit," Leo grinned. "You know me, I play the percentages even picking a seat.

"I don't think I ever met the dame before, but she's so nervous her hand is shaking on the arm of the seat.

"Finally I said to her, 'What the hell is it with that shaking?'

" 'What the hell is it you are doing with that rapping on the arm?' I said. 'You're making *me* nervous!'

"The dame don't talk, you know, she don't speak up; it turned out later, so they told me, this was her first trip. Hell, if they'd told me that, maybe I could have comforted her. Instead I said, 'What are you worried about? It goes up and comes down either safe or in a heap, so why worry?'

"I guess she never had any bum talk like that to her. She gets calm. Then they bring the food. I'm a steak guy. A meat and potatoes guy. I eat mine real fast, then I notice the salad.

"I said to her, 'What is it with you and Gaylord Hauser, Howser, Hoosier, whatever it is, and the salads?' I got an expression, 'Salads make your bones soft.' She talked a little and quit shaking. Next thing I know we were in Newark, and it's jet dark, and they got two cabs for about 50 passengers.

"A guy comes up to me and says, 'Leo, you want me to save you a cab?' So I give him a sawbuck, and he saves me a cab.

"Greta gets in and also another lady we can drop off, and Greta says, 'How do you do these things?' She didn't see me give the guy a saw.

"I said, 'You gotta be alive or you'll finish in the second division.'

"I took her to her house and I said, 'How was it, honey' It wasn't so bad, was it? Just remember what I said: You either come down safe or all in a heap and it don't matter; if you worry about it, there's nothing you can do about it.' She didn't hardly say anything but 'Thanks.'

"I called Laraine"—his wife, Laraine Day—"and told her about the trip, and she says she likes her. Usually I sleep on a plane, but this time I stayed awake and talked. She's a wonderful woman and don't talk back to you like some ballplayers. Hell, I wish she could play second base."

15

KIM NOVAK'S SECRET CHEESECAKE

Cheesecake. What was *cheesecake?*

Cheesecake was defined in two dictionaries as slang meaning "a photograph of a pretty girl scantily clothed" and a "picture displaying a woman's shapely body" when I set out for Hollywood in 1954 to interview a "very hot new actress" who fairly smoked with sex appeal, curvy Kim Novak.

"Be sure to get cheesecake," a photographer friend advised me, lending me a Roloflex. He failed to warn me that Harry Cohn, the fiercely tyrannical president of Columbia Pictures, had sternly forbidden Kim to permit photographs of her body "scantily clothed."

I got the message soon enough when the blonde, bubbly, and sensationally scenic beauty, very leggy and with a chest seldom equaled in this age, arrived at the hotel with a woman press agent whose opening admonition was "Remember the rules! No cheesecake."

"Why not?" I asked.

"Harry Cohn would beat you to death. He wants to keep his little Kim dignified."

Kim, only 21 then, who had been discovered when she visited Hollywood with a refrigeration show, smiled bashfully and tossed back her silver-blonde hair. Already she was being courted by rich wooers.

Harry Cohn regarded her as a bombshell he was not yet ready to detonate.

I was happy that my wife was with me. She followed through on her announcement, when I became a columnist, that she would be "not the girl he goes home to but the girl he goes home with."

Welcoming Kim to the hotel, the tennis court, and the swimming pool, she watched as I took several innocent pictures and chatted with Kim while I talked to the publicist.

Curvaceous Kim seemed compliant, obedient, well disciplined, but she was independent and a rebel with a cause—and the cause was Kim Novak.

"I could come back tomorrow—when *she* [the woman press agent] won't be here, and we could get some more interesting pictures," she volunteered to my wife.

Kim was ready for cheesecake, and so was I, and the devil with Harry Cohn who wanted to keep Kim covered up.

On a warm Sabbath noontime we commenced our secret conspiratorial safari for Cheesecake à la Kim. She came in slacks and an off-both-shoulders shirt, which she lowered as a starter.

Quickly we moved our operation to the bathroom, ever the principal bastion of cheesecake. I remembered Paulette Goddard telling me a decade before that her directors were always attempting to film her taking a bath.

There are so many things a girl can do when she is sitting in a bathtub posing for pictures, especially if there is no water in the bathtub.

She can sit there pretending to be entirely naked, of course, scrubbing her chest, washing her ears, drying the back of her neck, and especially always leaning forward, with her bosom not quite but almost on the rim of the tub.

And then she must get out of the tub, and that involves pulling around her a towel that isn't half big enough. If the girl is Kim Novak, with her measurements, the towel is very, very inadequate.

All this we did very clandestinely with a feeling of naughty children, making jokes about our secret cheesecake. And what would Harry Cohn think of *this* pose?

Finally Kim Novak, who has posed getting out of a towel about as many ways as one can get out of a towel, said, "I wish I had something more to wear than a towel."

"I could lend you my white fox fur," my wife said, bringing one out of a suitcase.

I've noticed that girls like furs even if they have nothing to wear with them. Kim got into my wife's fur—with nothing else—and we returned to the bathroom to see if we could improve on our earlier adventure there with just a towel.

I noticed my wife getting nervous.

She was wishing she hadn't been so generous with her fur. Kim would be perspiring in it. She was wishing she could switch her to a cloth coat.

Kim's boyfriend of the moment, a theater owner, Mack Krim, came to collect her, and together we totaled up the crime. Kim had said breathlessly, "Oh, thank you."

We had some sexy pictures, not nude, but thought of as seminude in those days, and while they weren't pornographic, they probably showed areas of Kim not shown before. What would we do with them?

Sell them, of course.

But Kim must be protected. If Harry Cohn got into one of his famous tempers, she must say the mean old photographer called Sunday and asked to shoot everything over. His camera wasn't working.

The pictures turned out to be sexational. Harry Cohn exploded and barred the photographer from the Columbia lot. When he found out that the photographer was also Earl Wilson, the columnist, who was in good standing with his press department, he decided the columnist was also barred. His fury increased.

Harry Cohn had so many battles that he tabled ours. Kim, ecstatic, sent us Christmas cookies and signed the note "Kimmie." No doubt about it now. With her secret cheesecake, Kim was a Sex Symbol, a bombshell ready to be detonated.

And so I watched pridefully as Kimmie, forgiven by Cohn,

was steered into stardom. With *Picnic* and *The Man with the Golden Arm*, she became a dramatic actress.

Her fame spread overseas. Invited to the Cannes Film Festival, she house-guested with Aly Khan at his chateau. She danced with Cary Grant, who reportedly nibbled her ear.

One day I got a "Dear Earl" letter.

"Don't you think you should take those horrid pictures of me off the market?"

I was crushed. Those pictures were like our love child. And now she disowned them. They weren't even hers. Just mine.

"Once you loved them," I reminded her.

"We're both older now," she said.

Cary Grant could nibble her ear, but I could eat my negatives. Somehow the years dragged by without Kim.

The Sexy '60s came along.

Brigitte Bardot's best friend was her towel. Marilyn Monroe permitted nude shots, which she posed for in a picture she never finished. Shirley MacLaine was nude in *Irma La Douce* but told me she insisted the negatives of the still photos be destroyed.

It got to be eight or nine years later.

On St. Patrick's night, 1963, my wife and I were on the dais in Dublin at a dinner beautified by Kim Novak, who was going to play Mildred, the Cockney waitress with loose morals, in the W. Somerset Maugham film *Of Human Bondage*.

Kim was going to play a couple of scenes in the nude.

Henry Hathaway, the director, explained that he had been showing the script to Kim and came to a part where they would use a "body double" for Kim in a love scene with Laurence Harvey.

"What's a body double?" demanded Kim.

Kim wouldn't want to go nude, so they'd hire a professional "body double."

"Who needs a body double?" our Kimmie exclaimed. "Who's got a better body than I have? I have a better body than you can find anywhere else!"

And so Henry Hathaway, who may have anticipated just such a reaction, bowed to the lady.

Sitting there beside me on the dais, talking to me for the first time since our coolness, Kim confirmed it all.

"I am not going to let there be anything between my audience and me," she said. "Nothing! I'm going to give them all of me."

Was this the girl who had disowned our little cheesecake pictures because they were tasteless and horrid? I managed to say, "You've changed your mind about nudity, haven't you?"

"I certainly have," she said. And with a laugh that was almost apologetic, she said, "Oh, Earl, why don't you start selling those cheesecake pictures of me again?"

It was my cue to be generous and forgiving. And I was. I didn't say what I wanted to say: "No, we're both older now, Kim, and the trend has gone toward nudity, and your cheesecake pictures don't show enough of Kim for today's market."

"I'll get to work on it," I said.

But our pictures were too virtuous for the day. Kim kept her promise. In April 1963 the director chased almost everybody from the *Of Human Bondage* set, and Kim and Laurence Harvey posed for the nude scenes, Kim unclothed from the waist up, clutching some bedclothes that "partly" covered her back and "partly" didn't cover it.

Kim's willingness to share herself with her audience wasn't very rewarding. Critic Archer Winsten said she gave Maugham's classic "a big try" but the way she kept her lover Harvey under her wicked spell wasn't convincing. The critics neglected to mention Kim's nudity.

However, Laurence Harvey gallantly noted that angle.

"I'm glad I became an actor," he was quoted after the bare scenes were shot. "It was worth waiting for."

The picture did receive one special attention. The Italian state prosecutor banned an Italian magazine for publishing five centerfold pictures of Kim clutching the bedclothes that partly covered her and partly didn't.

Now, 20 years after her famous figure evoked all that excitement, Kim laughs and says, "I did, too, have something on—a sheet."

She has kept her shape shapely and has never let her curves get out of control like some celebrated beauties. She teaches an exercise class at Carmel, California, where she has a ranch and lives happily with her husband, Dr. Robert Malloy, a leading animal authority and veterinarian. They honeymooned on horseback. They go several months a year to their place in northern Oregon where they're far from telephones and agents.

"Kim goes to bed at nine and gets up at five," a friend said.

"Make that 6," Kim said.

Seeing reruns of Kim in *Vertigo, The Eddy Duchin Story,* and other films, producers try to cast her in pictures or TV, but the vivacious blonde ("a natural blonde," she says) doubts there'd be the excitement there was when her sensational figure was first unveiled.

SECOND INTERMISSION

Things people said:

"Premature Baby: One born before its parents get married."

Groucho Marx turned down an invitation in this classic manner: "I have a previous engagement, which I am going to make immediately."

Honest Admission: "I married my boss. Of course she was nice enough not to tell me until after the ceremony."

"Zsa Zsa Gabor," said Oscar Levant once, "has discovered the secret of perpetual middle age."
    Levant also said, "I knew Doris Day before she became a virgin."

Jack Benny's radio and TV programs emphasized his alleged thriftiness, which was not true. Dennis Day, the singer, said on the program, "Jack Benny has found a new use for old razor blades. He shaves with them."

"A columnist," said Morton Thompson, "is a newspaperman who got a break that turned out to be a fracture."

Just joking, Dolly Parton said, "I get tired of carrying these things around. Someday I'm going to let the air out."

George Gobel asked Garry Moore if they were having a drink before doing Garry's TV show. Garry replied that he never drank before the show. "You mean," said Gobel, amazed, "you go out there all *alone?*"

"Elizabeth Taylor ran out of men. She started marrying men she'd already married." (Seaman Jacobs).

Joey Adams told of an actor's club "where the average age is deceased."

Johnny Carson: "I'm a great admirer of Don Rickles. I can't wait to hear his joke."

President Gerald Ford took frequent falls, and one journalist said his favorite song is "Stumbling." His defenders, however, denied he was slipping, and one said, "He can get in to see Secretary Kissinger any time he wants to."

Satirist Mark Russell: "I heard from my bank. They want their toaster back."

"Jackie Onassis is making Aristotle Onassis a millionaire. Before they got married, he was a billionaire."

Al Pacino's Broadway show about Vietnam was called by one critic "a casketful of laughs."

Beatlemania had a loud audience at the Winter Garden, and a narrator warned the audience not to smoke: "You understand what kind of smoking I mean." (1977)

A Broadway producer said, "There's no business gives you the business like Show Business."

President Jimmy Carter's banker friend, Bert Lance, was criticized for using the same collateral over and over to get money. Bob Hope said, "I know a prominent lady who has been using the same collateral over and over for years to get money."

Silly Simile in 1980: "Busier than Nancy Reagan's decorator."

"It helps to be a success in Hollywood if you've been indicted." (Broadway Producer Harry Rigby)

Misprint in the Travel Notes:
    "The Duke and Duchess of Windsor left Jamaica and returned to Nausea."

"All the money I earn from this show will go to a needy family of which I am the head." (George S. Kaufman)

"The only woman who ever looked good in a veil was Salome."

"What contemptible scoundrel stole the cork from my lunch?" (W. C. Fields)

"I took a look at Jane Russell, Howard Hughes's sweater girl, making her singing debut at the Paramount. I'll say this for her. I couldn't take my eyes off her voice." (Earl Wilson)

"America would be a wonderful place except for the Americans." (Gina Lollobrigida's son attending college in the United States)

"It's hard enough to write a column every day without being expected to get things right." (Jack Martin)

"Jaws: Howard Cosell's autobiography?"

Gadabout girl, talented actress Sylvia Miles, inspired the observation, "She'd go to the opening of an envelope."

"They're against Ronald Reagan because he's an actor. He's not an actor, and has 40 pictures to prove it."

A comedian at the Playboy Club, Jackie Gayle, was overhead saying, "I was just talking to the guy who parks our cars, and I said, 'Spiro, . . .' "

"Streakers" were flashing their private places in public places, and Angie Papadakis reported a California preacher carried a sign, "Streakers, repent. Your end is in sight." (1974)

"You can be on the cover of *Time* one year and be doing it the next." (Marty Allen)

"Any country with a population of 300 million that says its favorite sport is Ping-Pong will lie about other things, too." (Marty Ingels, 1971)

Pregnant teenagers were newsy. One pregnant teen told her parents it happened when they were at the movies.
   "Where were you when we were at the movies?" they asked.
   "Oh, I was home. I wasn't allowed to go. The picture was only for adults."
   Another teenager said she didn't know who the father was. "And it's your fault I don't know."
   "Our fault!"
   "Yes. You wouldn't let me go steady."

"Journalism is the most underpaid and oversexed profession in the world." (Liz Carpenter)

"Jimmy Carter is doing the work of two men—Laurel and Hardy." (Milton Berle)

Teenage language of love: "What happened to your old lady?"
   "Oh, we weren't cuttin' it and she split."

The Inflation Song: "I Wonder What's Become of Salary."

Martha Mitchell told black pianist Dorothy Donegan, "When I was little, I had a black mammy."

Dorothy replied, "So did I."

He's a good-looking star with broad shoulders and a fine head of hair, and he's perpetually falling in love with a leading lady and leaving his wife of many years—but he always returns to her after tiring of the new one. In Sardi's his wife's friends say, "He keeps coming back like an unclaimed letter."

Before Liberation: "To get a husband a girl must play tennis, bridge, and dumb."

"You're getting on in years," said columnist Jim Murray, "when a little old lady helps you across the street and the little old lady is your wife."

Dear Louella Parsons, Queen of the Hollywood columnists, was also filmland's most prolific writer. The saying among the studio publicists was "she can spell anything but words."

"A practical nurse is one who checks into surgery and checks out with the surgeon."

"Of all the remedies that absolutely will not cure a cold, whiskey is the most popular."

Some of Today's Music: "A fate worse than deaf." (Leonard Levenson)

Rodney Dangerfield suspected his marriage was in trouble the first day: "Her parents sent me a thank-you note."

"What is the only time a woman wishes she's a year older?"
  "When she's pregnant."

"You're as popular," two Lambs Club members kidded comic Jack Waldron, "as a wet dog in an elevator."

Joe E. Lewis, who often drank to excess, went around town with Bob Considine, who introduced him as "my blind date."

His son, a sociology student, said he wanted to clean up the mess in the world, so Van Harris, the comedian, said, "OK, let's start with the mess in your room."

A man who wishes to remain anonymous broke his hearing aid, and said, "For a couple of days it was almost as nice as being single."

16

HOW TO HANDLE SCANDAL

Once in my news-digging chores I ran across some scandal about Rosalind Russell.

Well, it wasn't very serious scandal. She was queen of the screen then and the stage too. When any major role came up for casting, Rosalind Russell could have it and was mentioned for it, unless it was a masculine part, and they could have adjusted that for her, too, although that was before Dustin Hoffman and *Tootsie.*

Roz was such an angel, so perfect, that this scandal didn't have to be serious. I might as well tell you what it was. But remember, it was only a rumor. The story was that Roz Russell had misled the world about her age—by as much as a couple of years.

Nobody had cared much about her age 'til she got to being offered every major role, and now some people cared and were circulating this rumor. But how could she fake her age? Didn't the sisters—the nuns—at the school she attended vouch for the authenticity of the age she gave?

That was just it! They did, and that was where the villainy was. The nuns who were still around, who taught when she was there as a student, were just so much in love with Roz, and so ecstatic and so much under the influence, that they believed every word she said, and if she said she was younger than their records showed, and the records must be in error, they would nod and laugh and giggle that she was right, and they would even change the records.

That's the way the story was passed on to me, and as much as I like Roz Russell, I was inclined to think it was a story for my column, but it would take a lot of investigating, and if it proved true and I printed it, I was going to make a lot of people angry and hurt some people, especially Roz Russell.

My wife and I talked it over at dinner one night at the famous Colony Restaurant, discussing whether I should look into the story and begin the investigation.

"That brings up another thing," I said. I had heard another story that maybe I should look into. There was a vice ring exposé involving a boy of good family, Mickey Jelke, making headlines daily, and now I had a tip about one of Mickey's highly respected antecedents having been in trouble years before. Should I begin investigating that also?

My wife suddenly said, "Do you think the public cares whether Rosalind Russell fibbed about her age?"

"*If* she did."

"Yes, *if* she did! Does the public care? Do they want to pin her down and get her true age?" my wife asked me.

"I don't know," I said. "Let's ask them."

So, in my column I put the question to my readers. Without using the names, I wrote about the two stories and inquired whether they wished to know. The mail response was such a resounding "No" that I forever remembered it and let it be a guide for me in deciding whether to work on certain scandal stories. In later years I talked this over with Roz Russell's widower, Fred Brisson, and was convinced the story wasn't true. But as my wife asked, "Anyway, did it matter? Did it really matter? Did anybody care?"

YOU CAN APOLOGIZE

Barbara Stanwyck was one of the hottest glamour ladies in the world and was accompanying her husband, Robert Taylor, on a tour, and I wanted to interview her. My appointment to interview Taylor at the Pierre Hotel was for about 3:00 P.M., and after about 15 minutes of talking to him, I grew restless and asked him right out, "Where's Miss Stanwyck?"

"I think she's taking a shower," he said.

He was not only handsome. He was judged one of the 10 best-looking men in the world. Tall, well built, black hair up in a widow's peak. His real name was Arlington Brugh, from Nebraska.

My appointment to see him was really a subterfuge. I would tolerate him, but it was Barbara Stanwyck I wanted to see, and I kept asking when she would be out, and Bob Taylor kept saying she was taking a shower.

Miss Stanwyck showered for about an hour and a half, and I tried to conceal my disgust, but the dismal truth was that my trick to get an interview with Barbara had backfired and I was now the trickee, with an hour and a half conversation with Bob Taylor, mostly me asking when she would be out of the shower.

I was younger and meaner and fresher then, and I wrote a column that was really nasty, alluding to how I'd got a runaround because Miss Stanwyck had been taking a shower—"she probably needed one" and that sort of thing—and it was printed the next day, and some people were amazed at my vindictiveness.

That night I went into the Stork Club and I saw Barbara Stanwyck—fully dressed, not in the shower—with her husband who was in a Navy or Coast Guard uniform—and I figured they were going to be smarting from the dressing down I gave them.

But they weren't. They were laughing. At my stupidity, I guess.

"We had an understanding," Barbara Stanwyck explained, sitting me down at her table, "that this tour was for Robert's service movie, *Tars and Spars,* and I was going to stay out of every interview—I wasn't even going to appear. And you were the first victim."

"The shower idea was not the best one we could have selected," she admitted.

I was so ashamed of my conduct. What could I do? I was just starting. Should I apologize? But columnists aren't supposed to apologize. They're supposed to refuse to run corrections, somebody had told me.

Next day I wrote a sincere column of apology as long as the first piece. The enthusiastic response in the mail, applauding the apology, taught me that you can apologize. The apology was much better than the blast. Some days I thought I should run more apologies.

17

ACTRESS
KEEPS
SECRET

You hope every interview will produce something, but I didn't expect much from Lilli Palmer, beautiful actress, Friday, January 23, 1953, in her dressing room at *The Love of Four Colonels*. 'Til lovely Lilli, one-time wife of Sexy Rexy Harrison, twittered, "Wonderful about them finding a new polio vaccine!"

"What?!" (Helen Hayes's daughter, Mary MacArthur, had died of it. The whole country was terrified of it.) "Who told you?"

"Anita," Lilli murmured. Anita Loos, the *Gentlemen Prefer Blondes* playwright. "Big secret. I'm not to tell anybody. They're going to announce it Monday. I have to go."

I didn't have one fact. Just an actress's rumor. But what a rumor. Why the big secret? Why Monday?

I tried my March of Dimes contacts who were fighting polio. Nothing. I called professors from hell to Harvard. I kept all my little notes.

Finally a professor in New England admitted sleepily that a "Dr. Salk" reported a "possible vaccine" at a secret meeting in

Hershey, Pennsylvania, and it seemed to be a "dramatic advance," but to announce it now would be "premature."

"The more premature, the better we like it," I thought.

I phoned Pittsburgh, Dr. Salk's headquarters. I just missed him. He had boarded an overnight train to New York. That was it. They were going to announce it at the Franklin D. Roosevelt birthday and March of Dimes dinner.

"Can we go with it?" the executive editor, Paul Sann, asked.

Our Monday first edition *New York Post* screamed, "NEW POLIO VACCINE, Exclusive by Earl Wilson."

I was so deep in my sea of notes I misread them and gave credit to "Dr. James Salk" instead of "Dr. Jonas Salk."

Oh, my, but the medical writers were mad at me for turning in the story when I got it instead of waiting 'til Tuesday, the day after the dinner. I learned later that Lilli Palmer got it from Anita Loos, and Anita heard it from her dear friend Helen Hayes. If she'd only told me that, I wouldn't have worried. She would have known.

It became the biggest story I ever wrote. And the last time I saw Lilli Palmer, now a big novelist as well as an actress, I thanked her again. She hardly remembered it.

"But I proved that girls can keep secrets," she said with a smile. "I kept one. I didn't tell anybody but a newspaperman."

18

GWEATER
THAN DEITWICH

Funny as she has been for almost a quarter of a century now in *Hello, Dolly,* the talented Carol Channing has been even gweater doing her impressions of the Blue Angel, Marlene Deitwich. When Carol, who has pretty legs, too, gets them caught in the legs of a chair she is sitting on, you suddenly hear Grandma Deitwich growling and spitting, "Gott in Himmel!" and we're back in Germany seeing the spoof of spoofs. When you total up the ticket sales, though, you may ask who was spoofing whom, because over the years Miss Deitwich has done pwetty good.

There's leggy Carol up to her thighs in silk stockings, feeling very hurt as she impersonates Marlene, asking, "Vouldn't you teenk dere'd be more opplowse for Marlene Deitwich? and just then her foot—that is to say, her beautiful foot at the end of one of her beautiful legs—is going to bring this whole contraption and Miss Deitwich, too, down on her beautiful behind.

Carol would have us believe that Marlene said, "Of course I dwon't objwect, darling," and that Lucille Ball said, "How can you do that to Marlene?'' and then did it to Marlene herself—an entire evening, on TV.

It's the fashion to rap Marlene, the only actress I know who has succeeded in getting younger every year, but we have to admit that she is the original—the one who answers the phone and says, "Miss Deitwich is not in. Her maid is speaking. Vot iss it you vanted?"

What beauty she had—in the legs, anyway—she broke so many hearts. A director of radio shows confessed to me once that he had made conquests of so many stars and he expected the same cooperation from Marlene the night after she emoted on his show.

When he had washed and cologned himself at the studio he proceeded to her apartment, where he hoped to spend the night.

Her man, or butler, or servant, or whatever took his coat and asked if he'd care for a drink while waiting. The director sat back, thinking how comfortable all this was going to be. Miss Deitwich emerged in something comfortable and had a drink, too, from the manservant.

Perhaps a half hour later Marlene thought to say that the man doing the "butling" was Rudolf Seiber, her longtime husband, which sent all the director's hopes crashing.

Marlene created much of the Marlene legend herself.

She was 65—did somebody say 68?—before she played Broadway, and it was a triumphant riot. I know. I was at her table when she got under it.

Producer Alexander Cohen told me that Marlene made sure that there would be flowers thrown on the stage at her feet at the end of the show by bringing the flowers there herself. They were kept in readiness at a location backstage. The ushers were trained and rehearsed so they knew exactly where they were to throw the flowers so Grandma would not slip and hurt her leg (as she actually did one night).

After escaping her dressing room with her life on opening night, Marlene somehow got on top of a car—on the roof—and, as police assisted, she perched there with legs crossed, throwing out pre-autographed pictures of Marlene.

I was one of the few hundred waiting at the Rainbow Room for Marlene to arrive for a black-tie party.

When Marlene and her mob finally arrived she pretended to be terrified of the cameramen and jumped under the table and rolled herself into a ball and only made it a more interesting photograph. Eventually she got out of the cocoon and sat down at our table, somewhere near me.

There was a man at the table whom nobody seemed to know. Except me. I had met him before in my line of work.

Marlene didn't introduce him to anybody. She didn't indicate she knew him.

That was Rudolf Seiber, her husband, whom the director had believed was her butler.

Mr. Seiber and I discussed Marlene's under-the-table performance somewhat later that night. "Marlene has many tricks," he said.

Let those who might doubt her appeal hear me on that subject. In 1960 my wife and I went to Hamburg, Germany, out of our way considerably, to see her and hear her do a concert at the Opera House. Burt Bacharach, the now famous composer, was then her accompanist. We saw her mesmerize that throng of Germans. It was such an incredible performance that we wanted her to know we had witnessed it.

It took us half an hour to get through the backstage crowd and into the back of the theater.

Burt Bacharach was waiting for us.

And there was Marlene—running. She was in a blonde mink three-quarter-length jacket, which showed off her legs nicely.

What was she running from? A fire? Something gone wrong?

No. Simply, the crowd in the theater wouldn't leave. She was taking bows; she was running to the stage to take another one.

Marlene was a perfectionist—she thought she was perfect and expected you to be. You've heard this story about her. You'll hear it again.

Marlene complained to a photographer about his latest batch of pictures of her. They weren't nearly as good of her as some he had taken 10 years earlier.

"Well," he said, "you see, I've gotten 10 years older."

19

WONDERFUL FAMILY

My dear wife Rosemary has tried earnestly to make clear that she doesn't take seriously my propaganda about her being "the Beautiful Wife" or "the B.W."; she insists that it started as a joke and continues to be a joke.

It began when I was launching the column. Writing about her, I said "the Beautiful Wife" with a parenthetical "Hope you don't mind, fellas; makes things easier at home."

Two paragraphs down, to save space, I wrote "the B.W."

The crazy unplanned thing caught on. She was beautiful, she was charming, she was smiling, and she was there. I first noticed it at theater openings, "first nights."

"Hi, B.W." "There's the B.W." One night a woman reader said, "Isn't that Earl Wilson?" My wife said happily that it was. The woman said scornfully, "But you're not the B.W.!"

My wife laughed. What a put-down. What was she supposed to look like? "Did she expect Garbo?"

The question "Are you the B.W.?" has been asked her a few thousand times since, and she often says, "No, but he says I am," or "No, I just have a good press agent." And when there's been time she's repeated the "But you're not the B.W." story.

She's also a very witty lady, and some of her pronouncements have called attention to the B.W., the conversationalist.

There was the time when I wanted to cover, or uncover, a nudist convention at Atlantic City and was told I'd have to undress like everybody else. Fearing that she wouldn't like me traipsing around in that interesting condition, I asked my B.W.'s permission.

"Thank God, one trip you're going on, I won't have to pack a bag for you," she said.

Everybody was dieting. "The hardest part of a diet is the first day, because by the second day you're not on it anymore," she said.

The B.W. is very good with children. When I took her and our son, Earl, Jr., then about four, to a nudist camp she steered the child toward the men's room, although at a nudist camp there's not much difference in the retiring rooms. Anyway, our son suddenly looked up and shrieked, "Oh, Mommy, there's a man with no pantsies on."

Our son wasn't doing well in spelling in school. "They give me all the hard words," he complained. (The teachers were obviously plotting against him.)

"They give you the hard words?" I said, looking at the word list on the blackboard. "How do you spell *cat?*"

"I don't know," he admitted.

"I told you, Daddy, they give me the hard words," said Sonny.

Our son, whom we called Slugger because he weighed four pounds when born prematurely, got bored with all the Mothers' Day and Fathers' Day observances, with the obligatory gifts.

"When is there going to be a Little Boys' Day?" he asked.

Our son was taught good manners by Rosemary's mother, Rosella Lyons, a tall, erect, rather severe gray-haired widow who came to live with us after her husband, Jack Lyons, died. She didn't drink, having had numerous relatives who ran saloons, but one night at a church bingo she won a bottle of whiskey and hurried home with it so her son-in-law could have a nightcap before he went to bed.

"The gorgeous mother-in-law," as we called her, kept close watch on our son's activities. One morning he started off to get to the school bus to Riverdale Country School with a copy of a nudist magazine in his hip pocket, taken from Daddy's desk.

Both boy and nudist magazine were apprehended by Rosella.

I was trying to become a writer and rented a storeroom for $10 a month to use as a study, office, or studio. Rosemary had become creative also and started taking painting lessons at Grand Central Art School.

"There were no available models around for me to try to paint," Rosemary remembers. "So I used the only thing that was handy—my husband."

We had a "house guest," Ann O'Neill, who was invited to my studio to take a look at the surroundings and the easel with me on it. Ann O'Neill looked at my likeness and said, "If it isn't Cabbage Head Wilson."

Rosemary left the field to Picasso and Dali.

Rosemary was very patient and understanding when I buckled down to write *I Am Gazing into My 8-Ball,* which quickly became a best-seller. I wrestled with the dedication.

"To the wonderful little woman who cooks my meals, darns my socks, and rears my son, my Mother-in-Law."

We were flying to London, Paris, and Rome, and I was trying to write columns from abroad. I was getting copy about Ingrid Bergman, Roberto Rossellini, and Gina Lollobrigida in Rome. We became friendly with Gina and her husband. We decided to have our son fly to Rome to join us for a couple of weeks. He was 12, and his grandmother thought he was too young to fly alone. She cried when she said goodbye to him at the airport.

Gina and her husband went with us to the airport to meet Earl, Jr., on his arrival. We would help him through customs.

There was a mix-up on the arrival time. The plane seemed to be late. We idled about the airport, waiting.

"Hi!" our son called out to us.

His plane was in, he had gotten through customs quite easily, and he was looking for us, thinking we must have forgotten about meeting him.

We wanted to be first of the tourists in Russia. And he was first of the nonembassy youngsters to get there. Krushchev and Bulganin were in power, and they attended a July 4 cocktail party at the U.S. Embassy in Moscow.

Drinks were poured as we stood about on the grounds. A woman who wanted to light a cigarette asked Earl, Jr., to hold her drink for her and he did. Just then Bulganin and Krushchev wandered up and saw the boy with the glass of alcohol in his hand. They stared and laughed and made some comment apparently about the American children taking to drink so early in life. The word *decadent* was heard, and also *Americaniski*. Later I asked him, "Who was that lady whose drink you were holding?"

"That wasn't no lady," he said. "That was my mother." That was his joke. It was another American.

Sure, we were supposed to be shadowed, watched, and bugged, but we never caught anybody doing it. While I was trying to write columns, Rosemary and Earl, Jr., tried to construct sentences in double-talk or Pidgin English that would confuse anybody eavesdropping. Sometimes they would simply speak at double the normal speed. One day I heard them saying, "Our father who art in Moscow."

"What's going on here?" I asked.

They were fixing up the Lord's Prayer for the Soviets.

Earl, Jr., told us that Russian maids who made our beds finished the chore by spitting on the bed. Somebody believed that was a Russian custom, "to settle the dust." Our son preferred to believe it was the Russians' expressing their opinion of us.

We had three weeks and "luxe" accommodations—four meals a day. Down in Tbilisi, birthplace of Stalin, I went out picture-taking one morning. I photographed a line of Soviets waiting for milk in some kind of a demonstration. I didn't know, nobody had told me, that the scene was not to be photographed.

A Soviet soldier hustled me over to the police.

I was scared. I'd had a similar experience in Yugoslavia. I'd had a written permit, but the policeman or militiaman there in Belgrade (a couple of years before) shook his head no. I must go with him. He couldn't read, I found out later. Street people gathered around, buzzing, shouting. Another Yugoslav soldier— who could read—let me go.

Now here it was again. A Russian soldier was pulling me to one of the much feared Soviet police stations. My next of kin were at the hotel asleep. I hadn't bothered to wake them. I had nobody to help me or speak for me. All I had was my passport.

"Americaniski!" I kept yelling, waving the passport.

My Russian captor babbled something that seemed to say, "Tell it to the judge." He pulled me into the station house with a big Russian flag on the wall and another soldier in command at a big desk. In my fear I let loose with "Americaniski" again with more wavings of the passport.

The top cop studied the passport, shrugged, and then, with a stream of Russian, scowled and let me go, finger-pointing at my camera and shaking his head no.

I was a free man! Back at the hotel, I woke up my family with this horror story of my crisis. Recounting it years later, I discovered they thought it was a dream they'd had.

Several years later Rosemary and I returned to Moscow for a Petrocelli Clothes men's fashion junket, attending a men's fashion show with Russian models. The vice-mayor was there in his obviously Russian-made new suit. My old schoolmate from Ohio State, Foy D. Kohler, was then the American ambassador.

A huge reception, a big cocktail party, followed the show. American capitalists, Russian communists, and fashion writers drank with arms around each other. All were happy.

"Any country that invented vodka," the B.W. said, "can't be all bad."

In all those years of traveling and nightlife, Rosemary has retained a sense of humor. She was wise to have said, "I'm not going to be the girl he comes home to but the girl he goes home with." It worked.

On our first trip to France I'm afraid I disappointed her.

I'd actually been studying French with Berlitz, and I had a few happy remarks ready for the first Parisian I met. The Hotel George V had sent a car and chauffeur and a porter to help with the bags.

We landed, and I was instantly busy trying to carry a portable typewriter while a camera strap was strangling me and my raincoat was trying to trip me as I undertook to change money after clearing customs. Frankly, I didn't know where I was.

But the ever-smiling B.W. knew where she was.

Breathing deeply and surveying the scene before her, she gasped excitedly, "Darling, this is Le Bourget!"

My first Parisian! I thought she was talking about the porter.

Straining to put on a smile through all my harness, I shot out my hand and let go with my Berlitz: *"Monsieur Le Bourget, je suis enchanté de faire votre connaissance."* ("I'm happy to make your acquaintance.")

"Not him, for God's sake!" howled the B.W. *"Le Bourget.* The airport where Lindbergh landed."

The porter was most amused at the case of mistaken identity and, as for my wife, she thought it was the funniest of my many goofs and laughed most of the way into Paris.

I seethed.

"If I hadn't had the camera and the typewriter—" I snapped.

"No, it was just plain stupid," the B.W. said. Even today she could probably be persuaded to tell the story again.

I've been able to get even only by telling how she wanted to have a class reunion in Kansas City on a trip back from California.

"You remember I went to school there," she said.

"Sure," I said.

"I'll dig up some of my old classmates," she said.

"You'll probably have to," was all I said.

20

EDDIE AND LIZ TAYLOR AND ME

Thank you, Eddie Fisher, for stating in your esteemed book, *Eddie, My Life, My Loves,* that I was the columnist who discovered that you were sneaking dates with Elizabeth Taylor while you were married to Debbie Reynolds.

You shouldn't have done it, Eddie—get discovered, I mean. Should have been discreet. Sneakier!

Well, now you straightened it out, we got the truth and the whole truth, and the Greatest Love Story Ever Told, the Great Triangle, the Great Quadrangle, is right there in the archives. My archives, anyway. I don't know about yours.

For I was important in that Great Quadrangle, Sexangle, whatever it was. Without me you might still be Mr. Debbie Reynolds and have missed being Mr. Liz Taylor. You wouldn't have wanted to miss that, and your book wouldn't have been so lively. I still think Richard Burton is going to punch you in the chops for that quote, "She's going to make me a star; I'm going to use her, that no-talent Hollywood nothing."

I'm surprised Violet Eyes didn't squawk about some quotes,

too; especially that one about "When are we going to make love?"

But, rushing right along, it was 1958, and Elizabeth Taylor, the most beautiful girl in the world, had lost her third husband, Mike Todd, killed in the crash of his plane, the Lucky Liz. Elizabeth didn't enjoy widowhood, and eventually her violet orbs fell on you, Eddie Fisher, Mike Todd's great buddy and pal (married to Debbie Reynolds), and you two shared your grief in her suite at the Plaza when you met in New York. Liz was going to Europe, and you were in town with your grief over Mike.

You got real frank in your book at this point and said, "Just held hands and kissed at first," but then you allege as how Liz practically popped the question at you.

Now, Eddie, here's where I come in, and I come in big. In case there's a movie or miniseries, you'll remember your old friend, won't you?

It's Thursday night, August 28, 1958, and I'm covering Broadway, and I hear certain things, and I think, "I better put this in the paper."

Labor Day Weekend is coming up.

I rattle out "The Lowdown on the Higher-Ups":

> Elizabeth Taylor and Eddie Fisher were dancing it up at the Harwyn this morning, Eddie having been Mike Todd's close friend and now sort of an escort service for Liz. They saw *Two for the Seesaw* the night before. Liz and her ex-husband Nicky Hilton are on the same floor at the Plaza, but don't be drawing any confusions from that because Nicky's around with Cary Latimer. When Liz flies to Europe she won't be with a guy but with Medora Tsuji, treasurer of the Todd organization. . . .

I didn't expect anything to come of it. But I protected myself. I did wonder about Debbie Reynolds out there in California alone while Eddie was dancing it up at the Harwyn—just holding hands and kissing.

Of course, Eddie, you told in your book how you two fell in

love and you two phoned Debbie to confess but she didn't want
to hear it; she was going to divorce you two years ago but she got
pregnant.

"We got to have privacy," you say. You and Liz go to Grossinger's in the Catskills, where there won't be any stinking press, just
hundreds of Labor Day tourists, and by a crazy coincidence, me,
a member of the press.

I took my Gorgeous Mother-in-Law and son for the holiday,
leaving my wife home with the schnauzer.

When I checked in, the weekenders were all asking, "What's
with Liz and Eddie staying private with Mrs. Grossinger?
What's up, Oil? What's the story, Oil?"

I was amazed myself. Eddie walks by with a happy face, and
Liz looks content about something, and the hotel spokesman
says, "Oh, them," as if he hasn't noticed them, "they're here to
dedicate a new indoor pool."

An indoor pool needs a dedication?

"I even went through the ceremony," Eddie said in his book.

We all rode over to the indoor pool in a bus on a rainy night,
and was it dull? It was!

But, Eddie, can I talk at you a moment? You had guts. In your
book you wrote, "But at least one reporter wasn't fooled.

"Earl Wilson wrote about Elizabeth and me in his column,
and then the hue and cry began.

"Exactly nine years earlier Eddie Cantor had 'discovered' me
at Grossinger's. Now I had been discovered again at Grossinger's, this time in the company of Elizabeth Taylor, and my life
would take a new and totally different direction."

You'd romanced Debbie up there, too, but you didn't mention
that. Grossinger's must be an aphrodisiac.

Liz and Eddie stayed indoors at Grossinger's over Sunday,
adding to the mystery and the speculation. We didn't have a
paper on Labor Day, so our tongues got a rest.

I took the Gorgeous Mother-in-Law and my son home to New
York Monday night feeling like I might have a big story and I
might not. Eddie wasn't talking; he was with Liz, wherever she
was. But the word was out how Liz was going to Europe and
Eddie was going back to California and Debbie.

On Tuesday morning in my New York office I got on the phone with the Rolodex numbers in California. I put in a call for Debbie's crowd.

Eddie had supposedly taken a plane to California Monday night, with Debbie meeting him at the airport Tuesday morning.

"Debbie met the plane, but Eddie wasn't on it," a source told me.

Not very nice, was it? Eddie must still be in New York, at Grossinger's, with Guess Who.

And there it is in my card file: September 2, 1958:

"LIZ TAYLOR. She's at Grossinger's with Debbie Reynolds' husband, Eddie Fisher."

September 5-6, 1958:

"She's out on the town with Eddie Fisher in NY . . . *having problems.* . . .

"Eddie says Debbie is home with the children." The Tip-Off to the Bust-Up.

The world press leaped on the story, and since I was journalism's only witness to any of Liz-and-Eddie's "handholding," I became an authority on it. Pictures of them smiled at you from the newspapers. I had broken a Hollywood story on my Broadway beat, and Hedda Hopper didn't like that. Eddie and Liz decided to go back to Hollywood and face their accusers. Liz was characteristically contemptuous of the rumors when the reporters got to her in California, and she called it "garbage."

Eddie tried to sneak in via Burbank. He thought it would be quieter that way.

Quiet! Eddie says Debbie was waiting in the hall of the house. She sat down on the floor weeping; he tried to pick her up; she got loose and ran up to the bathroom and locked herself in. She wouldn't come out; she wouldn't listen. Eddie was in love with Liz and it was over, and the all-American boy walked out of his house and out of his marriage (and I had seen it begin less than a week before).

Lucky I had used that mention when they were dancing at the Harwyn. Suppose I hadn't? What if I hadn't gone to Grossinger's?

Debbie's chums ganged up for her against Liz, and she played the role of the abandoned housewife with her daughter Carrie crying on her shoulder as she talked about that wicked old Liz. As Eddie saw the story unfolding now, Liz was the seductress and Eddie was the weakling who couldn't resist her. Eddie may have just been holding hands and kissing, but now he saw it as the "juiciest scandal to hit Hollywood in years."

Nor did I know that with my little typewriter and my "Lowdowns on the Higher-Ups" I had started another saga that would play for a decade or maybe two with another villain (or hero) waiting in the wings, not yet introduced, Richard Burton.

We couldn't foresee "the Cleopatra Scandal" and the ruination of the Coca-Cola boy, Eddie Fisher.

I keep asking, lest you forget, suppose I hadn't printed that item about Liz and Eddie dancing at the Harwyn, supposing I hadn't gone to Grossinger's, suppose I hadn't seen Liz and Eddie dedicating that indoor swimming pool?

Maybe Debbie Reynolds would never have screamed out loud; maybe there would never have been a public Liz-and-Eddie romance; maybe all of it would never have been.

Aren't you glad there are gossip columnists?

Eddie said further in his book, which I never saw printed or hinted at elsewhere, that as he was walking out of the house and the marriage "I smelled the overpowering odor of lima beans, my favorite food. Debbie was trying to save our marriage with lima beans."

(As a lover of lima beans myself, in fact as a lover of any beans, never having met a bean I didn't like, I could understand, but I don't suppose there are many who feel about beans as Eddie and I do.)

Eddie's version is that he and Debbie were not happily married, that he and Debbie were practically broken up before Liz came into the picture, that Liz didn't break up a home because there wasn't any home there to break.

Their sex life was nothing, Eddie said.

Debbie wasn't interested in it, Eddie thought. He talked to his friend, Rory Calhoun, who said, "Give it time."

They fought over income tax. Eddie said Debbie refused to sign a joint return, which would have been a big saving, because

The lovely English eye-opener, June Wilkinson, had it and flaunted it.
(Pajama Tops *Press*)

Anita Ekberg, then a sensational Scandinavian model, attended a Miss Universe contest as a visitor and stole the show. She was "discovered" by Bob Hope and went on to liven up Italy in *La Dolce Vita*. (*Artists' and Models' Ball*)

French lover Charles Boyer wore toupees on the screen to preserve his romantic image, but bared all in interview with Earl Wilson. (*Gary Wagner Photo*)

Joan Crawford kisses Wilson who manages to hold onto his notebook anyway. What a way to make a living! (*Gary Wagner Photo*)

The late, great comedienne, Fanny Brice, hands Earl Wilson a flower to celebrate the publication of one of his books in the long-ago '40s. Wilson sports a permanent wave as a stunt. (*Gary Wagner Photo*)

Eddie Cantor lifts his chin
disdainfully at pal George
Jessel. That's Henny
Youngman peeking over
Cantor's shoulder. (*Gary
Wagner Photo*)

Handsome Bill Holden at the
doorway of one of his favorite
New York oases. (*Bill Mark
Photo*)

Anthony Franciosa and Ava Gardner were in a happy mood when they starred in *The Naked Maja*. (Naked Maja *Press*)

George Gobel and Earl Wilson have been told that they're look-alikes—both resent it. (*Tim Boxer Photo*)

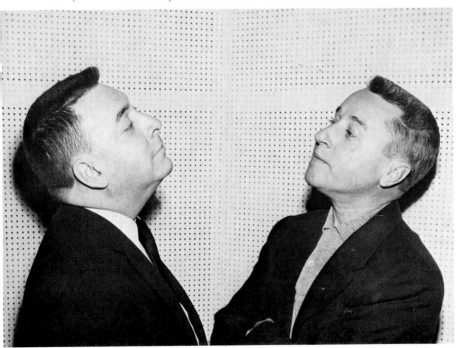

The entire Gabor family—Eva, Sari (now Zsa Zsa), Magda, and Mama Jolie give Wilson a mass interview. (*Tim Boxer Photo*)

Zsa Zsa Gabor, who was a brunette when she was still known as Sari, was a beautiful blond when this photo was taken with Mike Todd. (*Tim Boxer Photo*)

Ever-young Maurice Chevalier generally did record-breaking business whenever he brought his one-man show to New York. When he did have a slow week he gave the guarantee money back to his producer. (*Gary Wagner Photo*)

Jackie Gleason was a little overweight from French wines and sauces when filming *Gigot* in Paris. Here, helping him celebrate the first day of shooting are Director Gene Kelly and Earl and Mrs. Wilson. (Gigot *Press— Paris, Jean Schmidt*)

Toots Shor, the saloon-keeper's saloon keeper clowns around with good pal Jackie Gleason. (*Bill Mark Photo*)

Marlon Brando was unhappy with the exploitation of his role as a slightly homosexual army officer in *Reflections in a Golden Eye*. (*Ray Stark Productions Press*)

Sophia Loren, one of Wilson's favorite actresses, has a lovely back—and a nice front, also. (*Joseph Levine Films, Michael Hall*)

Hedy Lamarr, the great beauty who startled her fans with nude scenes, sits for a gag picture with columnist Wilson as her movie-star husband, John Loder, glowers. (*New York Post Photo*)

Heavyweight champion Joe Louis tells the showgirls that they'll have to be satisfied with just his autograph. (*New York Post Photo*)

Mae West comes across with a sly wink as she delivers the line, "I didn't get these furs to keep me warm, but to keep me quiet." (*Gary Wagner Photo*)

Elvis Presley, always polite, called Earl Wilson "sir." He liked jokes and encouraged Wilson to put on a fake mustache and wear a big-brimmed hat to resemble his manager Colonel Tom Parker for this picture. (*Presley/Parker Productions*)

Comedy king Harold Lloyd and ice queen Sonja Henie with Wilson and his wife at a Hollywood party where Sonja, the hostess, positioned herself at the front gate and turned away anybody who wasn't invited. (*MGM Press*)

Bob Hope played the role of the sloppiest GI in a USO show in Vietnam. Columnist Wilson interviewed him as part of sketch seen by as many as 50,000 servicemen per show. (*USO Press*)

Would you believe an interview with Dr. Albert Einstein? The occasion was a 1951 luncheon for the American Committee of Hebrew University in a New York City hotel. (*New York Post Photo*)

Marilyn Monroe shared a little gossip with columnist Walter Winchell at a cocktail party. (*Earl Wilson Photo*)

Elizabeth Taylor and husband Eddie Fisher posed for this picture before their breakup. (*Sam Siegel Photo*)

Liz Taylor and husband
Richard Burton have supper
after the show with John
Springer, their press agent at
the time. (*Sam Siegel Photo*)

Wilson never passed up a chance for
a dance with a lovely girl. Here, he's
cheek-to-cheek with Kim Novak.
(*New York Post Photo*)

Gorgeous Kim Novak was seen in *The Amorous Adventures of Moll Flanders*. (Moll Flanders *Press*)

"Papa" Ernest Hemingway, winner of the Nobel and Pulitzer prizes for literature, hosted a drinking session at LaFloridita, in Havana after surviving two plane crashes. At left is Earl Wilson, Jr. and across the table are Earl Wilson, Sr., Mary Welch Hemingway, and Rosemary Wilson. (*LaFloridita Press*)

her accountant didn't want her to be responsible for any debts he might incur.

Eddie swore at her under his breath, he said, and she slapped him.

Eddie also remembers that while they were discussing a million-dollar settlement—Debbie to get $40,000 a year, the house, three cars—Debbie also asked "Is there any chance of our getting back together?"

Negative!

So Violet Eyes and All-American Boy began living in sin (unmarried) in Bel Air, waiting for the wheels of justice and morality to grind out a divorce from Debbie, which Debbie was in no mood to hasten.

Some of their moralistic chums cut them off the list of invitations to their drunken parties, which gave them more time for bed. Eddie lost his TV show, which might have been partially due to his sinning with Elizabeth.

Then Elizabeth converted to Judaism (to the Reform faith). It was getting to be a popular thing to do.

Eddie was picketed by some ex-fans when he played the Tropicana in Las Vegas. There were "Liz Go Home" signs. At last they were married by a Jewish rabbi at a ranch in Las Vegas. They had been living together for months. They flew to New York on the way to Europe and stopped at the Waldorf Towers, which mistakenly gave the honeymooners twin beds.

Eddie brought the next scene in this Greek tragedy on himself. Chancing to pick up a script of *Cleopatra,* being produced by Walter Wanger, Eddie told Liz, "You ought to do it for a million dollars."

"You really think so?" she asked.

"For a million," he repeated.

Eddie swears that Walter Wanger called Liz and she didn't even ask him what he wanted.

"I'll do it for a million dollars," Liz said.

"I'll get back to you," he said.

He got back to her and said, "You've got it."

And that brought on and in Mr. Richard Burton, who one day would order Eddie Fisher out of Elizabeth's villa in Italy, telling him in effect, "Your wife prefers me. Blow, Sonny. Get lost!"

Eddie claims Burton put her through an act like a trained dog, asking her in front of Eddie, "Who do you love?" 'til she answered, "You."

Traveling in Europe at this time, I saw Eddie and was invited to a birthday party by him and saw the sham of a marriage he was having with Liz while Burton was breaking it up. Eddie says now that Liz was his all too willing slave.

Still, Eddie was such a VIP that it was difficult to get him on the phone—but he remembered our acquaintance from his beginnings as a production singer at the Copacabana and talked to me—but he couldn't admit the shameful depth he had fallen to.

Somebody gave him a gun and suggested he use it on Burton. Trying to hang on to her, he gave Liz a yellow diamond ring for her 30th birthday; $10,000 worth, he said. His "varsity" of men friends constituting his entourage feared he might commit suicide. He was beaten; he was desolate; he was devastated.

I felt pity for him, and again I had to write the bad news about Eddie for my papers.

My Beautiful Wife and I felt a special understanding of Eddie and girls. We had been with him in Hollywood on one of his first dates with Debbie years before. Later we were with him in London when he sang at a charity affair made regal and glamorous by the presence of young Princess Margaret.

It was a black-tie affair, and I darted about the ballroom at the Dorchester, checking names.

I must have become quite visible because the young dukes and earls kept calling to me, "More champagne."

It was not the first time I was taken for a waiter.

Eddie sang his heart out for Princess Margaret that night, and he said later that she asked him to dance but he was too bashful and refused.

We took him to supper at a club, and he admitted he was smitten.

"I'm in love," he announced dreamily. "I'm in love."

With Princess Margaret!

A few years later we invited him to a cocktail party in New York where Ernest Hemingway tutored Toots Shor in the art of hand-kissing, saying above the elbow was out of bounds.

My wife and I reminisced with Eddie, and we reminded him

of the London experience. "You were in love with Princess Margaret," I said.

Eddie turned and kissed the girl he was with.

"I have my own princess now," he said to the girl with him, Debbie Reynolds.

But that was before Liz and that was before Burton. And after Liz, Eddie didn't wait long before impregnating Connie Stevens a couple of times.

The absolute truth is that Eddie Fisher liked girls, but he didn't like girls any more than Elizabeth Taylor Hilton Wilding Todd Fisher Burton Burton Warner liked boys.

Elizabeth was the woman he couldn't handle. But who could? Las Vegas writer Ralph Pearl said, "Marrying Liz Taylor is like trying to flag down the 20th Century with a Zippo lighter." That was his opinion stated in his newspaper column.

But I still think that you should give a vote of thanks—it can be sitting, not necessarily standing—to us gossip columnists for reporting about Eddie and Liz dancing it up at the Harwyn and dedicating an indoor pool at Grossinger's. For there might never have been a Liz-and-Richard love affair, and that would have been a very dull world indeed.

And if you want to drop off a Pulitzer Prize, there's always somebody home.

21
ALL THE
NUDES
THAT'S FIT

And so I became a nudespaperman.

I was the politest little boy, who tipped his cap to teacher but had private thoughts about her. What did she have under that shirtwaist, and wasn't that a cute bump 'neath the middy blouse? When she took off her bloomers, was she as enticing as those sexy models in the Sears Roebuck catalog?

It never occurred that researching such things could be a profession. Even while studying journalism at Ohio State University and covering the Ohio legislature part-time, I dreamed of being a Washington correspondent—not an authority on breasts, navels, and backsides. Suddenly one day I saw a nudist and had a career change.

I improved on *The New York Times* slogan, making my battle cry "All the nudes that's fit. . . ."

Nudism had been with us since Adam, but it wasn't until about 1933 that I investigated rumors of a nudist camp near Akron and, stepping on a dry twig, scared the nudists. I wrote quite bravely at the time that "all I saw was a thighbone glistening momentarily in the sun."

But now I was a New York columnist, and somebody carelessly proposed that I cover, or uncover, a nudists' convention at Sunshine Park near Atlantic City.

"Skeeterville," as Sunshine Park was called by nudists in a rival camp back in the '40s, welcomed me providing that I come naked like the other skin folk.

"Take my clothes off?" I asked nervously.

"All of them," declared Reverend Dr. Ilsley Boone, executive director of the American Sunbathing Association.

I drove over on that coolish summer day, rang the bell at an administration building, and, quoting myself:

"Through the door I could see, bouncing across the room, a beautiful completely nude brunette of about 18 who reminded me in a couple respects of Jane Russell."

(Later it would have been Marilyn Monroe and, still later, Dolly Parton).

"She opened the door, looked me up and down, and I did the same for her."

Though it was summer, there was a fire in the fireplace. Several naked sunbathers turned their backs and derrieres toward the fire. These sunbathers were getting no sun. This was my first inkling that nudists don't go naked just for the sun.

Into this small naked group charged the Reverend Dr. Boone, also the naked managing editor of *Sunshine and Health;* also Dr. Boone's daughter, national president Mrs. Margaret A. B. Pulis, wearing principally a sweater reaching to just where sweaters usually reach to.

"Well, well, well, Earl," shouted the Reverend Dr. Boone, "I can just see you're itching to get your clothes off."

How he could see that I don't know, as I hadn't taken a stitch off. However, his daughter, the naked sweater-clad Mrs. Pulis, directed the naked managing editor, Ralph Sanderson, to escort me to a guest room, where I would get into my nudist costume—my sneakers.

That's exactly all I would wear.

Yes, sneakers are vital to a nudist. In his shoes he deposits keys, money, cigarettes, notebook, even his nudist convention badge. Where else can he wear his badge?

Wait! I forgot my baseball cap!

And now, in my baseball cap and sneakers, I started downstairs to face the ladies, and now I was scared. I didn't know what to do with my hands.

Where did I carry them? Fore or aft?

I tried both fore and aft, and that didn't solve it. If fore was covered, aft wasn't, and if aft was covered, fore wasn't. Arriving downstairs, I noticed something more about nudists. They didn't actually face you. They stared at you in the forehead somewhere. They couldn't face the issue.

Up stepped the lady in the sweater that came to just where sweaters come to, Mrs. Pulis, saying, "I think you ought to wear something."

"About time," I giggled.

She handed me an ID card, the size of a price tag, which stated that I was a nudist in case anybody looking at me couldn't tell.

Now I had on three things: sneakers, baseball cap, and ID card.

"Mr. Wilson," said Mrs. Sweater, "how would you like to drive over to the nudist singfest?"

A naked singfest, a nude sing-along with Mitch. Frankly, it was something I had long dreamed of. Still, I could envisage problems. We were going to drive over? Naked? Nude in the car? Who was going to drive? Much more was going to be stripped here than the gears.

"Oh," whispered Mrs. Sweater, "I'll bring a towel or a pillow for you to sit on."

Perhaps you have been in a car naked. Perhaps you haven't. I drove, raw, sharing the towel with Mrs. Sweater, who shared part of another towel with the naked managing editor. Driving a high-powered automobile in the nude is *different.* There are all sorts of dangers you become aware of when you realize you don't have any pants on.

But we were not to visit the singfest yet. First we saw an all-nudist movie, *Why We Became Nudists.* The picture was already on, and I exposed myself publicly for the first time when I tried to escape the glare of the projection machine.

The glare caught me, however, and I showed my all and everything else. The splinters on the wooden plank seats that we sat on contributed to making the movie less than an epic.

When the movie was over I saw mass nudity, and it over-whelmed me. They jumped up and ran around the recreation hall, some joining the singfest (with a three-piece nudist orchestra). Some just stared at each other's foreheads and talked about tennis tomorrow (mixed doubles, of course) and lamented that it was too chilly for skinny-dipping.

I saw nothing sinful or sexy, I saw nothing wrong, and as a newspaperman (nudespaperman) I was looking for something wrong.

Back to our towel and our car went Mrs. Sweater and naked managing editor and I. Soon I was hopping into bed in my cheery little guest room, feeling a bit too cool, and wishing that my wife had packed some pajamas.

All I had to wear to bed was a towel.

It made breakfast very simple. Off with towel, a little powder on the vaccination mark, and onto the chow line. Should I put on pants for breakfast? Not at a nudist camp, man!

And what a scene it was. Fats and leans, longs and shorts, a few graybeards, not many kids, about five times as many females as males, about 80 nakeds all together, including an elderly fellow with a long black beard who recited an old joke.

"A beard's useful in a nudist camp," he said. "Somebody has to go for coffee."

The sight of all that naked femininity, some scrawny, some overripe plump, unwhetted my appetite. I was just thinking that a woman in an unkempt nightgown would look better than some of these complete nudes. I proceeded to the dining room where a modest-type waitress made me feel better.

She had on a very small tea apron down around her G-string area.

"I thought I wanted some grapefruit," I heard a man say. "And then I thought I saw some grapefruit right here. Then I saw that wasn't grapefruit, that was a lady."

He lost interest in grapefruit.

I concluded somewhat sadly that the human body, when completely bare, is not very pretty, and it would be wiser to look at it one section at a time. Certainly the nude women at breakfast packed no sex appeal.

An exception might be the well-built receptionist looking

about 18 who admitted me at the front door. "What has happened to her?" I inquired.

"Ah, she's getting married!" they said.

"To a nudist, naturally," they explained. "She met the boy right here. Both their parents are nudists. They had their first dates in the nude. And people still ask them why, since they've seen all of each other and there's no mystery left, are they getting married?"

The quite obvious answer is "They couldn't wait to see what the other looked like with clothes on."

In a more serious vein, Mrs. Pulis, the sweater lady, told me that her father, the Reverend Dr. Boone, had heard about nudism years before and gone to Germany to look into its popularity there.

"He was going to be either for it or against it. He decided to be for it, and he gave up some of his church duties to promote nudism. We thought Daddy was a little peculiar, but we looked into it, and we decided to be for nudism, too."

Mrs. Pulis, a newspaper correspondent, lecturer, and writer, ran for president of a local Parent-Teacher Association. She made a clean breast of her nudism, so to speak, so her opponents wouldn't bring it up against her in the election.

"People who come to see me at my house have the idea that they are supposed to take their clothes off," she laughed. "We wear clothes when it's advisable and when it's chilly."

And so I was never able to write anything scandalous about nudism. I discussed the mysteries of nudism with many deep thinkers and also some shallow thinkers. One of the shallow school said, "Despite all the nudists' claims that they do it to get the sun, think it over. I have never seen or heard of a blind nudist!"

Ah, but time marches on. All that was three or four decades ago, and I would have thought that nudity on the stage, in the movies and on television, and in public would have silenced all discussion of it in this enlightened era.

Instead, in the year 1983, the New York state legislature passed and Governor Cuomo signed an anti-nude-sunbathing law that threatens naked bathers with 15 days in jail or a $250 fine for epidermis exposure.

Guess who deplores that as being the silliest bill passed this year?

The New York Times nudespaper, that's who.

With no reference to "All the nudes that's fit to print," of course. But Columnist Sydney H. Schanberg, on July 8, 1983, dealt at length with the distinction of "toplessness" as opposed to "bottomlessness," which was part of the battle.

Nudespaperman Schanberg declares that you can't go naked on a beach in New York without fear of getting a summons but "it's okay to plunk down a few dollars at a porn parlor on Eighth Avenue to watch a live performance of people dressed only in hip boots."

Thank you, brother *Times*. Now, if you can find a blind nudist. . . .

22
WE TALK
FUNNY
IN OHIO

My wife and I were having our usual argument about the population of my hometown, Rockford, Ohio, me claiming it was over 1,000, and she saying it was much less. So, while sitting in my Broadway office, I phoned the Rockford post office, which should certainly have the census figures ready for anybody who asked. The operator at the next big town nearby, Van Wert, Ohio, said the Rockford post office didn't have a phone.

"Should I try the Rockford police department?" the Van Wert operator asked, not betraying any surprise at the post office being phoneless.

"Yeah, yeah, try the Rockford police department," I said. I had visions of the Rockford police department.

A woman answered the call to the police department.

"Is this the Rockford police department?" the operator asked.

"He ain't in," the woman said.

"When will the police department be in?" the Van Wert hello girl said.

"He'll be home for his supper in about 15 minutes," the lady stated. The police department used to be a plump old fellow named Tom Cook. I don't know who the police department was at this time. Anyway, the operator in Rockford (her name was Mabel, and we used to be classmates) said she knew the postmaster—he had a phone in his residence. Should we get him?

Well, in a small town you know everybody. We got the postmaster on the phone at his home.

"Blaine," I said (knew him from my boyhood there), "you don't have a phone in the post office?"

"Earl, you remember how it is," he said. "We don't have free delivery in town. Only in the rural area. So everybody comes to the post office to get mail in boxes or at the general delivery window. Well, if we had a phone, nobody'd come to the post office. They'd just ring up and say, 'Blaine, have I got any mail today?' We'd never get the mail sorted, let alone have time to read all the postcards."

Well, the population was over 1,000, but not much over, and now they have free delivery of mail by letter carriers so they have a phone, too.

I told this story many times and told my mother that I had inherited some speech eccentricities from her. Ohio's not quite southern. Jonathan Winters, as a shine boy, said "Whurz? the fahr? He was drivin' so fast his tarz were on fahr." "He got a shoeshine from an ole boy that said Shann em ratt up and make um look rell good. Spayshul shann jes for you."

In northwest Ohio they have a tendency to put an *a* or an *uh* before a verb with an *ing* ending.

I asked my mother if she remembered my birth, and she said, "They gave me a shot and I was out, but when I come to, you was asquallin' and uhsquallin', and uhsquallin' "

"You see, you said 'uhsquallin','" I said. My mother shouted me down. "You been uhsquallin' ever since," she said.

23

IN BED
WITH
ANITA EKBERG

When the beautiful Swedish actress, Anita Ekberg, literally caused New York traffic tie-ups simply by overflowing her C and D cups when she went strolling, it was imperative that I interview her and do the authentic, in-depth, inside story.

The "Swedish smorgasbord" measured 39 inches around the bust, whereas most girls were happy with a 36. Anita was tall and exquisite and usually wore her shoulders bare.

Miss Ekberg had stolen the Miss Universe pageant just being a guest, not an entrant, and had promptly gone on TV with such connoisseurs as Bob Hope. *Playboy* seized her for nude pictures. Anita definitely fit into Part II of my own research, which was labeled "Booze, Bosoms, and Behinds."

As queen of the Art Students League's Dream Ball, an undress affair, she had received mountains of publicity about her mountainous measurements.

A life-size picture of Anita in and out of a bikini was selling neck and neck with a picture of Marilyn Monroe at a Broadway novelty shop.

"Vott a dreadful t'ing dey do," Anita fumed. "Dey get $2 a picture. I get nudding."

I had met Anita when she was exposed nationally on the Bob Hope show. Now she was publicizing a movie, *Blood Alley,* with Lauren Bacall and John Wayne. Miss Ekberg played a Chinese coolie—bare-shouldered.

I invited Anita's extremely able personal publicist, Mal Braveman, to bring her to our apartment at 600 West End Avenue. That was not unusual. I had interviewed a young barefoot actress, Debbie Reynolds, in our living room once. And once, when I interviewed Monique Van Vooren there, she persuaded me to arrange an introduction to Elvis Presley for her.

My wife Rosemary, the B.W., was not present for Anita's visit. She had gone to Florida to be with a woman friend whose husband had just died.

When Anita arrived with her press person she was all I expected and a little bit more. She was *big,* but in one department she was a disappointment. She was not bare-shouldered. Because she had thought of this as an interview rather than a photo session, Anita had worn a suit. A suit covered Anita's best features.

This bothered me as she sat on a couch, showing her beautiful legs, and I asked her about a poem some reader had sent her: "Ekberg/Is no iceberg."

Yes, the stories were mostly true. When she shouldered down Broadway, pedestrians yelled and taxi drivers leaned on their horns. Cars smashed into each other. Cops shouted, "You're stopping traffic, idiot." When she lounged past the Stage Barbershop, which she'd heard about, two barbers ran out into the street to ogle her and whistle. They returned to the shop when she had passed and in their confusion began barbering the wrong customers.

Anita was also famous for a nude statue—a bust of her—by Cuban sculptor Joseph Dobronyi. At issue between Anita and some suitors was whether she posed in the nude for him, and when, and why. And for how long?

After the interview I turned to the photography problem.

I took a few shots of Anita Ekberg in a suit.

"At least I'll have a unique picture of Anita Ekberg," I

thought. "The only one of Miss Ekberg showing absolutely nothing."

"Let me show you what we could have taken if you'd brought a change of costume," I said, leading her into a luxurious white bedroom, indicating the big fluffy white bed where the B.W. and I slept.

Anita's prodigious parts would have looked well, and I told her so.

"Too bad you didn't bring a slip, a pajama bottom, or a large handkerchief," I said sadly.

My wife would have thought of something. How tolerant my B.W. was.

"Too bad," I said.

"Yes, too bad," mused Anita. I think it was she who had the idea first. "Maybe I could wear one of your wife's. . . ."

Anita had spied one of my wife's closets with its feminine finery. We had 11 closets, and one of them was almost big enough to live in. Anita had found one attached to a dressing table, it was a wife's pleasure and treasure.

As Anita dived into the sheer, seductive negligees and nighttime glamour, I dived into my camera bag. Photographers carried a lot of gear in those days. Flashbulbs, cartons of them, and light meters, and tripods, and more flashbulbs.

Anita, as one of nature's children, and accustomed to her special type of modeling, gave no thought to the fact that she was more or less naked during her plunge into my wife's pretties. She was really performing a strip tease that wasn't being appreciated.

"Hold still, Anita. Let me get you in focus," I cried. (This was in the days when they took pictures in focus.) If she was in the raw, I hardly noticed. I worried about the shutter speed, too.

Mal Braveman, the press person, cheered from the sidelines.

"Get in bed," I called to Anita.

She nodded, all over. Clever girl. She knew these pictures had to have the subject in bed. My wife's garments were about half as big as Anita, who was an Amazon, and Anita was exposed in sections she wouldn't usually be exposed in. Now she pulled down the bedspread and the bed covers and stretched out languorously in bed—and sighed.

But Anita didn't quit. Bouncing right out of bed, she climbed in and out of more and more intimate apparel. Stepping revealingly out of one tiny extravagance, she would drop it into a growing pile of my wife's lingerie and hop back into bed and sigh again.

We finished—because I ran out of film. Anita, looking OK in a suit if you liked suits, departed with Mal. I looked around at the wreckage. A pile of crumpled laundry lay there.

My wife's. Oh yes, my wife!

I'd done nothing wrong, but I might be open to criticism from some quarters, allowing another woman to wear my wife's wardrobe, especially her very private things.

I'd better call her right now in Florida and confess everything before Anita and Mal blabbed it around.

And that's what I did. But I softened the crime considerably, saying, "Anita borrowed one of your slips or whatever they call those things."

I tried to put myself in her place. It was a miserable thing to do. She should be angry.

And she was. She said, "Earl Wilson, if you got flashbulbs over my pretty bedroom, I'm going to be so mad at you."

Oh yes, the flashbulbs, too. And the pile of finery.

I forgot to mention that our maid Daisy was out in the kitchen all the time, though I didn't notice her. She was probably slyly watching. When the B.W. came back to New York, she found everything in place in her closet, looking quite normal. Daisy trotted over to her closet with all the pretties.

"Oh, don't you worry, Miz Rosemary," Daisy said in a voice not fully approving of what had transpired. "After that woman wore them things, I washed everything right out."

24
EDDIE
THE BARBER

The street called Broadway is peopled with actors, and you know actors are proud of their hair. I mention Ronald Reagan as an example. Actors and their understudies and acolytes shine with happiness when the hair stylist gives that final touch to their luxurious locks.

Broadway barbershops may be more famous than churches. You might remember that a couple of prominent citizens got shot in barber chairs when their bodyguards stepped out for coffee.

Frank Costello, the mob boss, used to get shaved at the Waldorf Men's Barber Shop, which also served J. Edgar Hoover, the FBI chief.

These two famous adversaries met accidentally on the stairs one day. Affable J. Edgar invited F. C. for a coffee.

"Thanks, Edgar," stammered Frank, a personable chap, "but I got to be careful who I associate with. That Crime Inquiry you fellows got goin', you know."

Customers collected good barbers. All the way from San

Francisco, Joe DiMaggio would phone Frank Garzaniti in New York to make a 10:00 A.M. haircut reservation.

Samson knew that in haircuts there is strength, and so did my friend, Maurice Uchitel, "the shoulder pad king," the one-time owner of El Morocco, who was rich from the garment industry. He didn't have money the way Aristotle Onassis didn't have any. He often took 20 or 30 to dinner but never more than 30 because he said that was bad luck. He was one of those men who had power.

Dashing, devilish, and daring, Maurice had attractive pearl-gray hair. He was the kind of Maurice that nobody ever called Morrie.

Maurice frequented the Dawn Patrol Shop on Seventh Avenue, which catered to the stay-ups, the Walter Winchells, the Ed Sullivans, the jockeys and disc jockeys, and the guys who knew where the action was.

Maurice liked a barber in the back, Eddie, an Italian with a difficult last name. "Where's Eddie?" Maurice would ask.

Eddie was a veteran haircutter, well known for liking to move to a new shop just for a change. *Ubiquitous* wasn't quite the right word for Eddie. Maurice didn't know what the right word was. He liked his haircuts.

Maurice followed him to new shops.

If he could tie Eddie down to one shop, Maurice would worry less about his hair.

Maurice was on the phone all day talking deals; even at the pool he talked deals. One day Maurice heard something vital.

The Dawn Patrol barbershop was for sale.

Maurice chuckled. Strangely enough, he'd never owned a barbershop, nor even a piece of a piece of a barbershop.

Maurice saw happiness unrolling for him.

Eddie the Barber! Buy the shop for him, install Eddie as the boss, anchor him there, and he'd always be there to give him a haircut. He'd have partners.

He found Eddie in and got comfortable in his chair.

"How'd you like to own your own shop?" Eddie was putting in that final pearl-gray wave on top.

Eddie brightened. "Ev'y barber dreams of havin' his own shop."

Maurice lowered his voice. "Keep it down. I may buy this shop for you."

"For me? You buy it for me?" Eddie didn't understand. He only knew that Maurice was rich and that rich men did crazy things. Eddie also knew vaguely about partners and that Maurice could probably afford to buy the shop.

"You let me run it?" Eddie inquired.

"Sure, you run it; it'll be your shop!"

"My shop?" grinned Eddie. "We change the name, yes?"

"Change the name?" Maurice hadn't thought of that.

"Change the name to Eddie's Shop. Maybe just Eddie's."

"Not just yet," Maurice smiled and nodded. "We keep it Dawn Patrol for a while. Good for publicity."

"Later we put up a sign, 'EDDIE'S'?"

Maurice nodded. He'd done it. He was going to own a barbershop, and he was also going to own Eddie. It was just an expression. The Broadway fellows said they owned the mayor or they owned the police department or they owned a columnist, but they didn't mean they owned them. It just meant they had influence or had some power in those places. It didn't mean they really owned anybody. It was this "power" that people talked about.

Except Maurice now considered he owned Eddie. He could call on him for a haircut whenever he wanted one, and Eddie had better be there. Maurice owned him.

Maurice kept his word. They had a party with lots of vino and Italian sausage and pennants flapping. Maurice had a flower in his lapel. He made a little speech. A lot of famous jocks dropped in. Maurice turned over the keys to Eddie, and Eddie was glowing talking about the new Eddie's. Eddie moved from the back chair, back near the shoeshine stand, to the front.

Eddie, of course, took it real big. He was ostensibly the "proprietor." He was popular. He'd been around. The other barbers hoped he wouldn't get a swelled head. Maurice kept smiling. Well, let Eddie think he was the owner.

One of those deals Maurice was always talking over on the phone lured Maurice to Palm Springs. Eddie hung around the front, trying to figure where the EDDIE'S sign was going to be.

Maurice's deals in Palm Springs took less than a week.

Returning to New York JFK Airport, Maurice told his driver (of the Rolls) to drop him at the Dawn Patrol. This was going to be pleasant.

He'd have his own barber, whom he owned, give him a trim in a shop that he owned when he went home to meet his wife, whom he hoped he owned. It was cozy. Just like he planned it. Eddie had better be there.

When the Rolls rolled up to the Dawn Patrol Maurice leaped out, shouting, "Hi, Eddie!"

Eddie was right there in front, grinning. Maurice embraced him.

"How was the trip?" Eddie asked.

"Fine, fine," Maurice said. Maurice was happy to see Eddie was idle. He didn't have a customer. He could get a haircut without waiting! He was feeling his power.

"Can you take me now?" Maurice asked.

Eddie didn't answer immediately. It seemed to Maurice that he gave him a different look than he'd seen before. Maurice, looking at Eddie, noticed that he was wearing a dark jacket.

"Oh, were you just leaving for dinner?" Maurice asked. That would explain the dark jacket.

Eddie stood erect at the cash register, with the reservation book in front of him, a businesslike gentleman in a business suit.

"Oh, I get you a good barber to give you a haircut, boss," laughed Eddie. "I no cut hair any longer since I'm the boss of Eddie's and own my own shop."

25

HUMOR—
PERSONAL, SEXIER,
MORE RIBALD

As humor changes—and it does, with amazing swiftness—you observe that it gets more personal, more physical, sexier, more ribald, and sometimes a little strained and less funny.

It gets slippery and out of control and unpredictable.

Rodney Dangerfield is a beacon of success in today's upside-down world of improvisational humor. If you like him, you may not know that thousands think him moronic.

"I don't get no respect." Is that funny?

I didn't think so the first few times I heard him say it. But when he'd said it hundreds of times in person, on radio and TV, in airports when you're waiting for your luggage, I began to feel sorry for the guy who never got no respect. His parents moved away and didn't leave no forwarding address; they rented out his room; his bride's parents sent him a thank you for taking her off their hands. Yes, it was amusing.

It was the repetition, the saying it over and over and *over*, and the ungrammatical part—it wouldn't have been funny if he said he didn't get *any* respect—that made me smile.

And Rodney uses sex. Oh, yes, he does.

He's a pretty sexy kid when he's growing up, and all the boys in his street gang wanted a virgin.

Well, the boys in my gang wanted a virgin, too.

But Rodney found a virgin. The boys in his gang got him a virgin.

It was an unbelievable emotional experience for him, the deflowering of the innocent darling, and he would never forget it. He hoped for a nice compliment from the girl and waited a little impatiently for her to speak up. But Rodney didn't get no respect.

He gently asked her, "How was it?"

She sniffed, "I've had better."

Rodney probably worked five or six weeks on that joke, trying it out in improvisation clubs and with his own writers and gag mechanics before tossing it off in a major TV appearance—and then overhearing some critic denounce it as dirty material.

Rodney and the few comic geniuses in his bracket have to concern themselves not only with sex and morals fashions, but with international politics and shifting geography.

Billy Crystal, speaking to a largely Jewish audience at Emory University in Atlanta, just kidding around, said that they had almost as big a crowd out for him as they had the night before "for the PLO dance troupe.

"College has sure changed since I was a student in Long Island majoring in cafeteria," he said. His girlfriend "finished up in shopping—at NYU." Those were "the scared '60s."

Remember the rock concert in Woodstock? Sex was open in the crowd, and one speaker harangued them, "You didn't come here to do what you're doing."

"Yes, we did," they answered him and went right on doin' what they were doin'.

"They were responsible for the Herpes epidemic," Billy thought.

Billy mentioned racial problems, too—little Jewish boys trying to compete against big black *men* basketball stars.

"Jewish kids not old enough to have body hair playing against these giants," he said. "The blacks were almost pros. They traveled by Greyhound bus. They had one bus for the players and one for the players' children—and there was still another bus for the children of the player's children," he said, but of course he was exaggerating about that.

Though Jewish people delighted in having children and were good parents, Billy said he wondered how his grandparents had been able to have active sex lives.

"The Orthodox especially," he pointed out.

"Every old photograph I saw of them, the men were never out of their long black overcoats."

The female invasion of the field of comedy, led by Joan Rivers and Bette Midler, produced some outrageous material and some that was mild. One comedienne put in three words a marvelous description of Warren Beatty.

"Jack the Zipper," she called him.

They were the children of rebellion, mouthing the naughty things their parents would have disapproved of them saying. Their audiences were 25ish to 40, who believed themselves smarter than the generation that preceded them.

Girls' allusions to sex sounded sexier because girls (often surprisingly young) were doing the alluding. They blithely tossed off the forbidden words and did it sweetly. One of the comediennes who worked her way up via the insult route trailblazed by Don Rickles took exception to insults fired back at her by some customers (who only wanted to be "friendly").

A fight resulted—one of the few that was strictly between girls, with no men allowed.

A girl didn't have to be pretty or sexy to be a comedienne. In fact, beauty often distracted. Seeing a plain girl trying to do a routine in a club, many another plain girl said, "I can do what she's doing." Besides, she also thought, "it looks like a nice way to meet guys."

Some comediennes were born.

"Where we used to have two girls in 100 comedians, now we may have 20," one cafe booker told me. He added, "By the time they've worked in these joints a year, they've really become experienced. You wouldn't want your brother to marry one."

WHAT WAS FUNNY THEN

Show Business oldsters like to tell how Milton Berle, clowning onstage, waved away the smoke coming from the cigar of a man down on the first row and shouted, "Don't you ever inhale?"

"Not when you're in the room," retorted the smoker.

So many are credited with that ad lib that I don't wish to add one more.

Wise showman, columnist, and millionaire Billy Rose, who knew so many stars enjoying their "hot second in history," said that the big laugh he remembered from the 1930s and 1940s was Jimmy Durante starring in *Jumbo* at Billy's Hippodrome.

Durante was accused of stealing an elephant.

"Where yuh goin' with that elephant?" demanded the sheriff.

"*What* elephant?" innocently answered Schnozzola.

A big laugh in Billy's day, it hardly got a snicker in modern TV.

Back in those days, Harry Houdini, the controversial magician and escape artist, appearing before a celebrity crowd at the Winter Garden, had a new trick.

Would somebody look closely in his mouth?

Houdini was going to place needles and thread in his mouth, separately, then close his mouth, and in seconds he would bring out the needles, magically threaded.

Houdini picked not a celebrity but an apparent nonentity.

"What do you see?" Houdini asked the man.

"PYORRHEA!" shouted the little man, who turned out to be Groucho Marx, without fake mustache, spoiling a trick.

Men's rooms have been joke locales.

Columnist Drew Pearson was reportedly attacked by Senator Huey Long in a men's room.

Afterward it was reported that a drunk in the same men's room wandered up to a urinal and said to a man more or less occupying it, "Are you Drew Pearson?"

The occupant replied, "Hell no, I'm just startin'."

When Gloria Swanson died in 1983 I found I was one of the few who remembered seeing her cause a sensation in 1951 when a whalebone stay in her evening gown broke through her dress and stood erect like an exclamation point during a love scene with David Niven in a play called *Nina*.

First nighters saw the little piece of white rising and nudged each other and began whispering.

Gloria heard the whispers but couldn't see the stay. Niven saw it but couldn't do anything. He went right on with the dialogue.

"Out of the corner of my eye I saw something," Gloria said. "I didn't know what it was. I was afraid if I pulled it I might pull the whole dress off."

The experienced trouper maneuvered expertly.

Swinging around, getting her back to the audience, in violation of the stage traditions, she gave the stay a gentle pull and tossed it over her shoulder onto the floor.

Gloria and Niven continued without interruption, and the whispering ceased. Constance Bennett, Hope Hampton, and others applauded. Niven had tried to help but only made the stay more visible.

Hadn't been such excitement since the monkeys in Billy Rose's show misbehaved right on stage.

THE BEST—LOWER CASE "Fred Allen"

The Great One, whom Show Business respected, admired, and appreciated, was Fred Allen, who came up from vaudeville where he started as "the world's worst juggler."

He was known as one of the really civilized wits of our time when he died of a heart attack almost in the doorway of his apartment building on Seventh Avenue in New York on St. Patrick's Day, 1956.

I regarded him as a friend and tried over the years to contribute to immortalizing his wit.

In August in those years I often asked Fred Allen to write me a "guest column." Designed to give columnists a vacation, they have since been scuttled. They were usually written by a press agent for the guest and promised to be dull, and kept their promise.

But Fred Allen enjoyed the mental exercise of pretending to be a columnist and wrote his own. Groucho Marx wrote his.

John O'Hara also wrote one for me, so incomprehensible that I could not discover what it was about. Unable to face him and say, "Thanks, but you must not have been feeling well," I never mentioned it.

I also abandoned guest columns.

Fred Allen liked to write letters. From playing around the typewriter, he got to tapping out noncapitalized words and began writing his name "fred allen."

So the postman would drop off a letter strikingly different because the words had no capital letters.

"how do you do it?" he would write from a favorite summer place.

"with gay abandon you write of falsies and their contents.

"i blush when i see breast of chicken on the menu. the first time i saw jane russell i wondered how she got her kneecaps in her sweater."

As NBC's big Sunday night radio comedian, constantly being censored, he naturally developed a cynical look at life. I believe he was the fellow who discovered a summer resort so dull that the tide went out and never came back in.

"there is a british nudist around the beach who wears a monocle on his navel," he wrote to me. "the new jersey mosquitoes are so big this year that one of them stung a greyhound bus and it couldn't get through the lincoln tunnel."

Fred Allen assailed the NBC vice-presidents who, he maintained, didn't know what their duties were, and by the time they found out, they were no longer there.

"Each morning," he said, "vice-presidents are given a molehill with orders to make a mountain of it by five o'clock."

Frequently these molehills were jokes that Fred wanted to use on the air.

Besides having an imaginary feud with Jack Benny, Fred Allen liked Bishop Fulton J. Sheen on TV and reported he was pleased that TV created a stained glass tube just for him.

"texas is still abounding in opportunity," one of his lowercase missives informed me. "in one texas town they struck oil, in a cemetery. four hundred dead people became millionaires."

His sense of humor enabled him to enjoy reminiscing about his days in vaudeville when he lived with other performers, including midgets.

"Midgets traveled in clusters on trains," he recalled.

"One midget in a lower berth complained that another

midget in an upper berth had insomnia and kept him awake all night by walking up and down in his upper berth."

He knew them all, including the gags about condensed milk and how they got the cows to sit down on those little cans.

The 17-year-old boy who killed his mother and father and asked for clemency on grounds that he was an orphan was also familiar.

"This last joke had been used by Artemus Ward 50 years before I got around to it," he said.

With that kind of joke serving some comedians very well, it's understandable that Fred Allen should write some material for himself.

George Burns was a contemporary. Burns was not yet with Gracie Allen but was one half of "Burns and Lorraine."

Lorraine chased Burns around the house with a hot poker (so Burns said in the act), but he ran into a closet and closed the door. She yelled, "Come out, you coward."

"Did you come out of the closet?" he was asked.

"Not me," Burns said. "In my house I'm the boss."

Fred Allen liked another performer of the day, a good-looking English boy named Archibald Leach. He was lean and brown with gleaming white teeth, a Prince Charming hero type. His curly hair and fine features in a show named *Polly* got him good reviews. But he was disgusted when the show closed and told Fred he was going to drive to California and try it there.

Fred wished him luck and told him he would be good.

Archie Leach didn't tell Fred he was going to change his name to Cary Grant.

Years later, when Cary Grant was a big star and part owner of Fabergé, he was in the audience when Dean Martin opened at a Las Vegas hotel. Dean acknowledged Grant's presence by saying, "He sent me a whole case of Fabergé, and you know, it ain't bad on the rocks."

I report happily that Cary Grant later got into the practice of complimenting me on humor from the shows that I printed and claimed he kept some of them to repeat to his chums.

"C.G." was the kind of guy Fred Allen enjoyed. He had taste.

"Some guys," Fred said, and he would name them if you asked, "have about as much taste as a yogurt sandwich."

26
WHEN I
WAS STUCK UP

Like some guys enjoy recounting tales of their amatory adventures and how they suffered when they carried a torch, I adore retelling the story of how I was stuck up on Broadway at 1:40 A.M. while on my way to an egg sandwich at the "Hookerama."

The yarn gets better every time I tell it, and the last time I heard it from me I was pretty brave, if I do say so myself.

You ever had that feeling at 20 minutes to two you have to have an egg sandwich (on white bread, fried hard, salt and pepper)?

I had a little office, a hideaway in the Broadway Theater, Broadway and 53rd. You remember seeing *Evita* there, and *Fiddler on the Roof,* and *My Fair Lady?* A lot of press agents and showgirls trooped in and out in the daytime. One day word went out I wanted a topless secretary, and Xaviera Hollander came in and typed topless to prove it could be done without anybody or anything getting hurt.

So it's February, 1969, and it's been snowing, and all is very quiet outside my window down there on the street when I get this urge for an egg.

The "Hookerama" is the name we gave to a small restaurant on the corner because that's where the hookers seemed to gather, although that was rumor because we didn't hang out there.

There had been a nightclub next door, but we said, "We only go there for the stabbings."

It was that club where some comedian said, "You've been a good audience, and I'm going to open the doors and let you see an accident."

There's nothing spooky about it as I descend the stairway into the front of the theater, the ticket booth area, although I am conscious of being alone as I unlock the front door of the theater, step out onto the sidewalk, and turn back to the door to lock it from the outside. I'm now on the sidewalk, about 10 or 11 blocks from Times Square, which has its own adventures around 42nd Street from time to time.

"What is it with me having a craving for an egg sandwich at this hour?" I was thinking as I stepped toward the street, dark and lonely. The usual hookers were absent. The snow had driven them inside.

I could now almost taste the egg, lots of ketchup, and hot coffee, on a snowy night.

Suddenly, from my left, two young men who must have been hugging the side of the building or waiting in another doorway jumped at me.

"Your wallet!" one of them snapped in a low but sharp voice. He thrust some hard object in my stomach. They seemed to be white boys, in their 20s, normally dressed, and very direct.

I was very cool. Friends said later I froze and was scared almost to death.

I assumed, although the young man holding that hard object against my stomach didn't say so, that the hard object was a gun.

A pistol, an automatic, a shotgun, a submachine gun, a guided missile, I didn't care. It must be a gun. This young man would not be out on the street without a gun, would he? It wouldn't be safe. The other young man assisted him by jamming his hand toward my inside jacket pocket for my wallet. The first young man jammed the hard object against my stomach with greater force.

"You must have been very composed," one of my admirers said later, whereupon another admirer said, "Decomposed is probably more like it."

Now it occurred to me that the one thing I wanted to do was cooperate with these two young men in their after-dark outing.

"J-j-j-just a s-s-s-second," I said and demonstrated to the second young man that men of stature like myself often thwart holdup men by not carrying their wallets in their jackets but in their left-side trouser pockets.

He was practically ripping the wallet out of my pants. The young man was still pushing that hard object against my stomach.

I must say I grew even more cooperative. With trembling hands I tore the money from my wallet—about $75—babbled something about "Can I k-k-keep the c-c-cards?" and these two young gentlemen then turned and ran. They ran to the right, carrying their booty and their hard object.

Yes, they ran one way and I ran the other way.

Then I saw them join a third presumably young white man who seemed to be a lookout waiting on the corner, although why they needed three men to hold me up was a mystery and also a waste of manpower. About 30 seconds would be the time required for me.

The three nice young men ran northward, probably heading for a subway, and I did not forget my egg sandwich but ran as fast as I could to the Hookerama, and yes, that's where the girls were.

I was feeling brave as I entered the little ham-and-eggery.

Yes, my intrepidity grew, it multiplied, as I pictured them running one way and me running the other way even faster. I strode to the counter, ordered an egg sandwich on white, fried hard and "a full bottle of ketchup."

My arrival was observed by one of *les girls*. The Hookerama is informal; no introductions required. A prostitute joined me at the counter. I know she was one because she said, "You want a date?"

I laughed at the irony of life. Business as usual!

"Just my luck," I said charmingly. "I meet a beautiful girl like you and I'm broke. I was just held up."

"Held up?" she cried indignantly. "Where, where?" You could see that this little lady was for law enforcement and against crime. She summoned girls from other booths, who marveled at me.

"But," one of them pointed out, "you have your watch. And they didn't take your ring."

"You know what I think," said the Stranger in the Night who had joined me at the counter. She was looking at my watch and ring. "I think those guys were amateurs."

"Amateurs!" I scoffed. "This guy with the gun, I guess he was the hit man, the leader of the mob. He was handlin' that gun pretty good. I guess it was a gun."

Milady beside me at the counter was philosophical. She shook her head reflectively.

"Amateurs everywhere," she said. "Amateurs are ruining my business, too."

27

WISH
I HADN'T

About 10 years after I'd been unable to get a writing job in Washington I went back there to act as master of ceremonies of a show for President Truman given by the White House correspondents—an evening I shall never forget because I got such stage fright that I ran around saying Dinah Shore should sing "Dinah" when the fact was she was then singing "Dinah."

While not being quite with it, I introduced Frankie Carle as a noted singer when actually he was better known for being in President Truman's racket—playing the piano.

After replying to a toast by saying, "Nobody's going to beat me out of a drink; I drink a toast to you," the President then told me, "You were a good toastmaster," which I could not wait to report to my B.W., who said:

"What else could he say?"

President Truman was beloved for his earthy humor and in one anecdote was pictured as saying to Bess Truman he was glad they were finally putting horse manure on the White House lawn.

"Daddy," spoke up daughter Margaret Truman, "I wish you wouldn't say 'horse manure.' "

Mama Bess said, "Let him say 'horse manure,' Margaret. You should have heard what he said before he cleaned it up."

I was asked to MC that show because as a columnist on Broadway I could facilitate bringing down certain stars of the theater.

I'd ridden with his campaign tours of New York City and knew how "Give 'Em Hell Harry" liked to pour it on. He had some gag writers supplying jokes even then, back in '48. He said an economist "is a man who wears a watch chain with a Phi Beta Kappa key at one end and no watch at the other." His face crinkled up in a grin when he said that. A Washington musician, upon hearing the election results in '48, said, "Oh, my God! Four more years of 'The Missouri Waltz!' "

He also claimed that he had weak eyes as a boy and couldn't play baseball so they got him another job.

"Cheerleader?"

"No. Umpire!"

I attained the dream of columnists—became syndicated—in 1944 when United Features took on my jottings. I made plenty of silly mistakes. But I didn't wait to be syndicated to make mistakes. One of my first chores on the cafe beat was to attend a party honoring the debutante of the year. I met a young lady named Oona O'Neill, who meant nothing to me at that moment. So, in my endeavor to learn all about her I could, I asked "What does your father do?"

"He writes," replied Eugene O'Neill's daughter.

Oona, who became Mrs. Charles Chaplin, and a friend, never minded my making that error.

While enjoying the success of my book, *I Am Gazing into My 8-Ball*, I cabled George Bernard Shaw, in a manner that he must have found preposterous, that I was sending him a copy and would like to interview him. He replied that he had more books than he could read the rest of his life and that he charged 10,000 pounds, or maybe it was 50,000, for an interview.

I thought he was kidding, but he wasn't. I hired a car and drove to his village and pounded on the door. He wouldn't see me. But I found he had a good heart, although I believe he didn't want it known. He suggested to the postmistress of his village that she might sell as souvenirs some postcards he'd written to her asking that she send him some postage stamps.

"They bear my signature, and you might get as much as a shilling for them," he said.

"I hate to tell you this," she replied, "but I've been selling them—and getting five shillings."

Winston Churchill saw me, after Bernard Baruch requested an interview for me and, after we'd talked about five minutes and I'd taken out a notebook, announced brusquely that nothing he said could be printed. He fired me cables warning me again that nothing could be published and, if it was, he would complain to my publisher, a friend of Baruch's. I couldn't understand his unfriendly attitude until Marquis Childs, the international columnist, explained, "He gets $1 a word for that. Why should he give it to you for nothing?"

George Bernard Shaw—well, I regret that I wasn't more humble. I would love to have known the old buzzard. Critics are fun. One of my dearest friends along the way was Irving Hoffman, publicist for the movies, friend of Walter Winchell and Irving Berlin, a demon when he didn't like a show.

"What's wrong with my radio show?" I asked him.

"You are," he said.

There was a fine lady whose first name was Ilka. She wrote a play. It was too tempting. He ruined her. He said "It made me Ilka."

In these days of conscientious young criticism it is hard to believe there was once a *Woman's Wear* reviewer named Kelcey Allen who made no secret of his habit of dozing at shows.

One night, before an opening, an actor entering Sardi's restaurant, known for its theater customers, saw Kelcey at dinner and sang out to him, "What's the matter, Kelcey? You're not asleep yet."

Kelcey answered, "You're not onstage yet."

President Truman, you might recall, disposed of a music critic in his own way when the critic panned Margaret Truman's singing. Truman wrote him a letter threatening to kick him in the jockstrap. The press found out, and so did the comedians. Truman was hailed as the great literary figure, a man of letters, who would rather write than be President. The National Press Club gave a father-and-daughter night at which I was again MC. Truman said in his own little speech that it was the best thing that happened to him all week but that he'd had a terrible week. He proved his humanness by asking each daughter there to give him her autograph.

He was proud of his daughter and phoned Tallulah Bankhead his thanks for "being so sweet to my baby" on Tallulah's radio program, "The Big Show."

"Do you call President Truman 'Dolling'?" I asked Tallulah.

"Dolling, I call everybody Dolling," replied Tallulah, "but especially Dolling Mr. Truman."

28

CHARLIE CHAPLIN DIDN'T SNIVEL

Although it was a hot afternoon late in May, Charlie Chaplin lit fire to some logs in the fireplace in his charming villa in the Swiss Alps and stood there warming his back.

"Would you like a sweater or coat?" he asked, quite seriously.

"No, thanks," I said. It was actually perspiration weather there in the town of Vevey, where he had a 37-acre estate and this rambling residence that some visitors said seemed a miniature White House.

He was going to take my wife and me walking over these sunny grounds.

Stepping gingerly to the door of a closet, he pulled out a winter coat with a caracul collar and got his arms into it.

"When you get to be 80, which I was April 16," he said, "time has its ravages." The year was 1969.

His voice was steady and clear, and there was a soft laugh in it. "I'm always cold. I hope to go to hell when I die so I can keep warm."

Pulling the caracul collar snugly around his neck, he said,

"But I'm sure there's no question about that. Now, shall the old fellow lead the way?"

His much younger, sprier wife, Oona O'Neill, wasn't going walking.

"The Old Lady has a runny nose and doesn't want to give it to you." Bundled up now, he motioned for us to follow him out into the sunshine, he in his overcoat. The whiteness of his hair was made more prominent by a brown hat he clapped on his head.

And so a little octogenarian should lead us.

"Nothing bothers me," he assured us. "I'm as strong as those." He pointed up to the snow-peaked Dents au Midi (the Middle Teeth).

"I go swimming in the unheated pool in the morning, although Oona says it's too much of a shock for my system. I play a little tennis with her. I can still beat her, too. I have a drink at six. Oona won't let me have one until then."

But maybe Oona was right. "I fell the other day in London running for a bus. I wanted to ride past the part where I was born. It's all being pulled down. I stubbed my toe; my face was all covered with blood; I broke my glasses. I was so embarrassed."

As we strolled down toward the pool, I watched to see whether he would shed the coat or any part of it. He didn't.

Proud as he was of his grounds, he was pleased, too, with his ability to continue working. He was writing, writing, writing. Not *acting!* "I don't want to squirt that stuff on my face anymore."

"I guess I'm just a little genius," he said, poking fun at himself.

Oona the Old Lady dominated his thoughts as we concluded the tour and returned to the villa, where the butler said that in the English tradition, tea would be served.

Small tea cookies were served, and I promptly dropped one, with all its jelly contents, on the floor. Our host dropped one of his tea cookies on the floor, too.

My Beautiful Wife insisted that he had dropped his deliberately so we wouldn't feel bad.

"There are plenty of chicks left in our nest," he said. "I would like to have some more, but I'm afraid Oona is too old for that sort of thing." Poor Oona had to hear that joke again and again.

Indeed, Chaplin said, his children were not very aware of his worldwide fame. He hadn't worn the little derby and twirled the little cane for 40 years—half his life ago.

"But don't the younger children want you to put on the outfit and do it for them?"

"No. They take everything for granted."

The Old Lady cooked every Thursday—no, it was Tuesday, cook's day off—and he showed us the kitchen, also his study where he worked.

"And there's the bad news there." He indicated a script half opened on a typewriter, a dictionary open beside it.

Some London newspapers were open on the floor beside an easy chair as though they'd been dropped there by somebody weary of reading them.

"You never quit working?" I said.

"No, the kids and the Old Lady say that's what keeps me going."

"Do you think so?"

"Whatever the Old Lady says."

Standing in the sun-drenched driveway, he said, "I might see you in New York—there's talk."

"Stay warm," I said.

And we rode away thinking how gracious he had been. I had interviewed him in London at the Savoy where he had an apartment or suite looking out on the Thames; I had interviewed him at dubbing sessions, at screenings, at restaurants in New York, in a lobby at the Broadway Theater in New York, and now at his home. Nobody could tell me he wasn't anything but a fine man.

Charlie Chaplin did come to New York three years later to receive the tribute from Show Business at Philharmonic Hall. All the old jokes about his age came to mind: "Oh, to be 75 again!" when he first looked at Sophia Loren.

I found him in a corner of the hall talking to a few friends. I went over. I stood watching. Chaplin the cool one was very moved at the tribute. He kept choking it back.

Oona was right there. "I mustn't snivel," Charlie Chaplin said. "Oona said 'If you snivel one more time...!' "

He bit his lips and his eyes got cloudy, but he didn't snivel.

29

PUT A HEAD
ON THAT

James Caesar Petrillo, the much caricatured and cartooned head of the American Federation of Musicians, was by far the best drinking companion I ever had, and all he did was tell the bartender, "Put a head on that."

The plump, gregarious, loquacious, occasionally pugnacious labor czar was always calling a musicians' strike—or threatening to, and that set the cartoonists to work. Jimmy had walls full of their caricatures, which emphasized that he had a beer belly.

In fact, there was a strike on (of elevator operators) that night of Labor Day, 1946, when I caught up with Jimmy at Toots Shor's bar.

It having been a holiday, everybody was playful, like there was no school tomorrow.

"What are yuh drinkin', Wilson? Put a head on that," Jimmy kept saying. Phil Baker, the radio star, played his accordion, and Petrillo sang "Ave Maria" and told about a monkey in a Chicago zoo that didn't like him. Somebody picked up a pretzel basket and passed it around like a collection plate, and somebody's shoe got in it.

"Get the hell outa here, you guys. It's 4:00 A. M.," Lenny the bartender said.

I went back next evening. There was the Music Czar, looking very rumpled and bloodshot.

"I don't know where I slept last night," he said. "Tried to walk up to my room at the Waldorf. Twenty-six stories. But couldn't cross no picket line.

"Gahdamn unions. They'll ruin the country. Hey, bartender . . . !"

THIRD
INTERMISSION

When Lyndon Johnson visited the Catskills, Dan Stampler said all the hotels had signs "LBJ shlepped here."

"The best way to win an argument with a woman is to hit her over the head with a mink coat."

Richard Burton said, "Elizabeth has been on a cooking spree, and we are going to lose all our kitchen help."

In white tie and tails, Averell Harriman, former governor and ambassador, had attended a diplomatic dinner and stopped at Toots Shor's on the way home. As he was departing, Joe E. Lewis said, "Well, so long, Ave, see you when you're better dressed."

Lauren Bacall, on Ronald Reagan's inaugural day, said, "This would never have happened if Hollywood would have given him better parts."

Henry Morgan's program was sponsored by a company selling elevator heels. Henry said he wouldn't be caught dead in those shoes. Forced to retract, Morgan said, "I would be caught dead, but that's the only place I'd be caught wearing them."

From my column, August 19, 1966: "If you think TV is bad now, imagine how much worse it's going to be in 20 years."

Asked why she wouldn't pose for pictures with a dancer, my B.W. said, "I decided years ago I should never pose with anybody but grandmothers and not them when they're Marlene Dietrich or Joan Bennett."

At Duke Ellington's funeral in 1974, I remembered the Duke telling me, "Joe Trent and I wrote a whole musical show in one night in 1923. It was *Chocolate Kiddies.* We wrote it in one night and it played the Berlin Winter Garden for two years. It made stars of Josephine Baker and Adelaide Hall. That's what comes from being illiterate."

"You were illiterate?" I asked the Duke.

"Sort of," the Duke replied. "Nobody had told us you couldn't write a show in one night."

Duke Ellington was a Great Lover. Young girls were always following him and vice versa. Once, in Chicago, he was an hour late for a concert. After a master of ceremonies had attempted an apology, Duke smiled at the audience and said, "Ladies and gentlemen, if you could have seen her, you would have forgiven me."

Ethel Merman, going into *Annie Get Your Gun,* announced "I'll wear my long low-cut gown and I'll show them a thing or two." (1946)

Jack Donnelly told of a woman who had so many facelifts, she was talking through her eyes.

While Jack Dempsey was sitting beside his swimming pool in Los Angeles, chatting with author-editor Gene Fowler, he noticed a stranger flailing about in the pool. Dempsey ordered him out. The stranger kept on splashing about wildly, and Dempsey repeated the command to get out. "Make me," snarled the stranger. The former world's heavyweight champion walked quietly to the edge of the pool, and the swimmer leaped out and said, "Come on if you want to fight." Dempsey broke up laughing. The "stranger" was a midget whom practical joker Fowler had "planted" in the pool as a gag.

A GI returning from the war in Europe said, "When I came back from overseas I was crazy to be with a woman. The first girl I saw I dragged back of the handball court. She beat me 21 to 7."

Otto Preminger invited a Hollywood friend, Ed Chodorov, to dinner. Chodorov said he couldn't accept; he had a dinner date that night with another Hollywood friend, a writer named _____. Preminger exclaimed, "He's not a dinner date. He's a lunch date!"

Zsa Zsa Gabor, once married to George Sanders, said, "Ve vere both in love vith him. I fell out of love vith him, but he didn't."

Texas Republicans, always critical of Lyndon B. Johnson before, during, and after his time as President, said, "An FBI man opened a gate at his ranch by mistake, and all the cattle went home."

Walter Matthau liked the way another actor described the crooked lawyer he played in *Fortune Cookie:* "He could find a loophole in the Ten Commandments."

"Why is it that panty hose look so good on a woman and so awful hanging over the shower curtain?" (Steven Kessler)

When the Queen of England visited California there was a problem of protocol. The Queen was wearing a hat, and Nancy Reagan was wearing a diamond Tiara." (Angie Papadakis)

Darryl Zanuck, who produced *Wilson,* said that Wilson, while governor of New Jersey, got a call that a close friend, the U.S. Senator from New Jersey, had just died. As he sat there stunned he was phoned by a prominent New Jersey politician, who asked, "May I take the senator's place?" Wilson replied: "It's agreeable with me if it's OK with the undertaker!"

When H. Allen Smith was a feature writer on the *New York World-Telegram,* he phoned in sick one day. He said he'd slipped on the ice and hurt his foot. B. O. McAnney, the city editor, asked, "How did he get his foot in a highball glass?"

During a heat wave, a Pecos, Texas, church displayed a sign, "You think it's hot *here!*"

Morey Amsterdam, the comedian, said he was so corny, when he died they wouldn't have to bury him, they'd shuck him.

While visiting at a friend's house in Florida, Eva Gabor wanted to swim but had no swimsuit. Thinking nobody would see her, she went in nude. A neighbor saw her and called, "Hello, Eva." Eva sang back, "Oh, hello, dolling! It's Zsa Zsa."

A Japanese man married an American girl, and they had a white baby. The father said "Occidents will happen."

Milton Berle, when acting as master of ceremonies, enjoyed introducing songwriters such as Julie Styne, Sammy Cahn, Hoagy Carmichael, and Jimmy Van Heusen. He'd say, "There's bad news. Richard Wagner is alive and well, living in London, and has a good lawyer."

30

HOW TO CONDUCT THE INTERVIEW

Having noted that I have had astounding success with the medium, students of journalism are always writing me letters asking, "How do you do an interview?" And I am unselfish enough to state that first you should get the subject in a friendly mood by asking them if it is true they were born out of wedlock, following through with an affectionate observation as to what went wrong with subject's facelift. Was the job botched by some butcher, or was the plastic surgeon from a long line of veterinarians getting vengeance in an ancient family feud?

A couple of simple icebreaker questions like this should elicit no end of what we call quotable quotes, and from then on it will practically write itself. The "born out of wedlock" question is one of my favorites. One famous poet told me he was illegitimate and had found out that he was from a long line of bastards and wanted to get that in print before some of the scandal magazines scooped me on it.

Generally, though, I do conclude that an interview based on a smart-ass questions (clinically known as the "impertinent interview") is a success if somebody calls from Hollywood and says the whole thing is a tissue of lies.

The word *tissue* is always used, referring to bathroom tissue that you wrote it on or should have.

You senior citizens may recall that three or four wars ago there was a family unit known as the Andrews Sisters who committed a song about the beer barrel polka to notoriety. The less said about their sex appeal, the less you have to retract. But they were hard-working ladies, and one day they invited me up to the Paramount Theater stage door to help them break their contract with Universal Pictures.

"Our pictures stink," one of the sisters said right off. I forget which one.

It may have been the fourth one, Lou Levy, who was married to La Verne, or maybe it was Patty he was married to; anyway, they called him the fourth Andrews Sister, and he was their manager.

"Your pictures stink." I wrote that down carefully in my wad of copy paper. I wasn't a columnist yet and didn't rate notebooks.

They said their last stinker outstank their previous stinker, which also rated very high in the smell department.

"The critics were right about our turkey before that," Maxene said. "And they were so mean telling us about our looks. They said our eyes were sunk in and we walked like football players."

"Yes," said Laverne—I think it was Laverne; it wasn't Lou (he slept 'til noon)—"we say, 'We're not happy,' and they say, 'That's all right,' and they pat you on the fanny. They patted me so much on the fanny I lost 15 pounds."

Well, I took my wads of copy paper back at the office and straightened it all out, except which one said what, and I said to myself that was an awful way to talk about somebody that's paying you a big salary.

Universal Pictures felt the same way I did and called the girls from Hollywood and said they had broken their contract and they were going to can them and hire the Smith Brothers to take over their personal appearances. So the fourth Andrews Sister said the girls never said no such thing as I printed and, if they'd said it, why hadn't he heard them say it. So the Andrews Sisters promised to shut up and got a little raise and some more pats on the fanny, and everybody was happy but me. It taught me something, too.

Always have a witness.

That was one kind of a Hollywood phone call, but there is another kind such as resulted from an interview I did with the famous Shirley Temple Black, the illustrious diplomat, when she was the world's most noted movie star, at age 16.

I had just begun to interview Shirley Temple, the whole world's sweetheart, at the Stork Club, when I happened to notice that Walter Winchell, the columnist, was there. This was not surprising. I happened to notice that Walter Winchell was talking. This was not surprising either. He was talking to Shirley Temple, whom I was supposed to be interviewing. He was telling her about a man he had known and loved for many years, named Walter Winchell.

Each time I addressed a question to Miss Temple, Walter Winchell would reveal something of a flattering nature to her about Walter Winchell.

He seemed to enjoy my discomfort.

"How you doing with your interview, bub?" he would say, making left-handed notes of his witticisms on a menu.

During an interim of one or two seconds, when Winchell was not talking because he was writing, somebody happened to mention Governor Thomas E. Dewey, who was running for President, and it developed that Miss Temple, at age 16, was a violent supporter for Governor Dewey, who, as everybody knew, was our next President.

"I even have a Dewey badge!" announced Miss Temple. Opening her bag, she plucked the badge from the depths and pinned it on herself.

Well, I wrote a column about that, inasmuch as the sayings of Walter Winchell about Walter Winchell were hardly newsworthy. And this piece of mine about the world's greatest little movie doll coming out for President Dewey was picked up by the news services.

Surprisingly, everybody in the country was not for President

Dewey. Some people were for Franklin D. Roosevelt, who was still running.

So about 11:30 A.M. next day I was wakened by a phone call from Don King at Selznick Productions in Hollywood.

Our conversation went like this:

"Earl, this is Don King in publicity at Selznick. How are you?"

"Fine. How are you?"

"Fine."

"Fine."

"How's Ted?" (Ted Thackrey, our editor)

"He's fine."

"How's your charming wife?"

"She's fine."

"Fine," Don King said. "Say Earl, did you have a column today about Shirley Temple?"

"Who?" I asked sleepily.

"Shirley Temple."

"Oh, yes, I believe I did."

"That column of yours on Shirley Temple. . . ."

"Who?"

"Shirley Temple."

"Oh yes."

"That column on Shirley Temple. Is it a pretty good column?"

"N-n-no. I didn't care too much for it."

"Is that column going to run here in the *Los Angeles Daily News?*"

"Uh-huh."

"You know, Earl," Don King said, "I don't think Shirley Temple at 16 should be telling people how to vote, do you?"

"No, I don't, Don."

"Well, Earl, it's been nice talking to you, Earl. How's your charming wife?"

"She's still fine."

"How's Ted?"

"He's still fine, too."

"Well, that's about all was on my mind, Earl. Somebody in

the front office said, 'Call Earl Wilson and give him hell,' and I
did, didn't I, Earl, in case anybody asks?"

"You sure did, Don."

"Fine," Don said.

"Fine," I retorted.

"And I'm going to tell them we had a very constructive
conversation and everything was just fine between us."

"That's fine, Don."

"Fine," Don said.

"And you can also tell them I'm going back to sleep and nothing could be finer than to wake up with a shiner. . . ."

"Fine, Earl, that's just fine. How's your charming wife?"

31
A HOT TIME
ON THE
OLD HONEYMOON

I guess I'd better explain what went on between glamorous Linda Darnell and me on her honeymoon when she was lying there in bed in her white satin nightgown, squirming around under the sheets, and I was talking pretty intimately to her.

"Uhhhh, where's your husband?" I asked her in my low, sultry, come-hither voice.

"Oh, don't worry about Pev Marley interrupting us!" she said in sort of a giggle that was also sexy. "He understands that as a movie actress I have to give interviews—even in bed—in my negligee. Oh," she laughed, "he'll be gone quite a while. . . ." Her voice drifted off.

"Good! I'm sure he knows he can trust you—and me, too." Linda's one of those hard-riding Texas beauties, very restless and always going, and she was tossing around in bed trying to get comfortable.

"Linda," I asked, "what color do you call your gown? Off-white?"

"No! Flesh! It's the color of me, of my skin. My suntanned skin. Do you like that color, Earl?"

"Do I!" I moaned. I reined myself in. "It doesn't have any shoulder straps, does it? Just bare shoulders. Linda, you naughty girl. I saw you in that film when you were in a load of hay."*

> *Miss Darnell, who had a "photographically perfect" face, appeared in *The Song of Bernadette, Forever Amber, Blood and Sand,* and numerous other important pictures. She died tragically of burns at age 43 in 1965 in a fire at the home of her secretary in suburban Chicago. (This column was published at the beginning of the sexual excitement over the brunette beauty.)

"Oh, yes, I was really in the hay, Earl. It was really me, an All-American suntanned girl. They made me so seductive. They kept making that low-cut blouse lower. My skirt they slit up and up and up, and it was kinda tight around the back of me. You know what I'm saying, Earl?"

"You were so sweet, but at the same time you were so *physical,* Linda."

"And they shot me from a lot of angles."

"And all *right* angles, weren't they?"

"I'm just glad you liked me in them," she murmured contentedly.

"You and your flesh-colored negligee! Anyway, there's one thing I have to ask you to do for me, Linda, as a special favor."

"What is it?" Her voice was like a coo, a pussycat's purr. Soft and sweet.

"Your measurements."

"My measurements!" Her laughter was sheer music. "You want to measure me. I heard about you, Earl. You want to put a tape measure to every hill and valley of my body."

"Just so I'll have it accurate, darling," I said. The word just slipped out.

"Wwwwwwellll, since you can get them from my press sheet. . . .' And she reeled them off. And then precious Linda, with that same pussycat purr, said, "Now, if you'll excuse me, I'm going to peel off this negligee."

"You are, Linda? You are!" And squirming out from under the sheets, she began pulling the sexy garment off.

"Shall I—uh—wait?" I asked.

"Why, no, I don't think that's necessary, dear," Linda said. "I hear Pev at the door now with the honeymoon dinner he went out to get us. He said he wasn't going to let me out of bed or out of the room or out of the mood the whole honeymoon. So you say hello to everybody you see there in New York, will you, Earl?"

"Sure, and you say hello to everybody there in Palm Springs, will you? Too bad we couldn't have done this in person."

For I was in my office in New York, and Linda was in her honeymoon hotel in California, and the phone operator said she had another long-distance call waiting.

32

BLOOD WILL FLOW IN HOLLYWOOD

When Ryan O'Neal knocked a couple of teeth out of the handsome face of his son, Griffin O'Neal, I jumped up and hollered, "Attaboy!" because it looks like we're going to have real bloodshed in Hollywood.

Maybe Ryan will even take a swat at Farrah Fawcett, his longtime lady, which would be a nice match, although Farrah might win if kicks to the groin were allowed.

Girls whose muscles are noted for decorative purposes—such as shapely Brooke Shields—would probably step out in front if it got to actual fighting and biting.

The charge that there are no roughhouse guys or girls left in the studios is frequently heard. Everybody knows that half a dozen major male stars are powder puffs, and it's gotten to the point where there's nobody left in the closet to come out. As for Broadway. . . .

It's been the Gay White Way for 50 years, but we didn't know the meaning of the word *gay* 'til the term *pansy* got tiresome.

Now it has become ridiculous. On a TV comedy show a boy broke down and blubbered the awful truth to his father.

"I'm straight," he sobbed.

"You're *what?*" exclaimed Daddykins.

"I have to face it," slurped the son. "My friends have started talking about it, and I wanted you to know, direct from me."

He stepped to the window and considered jumping out. "I'm a heterosexual," he confessed.

The grief-torn father remembered there were vague, whispered rumors a generation ago that there was a black sheep in the family who was straight, or "went straight."

The battling Ryans did some plain speaking about the flaws in their respective characters. That's what we need and suffer a lack of. In a way Joan Rivers's plain speaking is fresh, but it doesn't have the zing of the old-timers I grew up reading and interviewing.

One of my gods was the Baltimore bard and iconoclast H.L. Mencken who, were he alive today, would not say simply that Ronald Reagan is a poor President.

"Woodrow Wilson," he once told me, sitting in the Algonquin quaffing beer with George Jean Nathan, "is a Presbyterian baboon. Hoover was a superior bookkeeper. Truman was an Eighth Avenue haberdasher. I voted for Roosevelt the first time, because how the hell could you vote for Hoover. Those quacks!"

Everybody he didn't like was a quack, and he hardly liked anybody. He had been a drama critic, but he got tired of "Sitting in lousy seats stunk up by prostitutes watching some baboons who thought they could act. Those quacks!"

That was telling them.

33
TOMORROW: Jokes by Computer

Computers have no sense of humor, yet next-decade jokes will be conceived by, written, and fouled up by computers.

I can envisage joke king Joey Adams at the north end of his enormous word processor, punching, punching, 'til he's punchy. He punches, "Who was that lady I seen you with?" He doesn't have to remember the answer. The computer has all that memorized. But today the computer is brain-fogged, and it goofs and delivers an answer to another straight line, "Why does a chicken cross the road?" which is "To get to the other side." It's very sad, and the computer gets docked because the answer was supposed to have been "That was no lady, that was my brother wearing one of the dresses they give the transvestites to wear in the homosexual musical hit, *La Cage aux Folles.*

Gene Barry, the former TV Bat Masterson, one of the lovers in the hit, sneers onstage, "There's *one* transvestite and one *plain* homosexual."

Producer Allan Carr has given Broadway this delightfully

preposterous musical about two male lovers (for 20 years) whose life and love get tangled when their son wants to get married.

Barry, the plain homo, got curious about heterosexual love one night (everybody was talking about it), and he tried it, just the one night, the one time, and a grown son is the result of his folly. Now the son wants to get married (to a woman!), and the girl's parents want to meet the boy's parents, and what a mess it's going to be.

George Hearn, the transvestite who stars in the transvestite show, is asked to clear out one night when the girl's parents drop in. Can't he pretend to be Uncle Al or somebody?

Well, that's the plot, and Uncle Alvin gets mad as a transvestite can get when he's handed men's underwear. He hurls off his wig and stomps out into the theater orchestra section, and I can feel his dress and smell his perfume when he shoots by.

You can see the enormous potential of this breakthrough for "crossover" humor. Men have long enjoyed dressing in women's clothes. Ray Bolger, Milton Berle, and Jack Benny did it for comedy effect, and it worked.

We are learning a lot about the future of humor in other ways. Tomorrow nobody's going to be stupid. Everybody'll be brilliant. No dumb showgirls, no dumb blondes, no dumb wives. No more morons. No more Polish jokes; no more meatheads.

Vera Milton, the malapropist who was supposed to be a dumb blonde showgirl, wasn't that dumb.

Vera was in a cab one night with a guy who was trying to wrestle her out of her sweater and bra, and he said, "Darling, you have marvelous potentialities."

Vera said primly, "Ssssh, the cabdriver will hear you."

Broadway comedy writers made up jokes about Vera. One was about a sophisticated chap who said to her, "You have the face of an old Gainsborough," and she replied, "You don't look so gahdamned good yourself."

Thirty years ago my wife and I took two girls from the Ziegfeld Follies out to a nightclub show to see how dumb they were.

Gorgeous blonde Pat Gaston said she wanted to marry a millionaire. She married Tommy Manville within a year.

"I'll make some money on my own," said the beautiful brunette, Barbara Hall, who won the top prize on "The $64,000 Question" as a Shakespeare expert and subsequently as Barbara Feldon had her own character on "Get Smart."

Still gorgeous and still blonde, Pat Gaston has just written her second novel, which is about the world that Tommy showed her.

Because I'm a columnist, people thought I must know something about beauty, so I became a judge at Miss America and Miss Universe and got booed at the Atlantic City boardwalk one year for not voting for Miss Kansas.

I was called "The Old Man of the Shes" from judging contests. But I couldn't vote for Miss Kansas, though she was beautiful, bouncy, red-haired, and lovely, because she eliminated herself when she came to the "talent" category.

"I have no talent, except to go home, get married, and raise children," Miss Kansas confessed. She had already won best swimsuit category, but if she didn't play the piano, violin, or write poetry, paint, tat, knit, sew, or sing in the choir, she couldn't win Miss America.

So we judges were booed. We voted for beautiful Be Be Shopp, who came from Minnesota and played the vibraharp.

Miss Vibraharp was an ideal choice. With her talent for playing the vibraharp, she felt she was already practically in Show Business.

I fear we forgot about beautiful Miss Kansas, who looked real nice in a sweater but had no talent.

Several years passed, and I was in Hollywood looking over the new crop of girls, and one day Alfred Hitchcock's new find faced me.

"We have met before," the young lady said.

"I was Miss Kansas," she stated.

"The girl I got booed over because I didn't vote for you, though I did want to."

Yes, Alfred Hitchcock said she was one of the most talented actresses he had ever known.

She was Vera Miles, chosen by Hitchcock to be his next star. She was delayed briefly, having gotten pregnant again—one of her talents, you remember. Grace Kelly and Vera Miles broke into the big time at the same time.

Vera Miles never stopped making good movies (or at least giving good performances) and was actually tremendous and remarkable considering that she was the little girl "who had no talent."

Now, about that humor of tomorrow. The computers will have to recognize that Harvey Fierstein and his *Torch Song Trilogy* and *La Cage aux Folles* have made homosexual and transvestite jokes acceptable.

Playwright Fierstein is justifiably proud of his accomplishment. The one-time drag queen has recovered from the suicidal trauma he suffered when he was failing and now considers himself gorgeous and desirable. As he gazes upon photographs of himself in drag, he admits he would go for her (the drag queen) himself if he didn't know that herself was him.

Talk about split personality!

But the jokes must go on.

Congressmen having secret sex lives, whether with secretaries who can't type or with underage pages, will always be joke material.

"If Ronald Reagan doesn't do something about the country's unemployment problem," remarked one comedian, "he'll have an unemployment problem of his own."

Along with ethnic jokes and racial jokes, there'll be dirty jokes. Henny Youngman has a collection of 300 obscene or vulgar yarns that a publisher wants to release to the world.

"But don't use my name, *please!*"

While there will be a stupendous increase in jokes about gays, thanks to *La Cage,* there will be hostility from audiences who don't think homosexuality is humorous. Some mature folk even believe it's too delicate a subject to be discussed openly.

"Nice Guy" Perry Como was doing an Easter fashion TV show a few years ago. Comedy writer Goodman Ace handed him a line: "I think that dress looks familiar. I believe I saw Milton Berle wear it on TV."

Always afraid of offending somebody, Como rejected the line. He wanted to keep the air unpolluted and uncorrupted. He killed a joke by Bishop Sheen saying he wanted to exchange a Christmas present.

"You sent me a tie!" the bishop pointed out.

Little Brenda Lee would sing. Perry would say, "Now I'll give you an ice cream cone." Brenda would say, "No, thanks, Perry. I break out."

Como killed that, too. It was bad taste then. Today it wouldn't be bad taste enough. The little girl would have to say, "No, thanks; it makes my herpes break out."

Because of drugs and war and new fashions in sex, humor tomorrow is going to be a very serious business—and let's try to keep finding something funny about it.

But maybe—I suggest as a deep afterthought—Vera Miles spoke in ironies, knowing that the really worthwhile "talent" is "getting married and having children."

Besides Milton Berle, Jack Benny, and Ray Bolger enlivening their personalities with women's clothes and various feminine fripperies, there have been Dustin Hoffman, Jose Ferrer, Jack Lemmon, Tony Curtis, and Robert Preston daring to play members of the supposedly more delicate sex.

And the anguished lament of Gene Barry and George Hearn in *La Cage aux Folles*—"Our son is getting married, to a woman! Where did we go wrong?"—will be one of the guideposts into tomorrow's world of comedy.

You will hear it echoed a thousand times.

34

GEORGE JESSEL'S
BEST STORY

You must have heard the famous story about comedian George Jessel trying to take the beautiful black singer Lena Horne to a nightclub and the race-conscious headwaiter barring their way because of Miss Horne's color.

Jessel was young and flippant then. Miss Horne, just becoming a celebrity, had been described by one New York critic, Richard Watts, Jr., as "the most beautiful girl in the world." Holding her by the hand, Jessel undertook to proceed past "the velvet rope."

The guardian of the portal, the headwaiter, stood there, tall and erect and stiffly formal, folding his menu before him like a musket.

He did not know the girl nor especially care who she was. He knew their rules. He glared down over his menu with a look of total indifference and said what New York headwaiters always said:

"Do you have a reservation?"

Always the customer would stutter or mumble or cough nervously and melt away. And no black got in.

But George Jessel did not melt away.

Still holding Miss Horne by the hand, he replied with astonishing confidence, "Yes."

"You have a reservation?" stammered the headwaiter, who had never been confronted with this reply. "Who made it?"

"Abraham Lincoln!" snapped George Jessel.

And, so the story went, George and Lena swept in past the confused headwaiter who had no answer. They were taken to a choice table in "the private room" and drank and ate happily there forever after.

What a precious story! It had occurred in the '20s. Jessel became the best known toastmaster, the favorite of Presidents; he was called "the Toastmaster General." Lena Horne became our best-known singer of sultry songs, and people marveled at the tale of the time she had trouble getting into a nightclub because she was black. Now any club would welcome her.

For close to 40 years I reprinted that story and never asked for details. A woman reader of my column saw it reprinted in a collection, attributed to me, although I did not publish it first, and asked me, "Where did it happen?"

Good question! I had always thought it was either the Stork Club or the 21 Club. But the problem of what to do with black customers had been so sensitive that I hadn't pressed it at that time.

I would straighten it out for all time. Lena Horne was able to answer immediately. She was getting ready to start her famous one-woman show. She said, "It was 21." George was quick to answer my letter. I was glad to get his reply because he was not going to live long. He was, I learned later, dying then.

Jessel's answer, published not long before his death, when he was 83, stated that we hadn't reported *exactly* what he had said to the headwaiter who asked who had made his reservation. Jessel had answered, "Abraham Lincoln, you son of a bitch."

And, he said, of course it was all said at the Stork Club.

He even remembered the headwaiter's name, he said, but that gentleman had been dead for several years.

But Lena Horne had said it was at the 21 Club. The Stork was at 3 East 53rd. The 21 Club was at 21 West 52nd. I wanted Lena's answer in writing.

Lena's great opening at the Nederlander May 12, 1981, was

spectacular for its celebrities and its enthusiasm. As I sat down front on the aisle with my wife, I was handed an envelope brought from Lena Horne backstage. Even as the curtain was rising, I ripped open the envelope and read the handwriting on yellow legal paper.

"Please forgive this note paper. . . .

"Anyhow—it was 21, upstairs. I've never been in the Stork Club. Was it attractive? I heard a lot about it when Miss Josephine Baker came over from Paris and couldn't get in because she was black. . . ."

So there you have the answer. In fact, two answers. It was at the Stork Club and it was at the 21 Club. Anyway, blacks are admitted now anywhere and everywhere, and George Jessel's story may have helped.

In view of these conflicting answers—Jessel saying it happened at the Stork Club, Miss Horne saying she had never been in the Stork Club—some thinking people have asked, "Did it really happen?" My answer is the same I have had to give after investigating other fascinating stories about events in the world of nightclubs and cafés: "Well, yes and no."

35

DAYS AND NIGHTS WITH HEMINGWAY

To call Ernest Hemingway while he was in bed with his wife, I had to have plenty of nerve.

They seemed to be comfortable in bed and enjoying each other in an East Side New York City hotel. It was his third wife, the ebullient Martha Gellhorn. They were recovering from the shots, the injections, required of them as they set off for Spain to cover a war for *Collier's* magazine.

My credentials as a reporter for the *New York Post* were of little help. I explained on the phone that I did magazine articles and thought they would be the basis for an article about the intrepid "Mr. and Mrs. Hemingway."

Hemingway laughed about that. An article in one magazine about a writer for another magazine. Besides, they were a little groggy from the shots, and they were leaving in a few days.

So, "Thanks a lot," and "Sorry."

The next day they phoned me.

"We talked it over," Martha Gellhorn said. "We decided we're all in the same business. We ought to do that for you."

I wrote the article with their help. Hemingway was right. It didn't sell. The other magazines decided that they shouldn't be running articles about other magazine writers. Some of them were clearly jealous of Hemingway. But I remember it as an answer to the people who thought Hemingway was a selfish, egomaniacal boor.

He had given quite a lot of his time to another fellow who was a nonentity who couldn't do much for him.

With that experience in my memory, I was quite elated in the summer of 1983 to read in *The New York Times* that the fame of Ernest Hemingway was suddenly increasing. His "critical reputation" was soaring to a new high. The literary world had a new appreciation of him.

"Well, well!" I thought. I should look up that article.

I found it intact, complete with rejection slips.

One editor had written that my article was "much too laudatory.

"It was so gushing, in fact, it seemed to me that Mr. Wilson might hope to be the fourth Mrs. Hemingway or the second Mr. Gellhorn," he added.

"A lot of people think that Ernest Hemingway is only a little less than God," another reader-editor had written. "And I think it's foolish to try to get people to revise their opinion downward."

I never told Hemingway how these cynical editors had looked down on my hero worship, but I got to know Hemingway much better in the years that followed and became one of the occasional guests at his hacienda outside Havana.

And here at my elbow are photographs of bearded Papa, the beard white, sitting with my wife and son and his later Mrs. Hemingway, Mary Welsh, at La Floridita, home of the frozen daiquiri cocktail—one of the times when he hired musicians and took us all boat touring.

Here are longhand notes and some typed messages from him going back almost four decades.

He dropped a lot of wisdom on me concerning his passion for the outdoors and exercise. He said pithily in his four-letter words:

"You eat good and you write good and you fuck good."

The first time I visited him in Havana I did not have the proper directions to his residence, the Finca Vijia, the Old Farm, at San Francisco de Paula.

He had written most of *For Whom the Bell Tolls* in Cuba, but in the then happy city they did not know of him. A cabdriver queried the bartenders and little coffee bars and card players about the famous one, but they knew him not.

A girl at a switchboard in the town of Cotorro finally said after much quizzing, "Oh, si, si, Señora Marta! Señora Marta Gellhorn!" She did the shopping and the phoning, and she was the boss of the hacienda. And so I came again to the Hemingways.

She was a bewitchingly attractive blonde who was always running about in one of their cars, and as for Hemingway, the villagers acknowledged that he was a considerable fisherman and hunter and spectator at cockfights, but, they asked:

"Has anybody ever seen him work?"

Since they didn't know he wrote, they left him plenty of free time to write.

There were an old Spanish gateway, mango trees, royal palms, and a tennis court, to which jai alai players were invited, to participate in a special game Hemingway had invented for those who loved the speed of jai alai. And there were a lot of cold drinks and Cuban wine drunk down by the pool.

"We have 24 cats," Papa said.

"You know what we call their hangout? The Cathouse."

He was in his early 40s then, but at times he seemed already old, with a kneecap of metal and a silver plate in one shoulder, mementos of World War I. He had a workroom and it was dominated by a large photograph of Martha in a bathing suit.

Hemingway boasted to me of the courage of Martha, who at 20 wrote a first novel about an adventuress who contracted syphilis. That disease was not mentioned in those days except when one spoke of Al Capone's having had it. An English publisher begged Martha to afflict Martha's heroine with a more seemly ailment.

"Syphilis or nothing," cabled Martha. The publisher acquiesced.

There's nothing a writer likes so much as other writers

starving to write. At Hemingway's Old Farm, sitting amid the bullfight posters, having a drink, laughing at his recollections of hard times, he gave confession.

"I went busted writing this book," he said, referring to *The Bell* as he called it. "I didn't have a nickel. You can always borrow, you know. Marty—." He turned to Martha.

"Shall I tell how you had to get an assignment covering the war in Finland so I could go on?"

"No," she said, but it came out that she had arrived in Helsinki one day before it was bombed and gotten a story about being given temporary bomb shelter on a golf course.

Somehow he always managed to hold on to his 30-foot launch, El Pilar, and go for marlin and tuna. "If I really go broke, I can make $35 a day hauling some of these rich fellows around," he often said.

He told me he liked to write standing erect at sort of a rostrum, and it was his custom to write from breakfast 'til noon when he would quit for the day and go out to play. He would do a paragraph over 20 or 30 times 'til he got it the way he wanted it. He was interested in the flow, in the rhythm. I asked him sincerely, and he knew this was not flattery, how he did it.

"I ran away from home and got a job as a reporter on the *Kansas City Star*," he said. "I'd be covering a trial. We'd get the court stenographer's transcript. But though the stenographer took down exactly what was said, I saw it wasn't exactly what was said, either."

Because of acoustics and accents, what people said with their mouths wasn't what you heard with your ears, he said.

"I began thinking about that and working on it and putting all those other things in."

And from that came the short-sentence, easy-reading style that flowed and was so easily parodied.

I asked him, like a student (which I was), if he took careful notes.

"If I take notes, I have to take down everything. I have a good memory, and I don't need notes, but if I take some, I have to take them all.

"One time I made notes was when I was hanging around a gym, looking for things to write about. I'd write down what gave me a kick—the noise the resin makes in the ring when a man shuffles his feet, the way an outfielder throws his glove after the last out, not knowing where it will land as he trots in. I'd trace the emotion I got in fishing, to see whether it came from the rising of the line of the water, or the way it tightened like a fiddle string, or the way the big fellow threw the water when he jumped."

Here I could see was not somebody posing as a writer; this was somebody working to be a writer and constantly write better. He grew furious at himself for being slow at finding the precise expression he sought and swore like a blue streak, as we used to say (God knows why).

And thus came arguments about how many obscene expressions were used in his writings. One newspaper hit on the device of using the expression *Anglo-Saxon* for an unprintable word. Hemingway himself employed "obscenity in your milk." And thus came a story that Hemingway's mother's book club had taken up his book at a luncheon meeting.

She knew what it was going to be like.

"I didn't go," she reported to him.

The critics should go and obscenity in their hats, was his opinion. He pictured how laborious writing was for him.

"Do you ever get in a rut while writing?" I asked him.

"Every morning," he said.

It seemed to me that the circle sitting around in the cool shade usually included a priest who had become a Hemingway friend. The critics had said that Hemingway had thrown the Ten Commandments out the window.

Let them say what they wanted to say; he had his religion. His religion was trying to write what he wanted to say. You had to respect that.

There was too much adulation and too many requests for autographs and too much boozing at the Floridita for any real talking. I looked for him and found him when he was in New York, and he invited me along. He went to George Brown's gym and did some sparring and bag-punching, often in his stocking feet. He got into a celebrated alcoholic fiasco with Max Eastman over who did or didn't have hair on his chest. It was silly business and proved Hemingway's analysis: "I can't work in New York.

"It's like coming into Dodge City after a roundup; everybody with nothing to do but spend all they got in the poke," he said.

Striding the streets of New York, with a rolling gait, dressed in clothes off the rack in case the stores had a rack, he didn't look like the author you might expect Hollywood was now spending a lot of money for.

One time, on one of those strolls, he casually mentioned that his father had committed suicide.

He was flattering to me. He introduced me a couple of times as "my biographer," which I didn't take seriously. He did have an effect on me, however, I discovered later.

He said, "My religion is my work" on one occasion. Several years later somebody wrote a piece about me and said I was criticized by a news source who said, "The trouble with you is that to you news is a religion." I replied, "I'll settle for that."

There were a lot of crazies pursuing Papa in the next few years when he was getting the Nobel Prize for literature, which he called "the Swedish thing." Pleasant, nice little Mary Welsh from the magazine world was now Mrs. Hemingway, and Senora Marta was gone.

The "crazies" were the constantly-under-analysis people, slaves to the psychoanalysis rage. Hemingway thought very little good resulted in the crazies he knew who went to the analysts.

"My favorite analyst," he wrote to me once, "is. . . ," and he wrote in the name of his portable typewriter, meaning *work*.

Cuba was just about 90 minutes away by seaplane then, and we seemed to be going often for gambling casino events at the Riviera and Tropicana. On one of those trips in 1955 I heard some scary rumors about Hemingway's health.

"Miss Mary" disposed of that. "Papa is feeling good and writing good and is about to put another book in the bank."

Papa proved his good health by inviting us to "dinner in town." It saved Mary the problem of getting dinner together— Papa was always quick to invite you to his house. "Anyway, I haven't been off the reservation for a week," he said.

"About putting a book in the bank?" I asked.

"I got three unpublished books in the bank," he said. "This'll be the fourth. I put 'em away and let 'em ripen."

It was his kind of insurance, he said. He could always take a book out of the vault and cash it. His beard was whiter now than when I last saw him, and he was truly picturesque and almost saintly when he looked out through the beard and the rimless glasses with waves of white hair as a backdrop.

Because of his father's act, he was always thinking of death, I suppose, but laughing about it, too.

"Sure, when you're 56, and had your back broken, and skull fracture, and kidneys and bladder smashed, well, you're not at your best. But I'm fine. I finished page 667 today. By February 1, I may have her done and in the bank."

He and Miss Mary had been in two plane crashes in Africa.

I told him that New York literary circles were greatly concerned.

"I'm sorry we got people so spooked," he said. "Miss Mary had never seen a plane burn up before. That is very impressive, especially when you're in the plane."

A British doctor had treated his cracked skull by pouring gin in it. Hemingway remembered the exact quote from the doctor. "Laddie," the doctor said, "gin is as good for you on the outside as it is on the inside."

Hemingway laughed tolerantly at the wire service reports that he'd been killed. Having learned that Hemingway had been double-whammied by the aeronautics experts, that his first plane had crashed and the second had burned, they gave him up. His obituaries were published around the world.

"They were flattering but not very factual," he said.

Going over his injuries later, it was as though he'd hastened through a hospital catalogue and said "I'll have one of each"— spine, spleen, kidney, liver, back, knees, legs, feet, bladder, and a busted head from pounding it against a plane window trying to get out alive.

When we visited the Hemingways in Cuba with the Carl Erbes after the two accidents, Hemingway pretended to be most upset that he had to reduce his drinking to two glasses of wine a day while his guests drank whisky in the usual amounts.

He spoke proudly of Miss Mary's fishing, hunting, and shooting.

"She's such a good shot," he said. "I must remember to take the shells out of her shotgun."

The idea of working in New York irritated him keenly, for he mentioned it again more colorfully.

"When I hit New York it is like coming off a long cattle drive to Dodge City in the old days. Right now I'm driving cattle, and it's a long tough drive.

"All my life I wrote in all kinds of different places."

He mentioned Paris; Key West; Kansas City; Sheridan, Wyoming; Big Horn; Madrid; Hendaye, France; Schruns, Switzerland; Juan Les Pins; and, of course, Havana, at Ambos Mundos Hotel and at Finca.

"I like it here, and I love my life with Mary and the fun she has on this hilltop.

"You find me a place in Ohio where I can live on top of a hill and be 15 minutes from the Gulf Stream and have my own fruit and vegetables the year-round and can raise and fight game chickens without breaking the law, and I'll go to Ohio if Miss Mary and my cats and dogs will agree.

"Best to you, Rosemary, and el Slugger."

"El Slugger" was Earl, Jr., then 10 or 12, whom Papa taught to shoot. At least he showed him to press the trigger and hit the bird at the gun club, so Papa said.

I was impressed that he cared so much for cockfights and wanted to be legal and that he wanted that breeze on the hilltop. "I wake up when the sun rises, read the Miami and New York papers, work 'til noon, have a drink. Then you fish or go shooting. Sometimes we go to a concert or picture or go to La Floridita."

And thus he drove the cattle all the way through to the Nobel Prize and the Pulitzer.

Although some critics thought he was overproud of being Ernest Hemingway, I thought he was modest in telling me in 1951 that he had taken steps to prevent publication of "the horrid story of my life." The biography that was planned would "stench out the joint," he said, and he had declined permission, and now New York and London newspaperman Sam Boal wasn't going to do it; they had "very nicely agreed."

"I am tying up everything," he said. "There are too many people involved in a biography, including myself," he said.

"Been working like hell. Did 1,007 words yesterday. The book is not scheduled until 1952. Am engaged in bettering it. The main thing is to keep healthy and keep going," he wrote on.

"Thanks for always being so good about everything. Tell Slugger the best system probably is not to learn the English language at all. Then he won't have to read you or me either."

Mary Welsh thanked my wife for offering to give them a reception in New York.

"No parties this trip, please," she wrote. "Papa is still on his two-glasses-of-wine-a-day routine, no more, and it is harder to stick to it when he has to be on an island surrounded by seas of jubilation."

His letters indicated he was on schedule, not worried about meeting deadlines. "Excuse note. Am working like hell" was a typical beginning.

"Never gone better. Anyway, it seems that way to Mary and me. But we are very interested parties. Love to your wife and pigeon-slaying Slugger."

Besides the big-time writing, Hemingway was doing some big-time fishing.

"Our game warden friend, Dennis Zaphiro from Kenya, who's been here since July, caught a 334-pound marlin a while back," Mary wrote to my wife. "But Papa and he are hunting a bigger one, every day, every day on the Gulfstream. About half as big as a buffalo," Mary wrote. "Buffalos weigh a ton or more."

It seemed difficult to picture Hemingway as a two-glasses-of-wine-a-day tippler, and we always recalled the nights on the Pilar when half of the barflies at the Floridita appeared to be with us on our cruise in the harbor.

Mary's letter asking for no parties succeeded in averting a tribute in Hemingway's honor, but we got him to a later occasion for a friend, which was memorable in that Hemingway was at that time drinking tequila.

Our bar seemed to have had only one bottle of tequila, and Hemingway quickly disposed of that. Panic-stricken, my wife and I worried what Hemingway would drink until we succeeded in getting a bottle rushed to us from Billy Reed's Little Club.

The Mexican firewater came with all possible speed, but we needn't have hurried.

Hemingway was drinking champagne and finding it an excellent substitute for tequila.

I treasured Hemingway for the sense of humor that few people knew he possessed. In the column I advocated the scuttling of the word *very*. I suggested that we mercy-murder *very*, simply leaving it out of written and spoken sentences.

"I see you are trying to get rid of *very*," he wrote to me. "That would be a mistake. *Very* has been around a long time, a very long time—and a very long time is a lot longer than just a long time. I'd be very much opposed to it.

"Your idea will be very, very unpopular, you'll see very soon."

He was right. The avalanche of letters upholding *very* began pouring in next day.

It was refreshing to find somebody less conceited than the normal. When I asked if they ever went to nightclubs to see the sparkling, sophisticated entertainment, Mary said that they tried to get in a couple of times but the headwaiter wouldn't seat them because Papa didn't have on a tie.

"Next time they wouldn't let me in because, though I had a tie on, I didn't have on a formal jacket. In that place I was a nobody," Hemingway said.

"Listen," he said, "I'm not so gahdamned important back in my home state of Illinois, either. One of my relatives, a moron cousin or somebody, told me a long time ago he sure did enjoy my book, *All Quiet on the Western Front*."

After Hemingway killed himself with a shotgun in Ketchum, Idaho, in 1961, after a long period of depression, I wondered if the psychiatrists whom he'd held in such low regard would or could have helped him if he'd cooperated with them. Mary Hemingway was quoted that she'd talked to psychiatrists about his mental condition. One of his letters to me continued our discussion of analysts.

He signed off, "Yours in couchlessness."

And a notebook I preserved has a quote from an interview with him pasted on the cover.

It says, "Ernest Hemingway on antipsychoanalysis: 'It's the biggest industry. Passed bubble gum three years ago. Some wouldn't cross street without consulting analyst.' "

Papa was certainly fond of Miss Mary.

One night he persuaded her to show her strength. He obviously enjoyed it when she picked up this comparative giant in her arms and carried him across the room.

The marriage of the Beauty and the Beard must have been successful for those years.

As evidence, I offer a letter from Mary addressed to us "My Dear Children" on the letterhead of Finca Vigia, San Francisco de Paula, Cuba, typed and dated March 31, 1954, stating that she fashioned him a special award after a decade of marriage.

As she told it, "On March 14th, Papa got a surprise with his breakfast, a diploma elaborately colored and fancy, headed 'Labor Omnia Vincit Improbus.' My favorite translation of that was 'It is improbable that labor conquers all.' "

The sheepskin also contained numerous citations for Hemingway "for service above and beyond the call of duty during the last 10 years.

"Made by me and signed as wife," she wrote further. "It seems utterly unreal, but it's 10 years since we signed those papers in Havana.

"Despite the picture business, Papa is really recovered now and doing fine—me, too."

Twenty years after Hemingway's death some of the literati came to bury Caesar, not to praise him. In 1981 *The New Yorker* magazine published an article by John Updike that was headed, "Hem Battles the Pack; Wins, Loses."

It appraised bushels of personal letters he had written to friends, many of them similar to those he had written to me, some longer, some deeply thoughtful, and some quite literary— but most of them obviously punched out hurriedly.

"Certain traits, not especially attractive, of Hemingway's pysche emerge through these letters," Updike wrote.

"He was an unabashedly unfaithful husband and of course antagonistic to his mother, whom he blamed for her lack of loyalty to his early published work, for his father's suicide, and for an obscure impression of himself."

Hemingway wrote to Maxwell Perkins, Updike continued, that he could not write anything about F. Scott Fitzgerald while his wife Zelda was alive "any more than I can write with my bitch of a mother still able to read."

Hemingway's letters added 400,000 words to his output, Updike estimated. He counted every word in his manuscript each day, "a habit left over from writing words for foreign dispatch."

"Through these last addled years, though the words kept sliding and bloating, not coming out right, he battled on, piling up manuscript.

"In February of 1961, invited to contribute a sentence for a presentation volume to be given to John Kennedy, he wrote all day, covering sheets of paper, and could get nothing to satisfy himself; [Carlos] Baker's biography reports that 'tears were cursing down his cheeks.' A few months later he killed himself.

"He had never believed writing was easy."

Easy?

The century ahead will resound with continuing debate whether Hemingway was genius or egomaniac.

He venerated violence. He could laugh telling how the brains spilled out of a German soldier he had shot.

It was the laughing, the roaring laugh, that I heard, a laugh as big as he was. Always talking of bigness. "The big one." The big book, the big marlin, the big dinner. But not big words. Never big words. Dropping us off at the hotel after the Floridita evening with the musicians, he was gentle, hospitable. He was looking for the words he hoped he would find tomorrow.

Laughing, he quoted the Bible, but respectfully, for the words. We agreed the Bible was hard on gossip columnists, on bearers of false witness. And I mentioned that package of power in Matthew: "Judge not that ye be not judged." How could a gossip writer live with that hanging above his typewriter? So, after reading all I have been able to find, I judge him not, remembering him as a gentle giant and friend. Ernest Hemingway was the man who often said he would kill himself writing—and did.

36

AVA, THE MOST BEAUTIFUL?

Two disputatious personalities collide within the loving framework of Ava Gardner.

Most women will agree that this simple, plain-talking, unpretentious "sharecropper's daughter"—a description she once hated—was in her time the most beautiful girl in the world, or right next door to it, and many will bravely state that with those cheekbones she still rates it, although now she is a sexy sixtyish.

One of those personalities was wild, impulsive, Irish, maddeningly independent, Southern, and don't-give-a-damn. The other was prim and cautious.

The first time I met her she was flaunting that pointed bosom that could move men to mayhem. She was already an ex-Mrs. Mickey Rooney then, bigger than he was, almost enough bigger to hold her husband in her lap. She had been around, around and back, with champagne and caviar and movie star press agents steering her even to the bathroom, and she was exploiting a movie called *The Huckster*.

We were taking lunch at Dinty Moore's, a famous corned beef

and cabbage restaurant where the proprietor also served a hamburger sweetened with a pinch of sugar. Irving Berlin came there, and so did all sorts of stars, and it was customary at Moore's to precede the lunch with a large drink.

A movie press agent named Curly Harris, well known in the area, was our host, and for a drink our fetching and beautifully leggy and gorgeously cheekboned film star ordered an old-fashioned, a bourbon old-fashioned.

A waiter set down the flat old-fashioned glass with the fixin's already in it but with the booze not yet poured.

I can only think that Miss Gardner must have been thirsty or moved by the atmosphere because she picked up the glass and took a swig of it.

"That's the best drink I ever tasted!" she exclaimed.

Curly Harris was not one to treat events like that with silence.

"You like that?" he laughed. "Just wait 'til you see how it tastes when they put the bourbon in it."

That I could not understand: how a lady who had been around as Mrs. Rooney had been around would not have discovered an old-fashioned.

But there were also other things about Ava I didn't understand. Once she cut off our friendship of several years because I wrote about her going barefoot. Why, everybody knew she liked to go barefoot. They knew because Ava Gardner told them— again and again.

It was a part of her life story that she never denied. And I had seen it myself: first opportunity she got, off with the shoes! She had traipsed barefoot over the acreage of her tenant-farmer father, Jonas Gardner, of Boon Hill, North Carolina, as a little girl.

Barefoot beauty! Why not?

"Can't wait to get these shoes off," she'd say, and though Mickey Rooney and subsequent husband Artie Shaw hated it, they couldn't discourage her from exercising freedom of the feet. Lover Howard Hughes was more understanding. He had bad feet and often wore what appeared to be tennis sneakers. Some years later, a biographer, Roland Flamini, found the legend had grown.

Lena Horne, by then accepted in Beverly Hills, gave a fancy

party. The sharecropper's beautiful daughter, Ava Gardner, had come in an evening gown—barefoot. She carried her shoes in her hands, just to prove she had some. She had walked over from her own house, and her feet were dirty, and she washed them and then put her shoes on.

"I'm taking 'em right off again!"

This was something I could understand perfectly because my womenfolk—my wife and my Gorgeous Mother-in-Law—were always padding around our place, Hillbilly Hall, barefoot—to my embarrassment.

"Ava's right," they would say.

Had she outgrown the barefoot girl portrait, or had she simply grown tired of it? I've found so many stars who weary of an image and want to kill anybody who brings it up again—especially when the image is falsely manufactured, but also when the portrait is done accurately and honestly.

But with Ava Gardner, a true great lady of the screen at last, maybe the smell of the tobacco plantations was not perfume anymore. Now she was the friend and playmate of flamenco dancers and bullfighters of Spain and a pal of handsome Italian courtiers. I wrote a piece about her fondness for living abroad— a flat in London, too.

I did not write the headline for my article. Somebody else did, putting the headline in one word:

"EXPATRIATE."

As I say, I did not write the headline. *Expatriate* is a word I do not use, being slightly scared of it.

It is a word that Ava does not use, either. She did not find it friendly. My article did not employ the word. But the headline writer had made up his own mind about it, and I was not there to check it.

Try to explain that to Ava Gardner. I had no opportunity. The next time I tried to make contact I found Ava Gardner was not talking to me. To my wife, yes. To me, no.

Maybe she was right. I guess she thought I had made her a barefoot expatriate.

When you're born with cheekbones, there's nothing much your competition can do about it, except hate you.

Oh, they can say they're a plastic job, and the cute dimple is also the result of an operation by one of the great beautifiers.

But nobody went around rapping Ava Gardner's beauty. Nobody was knocking her. Oh, I don't say that Nancy Sinatra, Sr., was thrilled when asked what she thought of her ethics. But Nancy, Sr., was pretty sure by this time that if it wasn't Ava Gardner, it was going to be Lana Turner or Marilyn Maxwell or *somebody*. And Ava, having been Mrs. Mickey Rooney and Mrs. Artie Shaw already, knew how to take care of herself in a gang fight.

MGM had indeed worked on the cheekbones to get the proper highlight and had made the dimple less dimply, and the exclamations about Ava's pulchritude came from more women than men.

One day in June 1950 I discovered I was in England about 20 miles outside London riding in the back seat of an Austin with Ava Gardner heading for her flat in Park Lane.

Ava was frequently breaking out in song and doing the lyrics of "This Can't Be Love" and jiggling her shoulders.

And she was bare-legged and had her shoes off. She was barefoot.

She was calling everybody Sweetie. She had just finished a supposed nude scene, swimming out to visit James Mason on a yacht in the picture *Pandora and the Flying Dutchman*.

We had been at Shepperton Studios, and Ava, supposedly skinny-dipping out to the yacht, had fallen into Mason's willing and waiting arms and smooched him deliriously. Afterward she bounced about in a towellike bathrobe and said, "I'll get out of this, huh, and get some clothes on, and we'll go into town."

Ava wanted to talk about Frank Sinatra, who was still married to Nancy, and I let her.

The first of Ava's Spanish bullfighters, Mario from Madrid, who also wrote poetry, had attempted to build a great rivalry between himself and Sinatra for Ava's hand (or bare feet). He was issuing bulletins about the love battle, and the papers were printing it.

Sinatra was ripping around Paris with his songwriter friend, Jimmy Van Heusen. A couple of weeks before, I had phoned Sinatra from New York, catching him at the Paris Lido Club, where he was pretty indignant about the whole thing.

"This boy means nothing—*nothing, nothing*—to this girl," Frank maintained. And he and Ava were very, very close, but had they talked about him getting a divorce from Nancy and marrying Ava?

"Not a word. Not a word!"

Not a word, honest.

"Everybody is talking about it but Ava and me—not a word."

And anyway, suppose they were managing to see each other in Europe. They were chaperoned, weren't they?

By whom? Jimmy Van Heusen?

I'm afraid I didn't get that.

I give you this detail to show you that there were tabloids in those days, too, and they strove to publish all the important stuff even as we do now.

But back in the back seat of the Austin and in her flat, Ava was pouring out confidences to me. She continued to see her former husband, Artie Shaw, and would always see him because he was a trusted friend.

She was not in love with Artie Shaw anymore.

"You know how I feel about Frank."

Practically everybody did know now.

"But I can't go around screaming that I'm in love with somebody who isn't even divorced.

"I think Frank is a wonderful person, and if I were in love with anybody, it would be him."

She was indignant at some malicious letters she was receiving suggesting unseemly conduct.

"I wish somebody would go a little further so I could sue!"

It was clear to me that she referred to rumors that she was pregnant. Frank and Ava later authorized me to deny those rumors in print.

Ava was going to be marrying Frank, and she would really be a household word. In my column I was writing about Sinatra's tiffs with the press. They grew more bitter with a wrangle with photographers at their marriage in Philadelphia. Frank enjoyed piling ridicule on the Fourth Estate.

On a radio program he said, "My voice was so low when I sang 'Ol' Man River,' I got down in the mud, and who do you think I found throwing mud down there? A couple of Hollywood columnists." He added that a couple of Hollywood commentators have quite a racket. "All day long they lie in the sun, and when the sun goes down, they still lie."

Let's pass up the Barefoot Contessa's mad marriage to Sinatra and all the brawls that went with it. Volumes have been written about Ava's unselfish loyalty and assistance to Frank in getting to do *From Here to Eternity,* which won him an Oscar. As a friend of Frank's from the days when he was a mere band singer with Tommy Dorsey, I was able to report and write accurately about the unbelievable success of the kid from Hoboken.

And my wife, Rosemary, was an insider and personal friend, too, because she had said one night at Meadowbrook with Dorsey, "That boy will be another Bing Crosby."

I had said, "Oh, sure!"

Ava and Frank became our good friends, and I remember one night Rosemary and I waited in our room at the Savoy in London for them to join us because it was Rosemary's birthday.

Well, they didn't come or call, and we waited, somewhat disappointed, and decided they'd forgotten, and we were just about to go to bed.

The phone rang—and it was them. They were downstairs.

"Sorry to be a little late."

It was too late to have dinner, and anyway, they'd had dinner, and it was too late to do anything but drink. So they came to our room—it was just a room, not a big suite—and Frank sat on the foot of the bed, and Ava sat on the floor, with her shoes off, of course, and we talked and laughed 'til morning.

It was lovely and sweet, one of those things you remember. They had the fights and the breakup after that, and then Ava went Spanish.

We saw some of it ourselves in Madrid and elsewhere in Spain where she was so big with the flamenco dancers and the toreadors and the all-night drinking.

Then that thing happened.

The vodka had been talking and Ava had been saying, "Sure, si, si, I would like to fight a bull."

She'd received bulls' ears from the fights and knew a lot about bullfighting as well as a lot of bullfighters. She was thinking of doing a movie about the woman bullfighter Concita Citron.

And so one day, when she was visiting a ranch, she got on a horse, and she was going to play like she was a bullfighter. It was perfectly safe, of course, a very harmless amusement. She would tease the bull with a lance that had a rubber tip.

But this was a young bull. The young bull may not have known the lance had a rubber tip.

Her perfectly safe horse kicked up its heels and threw her to the ground, and the perfectly safe young bull charged her as she was trying to get up. The bull got her in the face—in the left cheek.

"Oh, dear God!" Ava was moaning and screaming and crying. What a disaster to that beautiful face.

As she was rushed back to Madrid to the specialists, the sad news spread.

A lot of Spanish veils and shawls and scarves were hauled out to cover the scar on the cheek when she rushed to see a plastic surgeon in London who may have been shocked at what he saw but gave her his word that in time it would heal and the mark would disappear.

Ava was far from cheered up by that. She was just going through the Walter Chiari and *The Naked Maja* phases.

Chiari was the slender, amusing Italian actor Ava had collected in Rome. He was obedient and respectful, not like the Roman Romeos we knew from the past.

Chiari was also trusting. He thought the American journalists were nice, asking him these nice questions.

"Do you sing?"

"No. All Italians sing; I am the exception."

"Is there anything going on between you and Ava Gardner?"

"I hope so."

"No, no. Is there anything going on between you and Miss Gardner now?"

"I weesh."

Ava helped him get on some TV shows. He didn't have the usual entourage, and I saw him often. One Sunday night he was on Steve Allen's TV show, which was a big Sunday night variety program with one major rival.

After he did the Steve Allen program I asked him, "Are you going to do the Steve Allen show again?"

"No. Next time, Ed Soolivan," he said.

Of course the American columnists reported that Ava and Chiari were going to get married. Chiari had never hoped for that. Ava had much grief in Rome doing *The Naked Maja* because she was constantly worrying about her damaged cheek.

She wanted to see the results of the daily shootings and claimed she could see the scar.

"You can't see it," the makeup people told her.

"I can see it," Ava insisted.

She claimed she could detect purple and red and green splotches and that it looked like a shell hole. Ava tortured herself for weeks waiting for the picture's finish to see how it all came out.

I was among those who went with her to an early showing.

We were scared for her. What can you tell, from the rushes? You need the finished product and an audience.

When a vital scene was shown I looked carefully. I couldn't see anything.

"It's beautiful," I said. "I can't see any marks."

"I can," Ava said unhappily.

The consensus was that it had been covered sufficiently that it was not visible now. Ava didn't agree. She went back to the plastic surgeon in London and had surgery to remove what she insisted were traces that hadn't been covered.

To this day Ava thinks the scar shows. To this day also she thinks I called her an "expatriate," and she thinks she didn't go barefoot.

37

GETTING REAGAN'S AUTOGRAPH

I'm writing this in the Keio Intercontinental Hotel in Tokyo before going to China. It's not a spy story.

I wish I had a spy story. Remember the assassination attempt against President Reagan and the wounding of press secretary James Brady?

About three weeks before that frightening event, which cculd have been so much more tragic, President and Nancy Reagan had a festive weekend in New York.

With motorcycles roaring and White House reporters following, and Secret Service men with little pins in their lapels only inches away, the Reagans went on Saturday night to see *Sugar Babies* starring Mickey Rooney and Ann Miller.

The show's proud press agent, Henry Luhrman asked me, "Do you want to go along when the President goes backstage?"

"Thanks," I said. "But I've no White House press credentials. And those Secret Service guys can be rough. And they're very suspicious."

"Stick with me and you'll be all right," he said.

I really didn't care to go. It was a Saturday night. I'd rather stay home with my wife.

But I kept thinking of Abraham Lincoln being shot in a theater, so I met Henry in the Mark Hellinger Theater lobby at 7:45.

Oh, it was exciting. President Reagan's friend who later died, Al Bloomingdale, was with him. The crowd gave the Reagans an ovation. I had to stand, on one foot and then the other. Then it was intermission.

"Follow me," Henry Luhrman said. The Reagans went backstage from inside the theater, but we hustled out the front door, westward a few steps to the stage door, and suddenly I was backstage and on the stage with the curtain down.

Ann Miller was waving a bottle of jelly beans.

President Reagan was saying to Mickey Rooney, "We have met before. You were trying to find the owner of a dog that had been hit. You had blood on your shirt. . . ."

A photographer, Judie Bernstein, pushed me forward.

"Oh, Earl!" cried Ann Miller, who seemed to be the hostess. "Here's Earl Wilson," she told the Reagans.

"Get in a picture with the President," Ann commanded.

I didn't remember ever meeting the Reagans, but the President gave me such a warm handshake and big smile, I was amazed at the great acting job he was doing.

"I mustn't take up any more of your time," Mr. Reagan told the cast, and they returned to their seats.

I went home and told my wife what had happened, which wasn't much. "Yeah, I saw some of it on TV," she said.

That's always a put-down for a print journalist.

Up to then I had been normal. But next day Henry Luhrman said, "We got a good picture of you and the President." It was good, too (for me!). A little jowly, frosty at the temple, with the President looking like he was really overwhelmed to see me, and Ann Miller between us.

My ego took over. It occurred to me that maybe I could get the President to autograph that picture. Other people did it.

Maybe it was kind of pushy, but I stifled my pride and dictated a letter to Press Secretary James Brady, asking about the possibility of getting the picture autographed.

A few days later the President was shot, and some TV news commentators said Brady had been killed.

My temporary secretary, Miss Lee Bohlen, didn't make a carbon copy, so we weren't sure what day we wrote to Brady but believed it was March 24 or March 26.

I think we should be forgiven for wondering during that historic and suspenseful time whether James Brady had received our letter.

We soon got a letter giving us our answer. The letter came back: "NOT KNOWN AT WHITE HOUSE!"

"Stupid postal service!" I said. Hey, wait! My fault. We had misaddressed the letter, to "James Blair." Probably due to the frequent mention of the Blair House.

Brady had never received our letter, it was clear.

My ego went back to work. In the following weeks the President and James Brady improved, and Lee Bohlen and I talked.

Would James Brady, now that he was out of the crisis, find this amusing?

"He just might," Lee Bohlen said.

Back to the dictation again, carefully addressed.

Silence again. One day the White House called.

"I have your letter to James Brady. . . ."

"Oh, forgive me. I guess it was bad taste. . . ."

"No, not at all. The news is better around here today. If you will send the picture. . . ."

Our housekeeper, Mavis, took it to the Post Office—and then you know what happened?

Nothing! We concluded that we were stupid to think that the President would have time. Oh, well, we had tried.

On Saturday, May 16, 1981, I was going through the mail preparing for our trip to China.

"The White House!"

Inside was the precious picture of the President with me and Ann Miller in a tall hat between us.

And there, in a bold hand on the lower edge of the picture:

"To Earl Wilson—With Very Best Regards [Signed] Ronald Reagan."

I rushed to my wife in another room. By now I was for Reagan for a third term. "Isn't that nice?" I said.

"It certainly is nice," she said calmly.

She kept looking at the signature this way and that.

"And I'd say," she said, "from some of his signatures that I've seen on TV, that this is one that he very well might have signed himself."

September 4, 1983

I succeeded in getting Ann Miller to add her autograph to the President's on the photograph later. Now I don't know quite what to do with the picture. I've no place to display it, and I don't want to lose it. It's going on three years now that it's been facedown in an envelope in a desk drawer.

38

THE
INTERVIEW
I FORGOT

I'd interviewed all the great actors and actresses—Garbo, Chaplin, the Barrymores, Helen Hayes, John Wayne, Brigitte Bardot, W. C. Fields. How was it possible I'd never interviewed the actor who was most important of them all, Ronald Reagan?

Now he was possibly the most prestigious man in the world. And I had overlooked *him*.

What could I do but admit the truth of the accusation? I had never interviewed the man who was President of the United States, though he was on my beat and very approachable? I made some remarks about how exclusive I was.

I didn't interview just anybody.

Even future Presidents of the USA had better have other things to recommend them.

One day a letter from songwriter Harry Huret of West Palm Beach, Florida, and Smallwood, New York, shocked and upset me. I *had* interviewed Ronald Reagan, approximately April 13, 1950.

I could tell in a minute that Harry Huret was right. He

remembered meeting Ronald Reagan and a beautiful blonde, Betty Underwood, at the Glass Hat café of the Belmont-Plaza Hotel, where I was conducting a radio program consisting of interviews.

"You were going to interview me," Harry Huret said.

"I had written a song to your wife, 'I Want to Dance with the B.W.,' but I also wanted to sing it. There was a union problem. Because we had no backup standby musicians, the union wouldn't allow me to sing the song. So I couldn't do my song.

"And so, Earl Wilson," said Harry Huret, "you turned from me, and you interviewed Ronald Reagan and the girl he was with, and also Gypsy Rose Lee, whom you had evidently invited.

"I think," Harry Huret continued, "that Ronald Reagan switched from a flaming Democrat to a Republican conservative that night. He didn't like the union's attitude about me being unable to do the song because of the union rules. He said, 'I'm sorry about that. It isn't fair.' "

After hearing from Harry Huret, I went back to my own files. Yes, it was all there. Photographs of Ronald Reagan and Betty Underwood toasting each other in nightclubs were found. Ronald Reagan was later President of the Screen Actors Guild.

How did I forget him, though?

"You remembered the blonde, Betty Underwood," one member of my family said accusingly.

"But you forgot the man," somebody else joined in, also accusingly.

A monstrous sidelight to this story is that I didn't remember interviewing Reagan but recalled vividly three or more interviews with Reagan's first wife, Jane Wyman.

Jane Wyman had given me that great quote, "You ask Ronald Reagan what time it is, and he'll tell you how the watch was made."

That could be interpreted in two ways: (1) that he was very boring or (2) that he was very thorough.

President Reagan was recently quoted as saying, "I wonder what I could have made of myself if I had really worked and studied."

Gee whiz, Mr. President, you might have made Secretary of State.

39

WITH INGRID—
IN ROME

It was dusk on the Via Veneto, long after the banks' closing time, but Ingrid Bergman would be waiting with a patient smile as her lover and husband, Roberto Rossellini, hustled in and out of the financial institutions, trying to borrow money.

"But so late?" I asked one of Roberto's men.

"He's borrowing to pay crews and actors and cameramen to shoot *tomorrow*. He's even borrowing film. And money for dinner tonight, too!"

And Roberto, open-throated, carrying a light jacket across his shoulder, would rush to us, display a sheaf of Italian currency, kiss Ingrid, and take us on a wild ride to his favorite pasta and wine.

It was life on a shoestring for the great Swedish star, and I suspect her happiest time.

Of all the great women, she was the wisest. When she died of cancer at 67, I remembered how we talked of happiness in a studio outside London years before.

Her face was smudged with dirt. She was playing a peasant in *The Inn of the Sixth Happiness.*

She was enjoying this make-believe Chinese hut.

"You are a basically happy person?" I asked her.

"I'm adaptable," she answered, and laid down a law or philosophy for all of us. This was several years after her Great Unhappiness, when she broke up her marriage with Dr. Peter Lindstrom and had Roberto's baby. Her loyal fans and the whole country, almost the whole world, seemed to have turned against her.

"You can't expect to have happiness all the time," Miss Bergman said to me. "You shouldn't, because you'd be a monster. You wouldn't be a human being.

"I'm grateful for the good things, but also for the unhappy things. Because, if you don't have some suffering, you don't understand it in others. You can't be patient and tolerant with others.

"You have to have sadness to appreciate what happiness is!"

Certainly the sainted Ingrid, our Joan of Arc and Joan of Lorraine, had suffered the worst of times. Gossip columnists Louella Parsons and Hedda Hopper were picking her reputation to pieces, bone by bone.

But they were right. They usually are. Please note that.

We had placed her on a pedestal too lofty to reach, but Roberto had reached her—or she had reached him.

And in August 1949 I was in Europe, hoping to be the first reporter to see Ingrid returning from her *scandale* in Stromboli with Roberto.

Based on our friendly relations, reporting her Broadway stage activities, I would have the courage to ask her whether she had indeed broken with her husband, whether she was marrying Rossellini, and whether she was, uh, expecting.

However, I also had a problem.

The very night that Ingrid, Roberto, and entourage were due to arrive in Rome from Stromboli I had an engagement in Naples—an appointment to interview "Lucky" Luciano, the ousted, deported, supposed king of the underworld. I'd set up a dinner date with him at the Excelsior Hotel in Naples, and Mr.

Luciano was said to be a stickler about dinner engagements and didn't like to have them canceled.

I had to juggle Ingrid and "Charley Lucky"—and it was a bit tricky.

Accompanying me to Naples on the Rapido was my wife, who was alarmed at the idea of my conversing with Luciano, even though he was thought to be a gentle soul (most of the time), owning pieces of the Stork Club and the Copacabana.

Arriving at the hotel on time, I phoned Luciano's room and was told to meet him at the hotel barbershop.

That scared my wife afresh. A barbershop, with all its cutlery, would be such a good place to dispose of an enemy.

"Lucky" turned out to be nothing like the mobster we anticipated. He looked like a farmer wearing glasses and took us to dinner at a waterfront restaurant called Aunt Teresa's.

By 9:00 P.M. he had convinced us that he was not the head of the Mafia and, besides, there wasn't any Mafia.

Disposing of gangland, we went to our room at the hotel and tried to find out about Ingrid. She was coming up by car from Stromboli and was believed to be stopping at Amalfi for the night.

Fine! Back to the phone booths. I would reach Ingrid by phone and get a scoop by long distance.

"Sorry. The switchboard at Amalfi closes at nine."

It was now 9:15.

Back I went to Rome on the Rapido next morning, hoping to catch Ingrid and entourage ahead of Hedda Hopper, who, I heard was also in Europe Ingrid-hunting.

Instead I met Ingrid's press agent, Joe Steele, who gave me the impression that he'd learned that Ingrid was still undecided about her future and wasn't certain she'd marry Roberto, and, as for the baby rumor—*of course not!*

I wrote that unexciting story and took it over to the press office to be filed and happened to steal a glance at a machine that was moving a story on the same subject by Louella Parson's Rome colleague.

It was the reverse of my story and, I suspected, correct, and supplied by Joe Steele, who was trying to slip an exclusive to Louella, who was back in Hollywood.

Losing my temper, I found Steele, accused him of many crimes, and demanded that he now arrange an exclusive interview with Ingrid for me in her hideout to which she had gone in Rome.

"I'll see if she'll do it," he said.

It was a little like the CIA. I'm not good at addresses, and this chauffeur took us on a twisting, winding route that left me with no idea where we were when we got there. But there was Ingrid—and she was all mine (for the interview).

The whole world was waiting (so I convinced myself) for Ingrid's words, which she now spoke to me from this secret apartment.

"Yes, I will marry Roberto.

"No, I will not retire.

"Roberto and I will make many pictures together." She could see herself in many movies with an Italian background; she could see them ruling the film world, "artistically speaking."

Ingrid had been so composed and firm, but now she asked me, "Why is there so much criticism of me in America because of this? Joan Crawford and Lana Turner changed husbands."

"It's because you were known as a devoted and loving wife."

"I was. If I had been a cheating wife, would that have been OK?"

And that got me around to the big question, which I had saved until the last in case she ejected me.

Was she expecting a small Robertino?

Ingrid gave a husky Swedish laugh and declared with seeming earnestness that she was not pregnant.

"It's even been printed in America, in *The New York Times*," she said, "that I'm pregnant." (I think she was wrong about that.) "And I told Joe, 'If anybody else prints that, *sue!'* "

And so I got my exclusive interview with Ingrid (and also one with Lucky Luciano), and it was front-paged very big. Hedda Hopper got to Joe Steele, and she got Ingrid, too (but I was first). Everybody was reasonably contented except Dr. Peter Lindstrom. Ingrid settled down in Rome with Roberto and his struggle to prove he was a genius. Joe Steele went back to Hollywood.

Ingrid finished this part of the story in her own book, *My*

Story, but I prefer my own version, which she personally told me later. Roberto took the rumors about the pregnancy very calmly. Joe Steele was, however, most indignant based on what Ingrid had assured him.

Joe Steele was anxious to defend Ingrid's honor and sue.

Ingrid was not one to waste words or money in cables.

One day Joe got a cable from Ingrid:

"If that rumor gets printed again, don't sue anybody."

Ingrid Bergman held her head up and walked around Rome with her pregnancy, and the attack on her morals worsened. Congressmen and columnists and TV star Ed Sullivan cried "Shame," and even I wrote a piece suggesting she didn't know how vicious American public opinion could be.

We didn't know how much she was hurt. They were going to blackball her and boycott her films, and the "Stromboli" picture she and Roberto made was a colossal failure.

When I was next in Rome I discovered her hurt. I phoned. She wouldn't see me or talk to me. I had been against her, she felt. I had not defended her.

Perhaps I hadn't. My wife phoned Ingrid, reached her, and tried to explain my position and feelings, as one woman speaking to another.

Ingrid responded by inviting us to visit her at Fiuggi, a mountain resort, where she showed us Robertino who, she said, boastingly, was four inches longer than other babies his age.

I tried to apologize for the misunderstanding.

Ingrid broke into that wide smile.

"I bawled you out good, didn't I?" she said, marveling at her fury. "So many people raised holy hands to Heaven, I became bitter and hard."

In later years, when America forgave her and showered awards and attentions on her, I followed her around like a little puppy dog. I guess Ingrid Bergman was the most honest great actress that I knew.

40

TERRY MOORE REMEMBERS HOWARD HUGHES

"I had a lot of loving but not a lot of lovers," Terry Moore said.

"And Howard Hughes was the best. He was gentle and kind and"—she paused a second to find the proper word—"unselfish."

"He must have been insatiable, too," I said. "Having all those starlets stashed in apartments all over Los Angeles. Was he a believer in conventional sex, or was he kinky?"

"*Kinky?*" Terry exclaimed. The sexy little blonde who appears to have come into millions from Howard Hughes's huge estate after her unceasing battle to prove she was married to the eccentric billionaire said, "If he'd been kinky, I'd have had nothing to do with him! I don't think Howard slept with so many girls."

"He just got them apartments?" I asked Terry.

"He liked collecting girls," Terry said.

"He had these pimps hanging around all the time," Terry said, naming some of Hughes's notable companions.

"They brought him girls he would consider for starlet contracts. He'd help them get places to live. He'd see some, and some he'd never see, and they'd leave."

One supposes he couldn't see all of them; just as the king couldn't see every girl in the harem.

Terry herself was an enigma. Her story was that she and Hughes were married on his yacht by the ship's captain in 1945 but that Hughes later got mad at her and burned the ship's log that recorded the marriage.

"I caught him with a girl at Lake Tahoe," Terry said.

"He wasn't having sex with her. I don't think he slept with a lot of girls. He liked to collect girls. He lied to me, and I found out about her. I left him."

Hughes had a technique for breaking dates, Terry said.

To get out of a date with a girl in Beverly Hills, he'd phone her pretending he'd been called to New York. Enlisting the help of phone operators, he'd convince the girl he was in New York. It didn't work with Terry. She claims her father and an FBI man helped her, and she caught him.

"He knew he could never get me back," she says.

But Terry was faithful to him—in her fashion.

The busy Terry had married football star Glenn Davis, Eugene McGrath, Stuart Cramer, and Richard Carey as well as Hughes and had a song in a nightclub act that referred to her love life.

"I said I had a lot of fun in the papers describing my nightclub capers but it was mostly in the press."

But Terry could look back on a lot of action in those years. She was a very bare 19 when she married Glenn Davis, and already there were rumors of fistfights over her affections, and the name of Howard Hughes was heard.

"But I didn't have a lot of lovers," Terry said. "I got a lot of lovin' from my husbands. I was like Elizabeth Taylor and Zsa Zsa Gabor. We married the guys." Terry says she still believes in that.

The Terry Moore I knew then was a brunette or brownette—light brown maybe—although other girls thought she was a brunette. Now she's a blonde. She was sizzlingly sexy. When she entertained GIs in Korea in a mink-trimmed bikini, with ermine panties, some Army officers thought she was just too hot for the troops and not good for the morale.

I was on Terry's side in that dispute. So Terry was a celebrity when Conrad Hilton took a junket to Istanbul for the opening of a Hilton Hotel.

The Turkish photographers rushed Terry when we arrived.

They wanted "leg pictures," then known as "cheesecake."

"I was wearing a Mother Hubbard dress," Terry told me a few days ago, recalling that international incident.

"One photographer hid in the bushes.

"He got a shot from a peculiar angle.

"It looked like I had no pants on. Of course I had pants on.

"Then they retouched the pictures and made them look worse. Somebody dabbed some white into the pelvic shot and it looked terribly vulgar."

The furor over whether Terry did or didn't have pants on mounted. I became a goodwill ambassador for Terry to go to the tabloid newspaper in Istanbul and straighten it out. They would publish the picture over and apologize and give Terry the negatives of the offending pictures.

The deal went through except that the paper didn't give back all the negatives. It kept back some of the goodies.

And Terry gets mad to this day about the retouching of the pictures. With the extra artwork, the Turks had now made it almost certain Terry was pantsless.

Terry wept. "It was a Moslem plot against the Mormons," Terry said. Her grandfather was a Mormon bishop, and he would never get over the shame of this. It would also hurt Terry in her Shakespeare studies, she was convinced.

Carol Channing was a guest star at the Hilton opening. Conrad Hilton had succeeded in getting both Louella Parsons and Hedda Hopper to this sensational opening.

It was decided that for the good of Mr. Hilton, the scandal about Terry's pantslessness would not be wired or phoned back to New York or California.

A "gentleman's agreement" to this effect was reached by the lady journalists, Louella and Hedda. Both columnists decided, however, to hell with the agreement and sent the story back home. I sent it back to my papers, too.

Terry, in her 50s now, says her new riches won't make her lazy. She'll work harder. She goes to an exercise class to keep in shape and has her own charity. She can be comfortable for the rest of her life on the interest from her inheritance.

She's not vindictive about any who doubted her claims about her marriage to Hughes. She says he "burned the log of the ship" containing information about the marriage. But witnesses supported her contention, and "now it's all over but getting the money."

Terry'll give 10 percent—"tithe"—to the Mormon church. "Howard was not a real Mormon, but he was a Mormon in his heart," Terry says.

"He liked the Mormons because they don't drink or smoke, and he didn't either."

Terry is not supposed to speculate about how much money she will receive from the Hughes estate over the years to come, but there is one fact about it that she finds of vast importance.

"It's tax free," Terry smiles.

"How can that be?"

"They," said Terry, "the other heirs and blood relatives, took care of the taxes for me, the widow," says Terry, the heroine of the remarkable story of Howard Hughes.

"Wasn't that nice of them?"

41

CELEBRITIES
ARE PEOPLE, TOO

The Earl Wilsons and Joey Adams and his wife Cindy Adams had been traveling in Europe. Now they were separating. The Wilsons, returning to New York, would take back a suitcase for the Adamses.

Early in the morning Wilson knocked softly on the door of the Adamses' room in a Copenhagen hotel. The door opened just a crack; the blinds were still drawn; the room was still dark. A woman's hand pushed out the suitcase. Wilson saw the woman less than half a minute, but he wrote a quick note to Joey Adams.

"Joey: 'Quick, get rid of that old crone you sneaked into your room last night. What a spook. I won't say anything, but those big-mouth hotel maids are telling people the old witch was your wife Cindy.' "

Cindy, who opened the letter first since it was addressed to Joey and marked "Personal and Confidential," took it good-naturedly. "What did he expect me to look like before I've put on makeup?" said she.

The Wilsons have always loved Jolie (Mama) Gabor, who seems to have been born 80 years old. Asked once, "Which of the Gabors is the oldest?", Zsa Zsa replied, "She vould never admit it, but it's Mama."

Jolie Gabor was fond of my wife, Rosemary, and repeatedly invited her to lunches and dinners. My wife wasn't a member of the Lunch Bunch and refused. But she told her that her own schedule was subject to change because "of my husband's deadlines." Jolie couldn't understand. "My husband has his deadlines, and I have to worry about them." Jolie, the Hungarian Dorothy Parker, replied, "Vy you vorry about your husband's dead relatives? You come out vith me and have fun!"

The stars I know are not preponderantly religious, although several comedians are known for their friendship with Israel. Alan King helped launch a hospital in his name in Tel Aviv.

Facing an overflow Jewish holiday crowd at the Concord Hotel at Kiamesha Lake, New York, in the Catskills, Alan King complained about the proselytizing efforts of the Moral Majority.

"Jerry Falwell is a charming man," King said. "He gave me a pamphlet with 92 points. If you do not believe these 92 points, you are not a good Christian.

"I don't need Jerry Falwell to tell me I'm not a good Christian. I knew that eight days after I was born."

When Richard Burton played Hamlet in New York the audience booed him one night, and he returned to the Regency Hotel in a bad mood. Elizabeth Taylor, suffering a cold, hadn't gone to the theater.

Burton sat down on a sofa beside Elizabeth, who was watching a Peter Sellers movie on TV.

"They booed me tonight," he confessed. "For the first time in my life I was booed."

Elizabeth tried to comfort him. "I'm sure that they were teasing you and didn't mean it," she said. "Let me watch Peter's last scene and then we'll talk about it."

And then, according to former Editor Lenore Hershey in her book, *Between the Covers,* Burton howled in anger and shouted

"I get booed and you have to watch this _____ movie!" And he put his foot through the TV screen, shattering the glass.

His foot started to bleed, a doctor was called, and Elizabeth was worried because Burton was in poor health. Burton canceled a performance and the audience accepted the management explanation that he had caught Elizabeth's cold.

Henry Fonda was usually gentle and polite. But once when I went to his New York town house to interview him, I took along a woman secretary and a tape recorder. Fonda got onto the subject of one of his daughter Jane Fonda's political mentors and some things Jane had said. "It's a crock of shit and you can quote me," Fonda said angrily. He liked his performance and repeated, "It's a crock of shit and you can quote me!"

"Where?" I said.

42

IN THE
DAYS OF
KING WALTER

When Walter Winchell was king of the Broadway gossip columnists, his jottings were accepted as the absolute truth by the press agents, although sometimes they were't true. Louella Parsons and Hedda Hopper had great power in Hollywood, where the stars seemed to ask their permission to get married or have children. Once in the 1940s Winchell dared print that then young Bette Davis had cancer. It was shocking—and it was denied by Miss Davis and her studio and all connected with her.

One of the most perceptive of the publicists, Sidney Garfield, walking into the press agents' hangout, Lindy's, saw his contemporaries huddled.

He knew what they were discussing. "That Bette Davis had better have cancer," he said, "or she's going to be in a lot of trouble with Walter Winchell."

Winchell joined the White House press on a trip with President Eisenhower and enjoyed it because he talked unceasingly about himself, with the working press powerless to stop him. Fellow columnist Bob Considine said he couldn't even get in a one-sentence reply and that Winchell barked at him, "Don't interrupt me by nodding."

Winchell shamelessly hustled around clubs, hotels, and restaurants, seeking compliments. They weren't always easy to get.

He approached one anti-Winchell editor and asked, "How did you like today's column?"

"Damn near didn't print it," the editor said. "Same guff you had on the air last night. We're trying to sell people the stuff you're giving them free. We shouldn't reprint stuff from radio."

Winchell retorted, "You reprinted Franklin D. Roosevelt's Fireside Chat, didn't you?"

In this same era, O. O. McIntyre's popular and successful New York column included "Thoughts while Strolling."

Fred Allen claimed that as McIntyre got older he gave up strolling and reported by looking through a magnified window.

Paul Lynde, the comedian who got famous on "Hollywood Squares," spoke with that Ohio twang that Ohioans found delightful and non-Ohioans didn't.

Paul claimed he dressed 250,000 chickens for his father's meat market in Mount Vernon, Ohio, and earned himself the nickname "the Chicken Picker." A girlfriend told this to her friends when he entered Ohio Wesleyan, and everybody in the block greeted him, "Here comes the Chicken Picker." Paul developed a definite hostility toward chickens.

His enunciation complicated his life, so he said. He could not pronounce the word *doll* in the preferred way. He would give it a soft *uh* sound. Thus *doll* would be pronounced "dull," and Paul was heard telling a girl, "You are a real dull." This was one of the reasons that Paul never married.

43

REAGAN:
The Joker
Goes Wild

In the late hours after the November 1980 national election, the new President-elect, Ronald Reagan, and his wife Nancy got into bed in their Pacific Palisades, California, home. Her teeth chattering, Nancy Reagan exclaimed, "Oh, God! Your feet are sure cold tonight!"

The President-to-be murmured modestly, "Oh, that's all right. You can still call me Ronnie."

It probably never happened, although it was widely printed that it did. It was a slightly used joke anyway, having been printed before about General De Gaulle, who implored his wife, "Shust call me Sharlshhh." De Gaulle didn't insist on being called God either. And we don't know how many were targets for that one long before.

As a former radio sportscaster with tonsils that had a long memory, Reagan was a tireless gag-borrower or switch artist. Had he been a comedian, he might have been called a gag thief, but as President he was admired and praised for injecting comedy into our national follies. After he was shot in an assassination attempt he told Mrs. Reagan, "Honey, I forgot to duck."

Sportswriters and boxing fans instantly remembered that those famous words were spoken by Jack Dempsey to his wife at the time, Estelle Taylor, after he had been licked by Gene Tunney in the classic heavyweight championship battle in Chicago.

Ronnie had appropriated Dempsey's remarks, which he remembered from his days as a sportscaster, and good luck to him. A President can always use a few laughs. In fact, the smart President laughs at himself so that others don't get the opportunity to do it first.

John F. Kennedy was one who laughed at himself first—as when he defended the appointment of his baby brother Bobby as attorney general, saying he needed a little experience before going into private practice.

Richard Nixon was on the other side when he said, in effect, "Your President is not a crook."

Gutsy David Frye, the impressionist, who had been satirizing Nixon before it became popular, conveyed a dour, saturnine picture of "Tricky Dicky" to the populace.

Frye had Nixon boasting, "My administration has taken crime out of the streets and put it in the White House where we can watch it."

Reagan came on the scene when the Billy Carter beer can humor and Jimmy Carter's *Playboy* interview about "lusting," had been used up. Comedian Marty Allen said, "You can be on the cover of *Time* one year and be doing time the next."

The former movie-actor-become-President waded right in, substituting himself for the victim. It was a nice change: a President knocking himself. He enchanted doctors and nurses, taking his injuries lightly, and hoarded risqué hospital stories that doctors passed along. When his press secretary, James Brady, was reported to be improved from his injuries, the

President proposed that he, Brady, and two other casualties "get four bedpans and have a reunion."

He never ran away from a suggestive story, but his timing and delivery were brilliant, as when he said, "There you go again" in a celebrated debate rejoinder.

As "other comedians" have favorite subjects, Reagan dwelt overmuch on his age, some people felt. ("Well, if I do, they don't!")

After telling the Washington Press Club that he knew it was founded in 1919—"It seems like only yesterday"—he gave his definition of middle age: "When you're faced with two temptations, and you choose the one that will get you home by nine o'clock."

The press corps enthusiastically announced it had discovered Reagan had a sense of humor, "the one-liner" variety. The Carters had been unbelievable.

"Suppose I went to a film studio," said a screenwriter, "and said I had a story about a peanut farmer who wanted to be President. He had a sister who was a born-again preacher, a mother who was in the Peace Corps, and a brother who urinated in the street and had a gas station. They would throw me out of the office."

He laughed. "They threw Jimmy Carter into office."

When Carter ran for reelection the comedians pictured the family as desperate. Jimmy—pronounced "Jemmeh" by some of the loyal—had tried to get rough by saying he would whup Ted Kennedy's ass if he ran for the nomination.

In the family deliberations Miz Lillian was listening to the real brains of the family, Billy, the six-pack man, map the strategy. They should desert Jemmeh and back Billy for President.

"I would get all the Arab votes and all the drinkers," promised Billy. Miz Lillian nodded to that argument but still was thinking of Jimmy.

"Do you think Jemmeh would be smart enough to run the gas station?" she asked.

His movie star polish and sophistication placed Reagan far above this level of gibe.

After the attempt on his life, he was able to demonstrate his apparent confidence in his recovery. "Wasn't it pretty serious?" asked one of the kin, to whom he replied, "It ruined one of my best suits."

"You'll be happy to know the government is running normally," he was told one morning by a cheerful aide, whom he then asked, "What makes you think I'd be happy about that?"

Sometimes he seemed to be the Milton Berle of the Presidents as he joked his way through his recovery, always remembering that as an actor he must never relax that warm smile.

With tubes and tapes sealing him closed in every exit, he could scribble notes to nurses telling them that if Hollywood had paid him this much attention he never would have left. He had jokes about the gynecologist and the teabag, about what Winston Churchill had to say about the joy of being shot at and not being hit. He retained hundreds of jokes, from long practice in Hollywood waiting to do scenes.

In the beginning they'd ribbed Reagan because of his age. Henny Youngman said, "He campaigned in an old-age home, and they wouldn't let him out."

Of course, Reagan was a Republican.

"My dad was a Democrat, but he stole so much money he got rich and could be a Republican," black comedian Nipsey Russell said. Nipsey was doubtful about how much help Reagan would get from the blacks.

"I entertained the National Committee of Black Republicans—three of the nicest guys you'd want to meet," Nipsey said.

Nancy Reagan was on the way to becoming the humor target of the family when husband Ronnie got his audience via his hospitalization. Nancy and her gifts, which were challenged by political or society rivals, stirred up Washington. It seems a long time ago now that politicians repeated the alleged quip:

"Nancy, what do you think of Red China?"

"It looks nice with a white tablecloth," says Nancy.

Nancy was always shopping for expensive garments and gifts. She had a horrible nightmare. She dreamed she was kidnapped, dropped off around the 14th Street cheaper stores, and forced to buy off the rack.

"She was the girl next Dior," commented witticist Robert Orben.

The National Press Club bar was the fount of political cynicism a generation ago. A kindly, gentlemanly friend, Radford Mobley of the Knight Newspapers, president of the club, taught me to listen to the great drinkers who were the top Washington correspondents and political columnists. From them I learned that politicians were 95 percent corruptible. I would have placed it at only 75 percent.

President Warren G. Harding's last trip was the source of gossip. George R. Holmes of International Service recounted how David Lawrence, founder of the United States News, had filed a story from Denver that Harding had for the first time in his life gone on the wagon.

"It was a good story," laughed Holmes, "especially since it wasn't true.

"But what were you going to do? When your editors queried you on it, could you write a denial story, that you had seen the President of the United States roaring drunk the night before?"

But that was shop talk.

There were stories like the one about the "New Priest."

He was nervous about his first mass. He asked the Old Priest for some advice.

"Put a little gin in a glass of water. It'll relax you."

The New Priest overdid it. After the mass he asked the Old Priest how he had done.

"You relaxed all right," said the Old Priest, "but there are things that should be straighted out.

"There are Ten Commandments, not Twelve.

"There are Twelve Apostles, not Ten.

"David slew Goliath; he didn't beat the shit out of him.

"We do not refer to Jesus Christ as 'the late J.C.'

"Next Sunday there is a taffy-pulling contest at St. Peter's, not a peter-pulling contest at St. Taffy's.

"We do not refer to the Father, the Son, and the Holy Ghost as Big Daddy, Junior, and the Spook."

Otherwise, it was a fine sermon.

44
JACK PARR
AND THE
WATER CLOSET

"What's a WC, Grandpa?

"A WC is a water closet, my lad."

"What's a water closet?"

Jack Paar made water closets famous—and infamous. He was the great bleeder and crier of American TV, a predecessor of nighttime Johnny Carson. Jack Paar staged a fascinating TV walkout against NBC in February 1960, because the network censored a joke he told about a WC (a toilet).

He really did cry on TV when he felt like it. He almost cried the time I called him a few years before and alerted him that NBC wanted him as a successor to Steve Allen and others who'd been doing "The Tonight Show."

"I need that job," Paar said that day when I got him at home. "I've been so down and so discouraged.

"I've been about to get out of the business."

"Don't call them," I advised. "Make them call you."

"Oh, they'll have to call me," he promised. But Dick Linkroum, the NBC producer, faced several crises that afternoon, and Paar got overanxious.

"Several times I went to the phone to dial NBC and got my finger to the dial, but I pulled back and didn't dial because of Earl's warning," Paar said later.

Jack Paar got the job and, with his crying and gifted interviewing and talent for controversy, he became as big as or bigger than Steve Allen, who had brought the desk and the couch into TV talk shows.

His public weeping was part of his magnetism. He also got friends and enemies confused, and in one instance included me, who'd suggested him for the job, in the pack of journalistic sons of bitches he was attacking.

But now for Paar's master stroke. He was a household word, a habit, a nighttime visitor that millions of women preferred to their husbands.

Finding a polite euphemism for toilet had occupied many American scholars and lexicographers. They were johns, outhouses, backhouses, three-seaters or two-seaters, and privies, from the French *privé*, which means "private." Most of the Americanisms beyond this group were downright vulgar.

In England you could "spend a penny," or "go to the loo," or "visit the ladies' or the men's." They also employed the term *water closet*, sometimes resorting to just the initials, WC.

But as Paar told the story before, during, and after he was on TV, many British people did not know of the abbreviation WC.

One of those who did know was an English lady, renting a room for a time in Switzerland, who very much liked the room shown her by a Swiss schoolmaster but couldn't remember having seen a water closet, a WC.

Straightaway to her desk she went and penned a note to the Swiss schoolmaster. Everything was lovely, but was there a WC?

The learned schoolmaster was puzzled. What was a WC? Some English idiom, perhaps. He went to a local priest for help. The priest had never heard of a WC, either, but swayed somewhat by his environment and occupation, he and the schoolmaster divined that the lady was looking for a place to pray. Yes, of course, there was one not too far off—a Wayside Chapel.

The schoolmaster promptly wrote to the lady about the availability of the WC (Wayside Chapel). The lady must have been so impressed with the arrangements suggested for her attending the WC that she passed them around. At least they were passed around among language classes in the United States and got the attention of a niece of Jack Paar.

Jack Paar did the only proper thing.

He read it on his program.

But the program was taped, and it did not get on the air in its entirety.

That is, because . . . well, here is the alleged letter:

Dear Madam:

I take great pleasure in informing you that the WC is situated nine miles from the house you occupy, in a grove of pine trees surrounding the lovely grounds. It is capable of holding 229 people, and it is open on Sunday and Thursday only. As there are a great number of people and they are expected during the summer months, I suggest that you come early, although there is plenty of standing room as a rule.

You will no doubt be glad to hear that a good number of people bring their lunch and make a day of it. I would especially recommend that your ladyship go on Thursday, when there is musical accompaniment.

It may interest you to know that my daughter was married in the WC, and it was there that she met her husband. I can remember the rush there was for seats. There were 10 people to a seat usually occupied by one. It was wonderful to see the expression on their faces.

The newest attraction is a bell donated by a wealthy resident. It rings every time a person enters. A bazaar is to be held to provide plush seats for all the people.

I shall be delighted to reserve the best seat for you where you will be seen by all. For the children there is a special time and place so they will not disturb their elders. Hoping to have been of some service to you, I am,

Sincerely,
The Schoolmaster

That's about how the classic letter was constructed by Paar in his own recollections and by Robert Metz in his book *The Tonight Show*. Jack bolted the show at midnight as soon as he was sure he was being censored. He and his wife hid out in a motel retreat he'd arranged for in Florida. NBC's embarrassment was acute. The headlines, the mystery, Jack's guts to "fire the network" and make the bosses come pleading to him, made it as exciting as a kidnapping. Jack the Crier, "Leaky Jack," cried all the way to his lawyer's office where he consented to accept a huge pay hike.

Jack Paar was king for a while, such a king as NBC had never confronted before, but one who was learning by watching and figuring out some improvements was Johnny Carson.

Jack used some of his time to make real estate deals, building a fortune and eventually investing in radio properties.

There were suggestions that the incident about the English lady and the schoolmaster was fiction and that the letter was also imaginary. Paar, of course, appeared to be sincere at all times. And he surely seemed to be honest when he declined to go on a Steve Allen Sunday night show opposing Ed Sullivan on CBS because, he said, he had been "living off Sullivan," doing eight $5,000 shows when he was unemployed.

"Sincere?" Peter Lind Hayes heckled Jack. "Sinceres and Roebuck!"

Nobody cried like Jack Paar. He could weep just remembering that he worked for Arthur Godfrey for a year and never saw him. "He had an unlisted floor," Jack said.

Some of his followers were pretty funny. One woman named Lillian often got mentioned by Jack when she came to the show. When he didn't mention her, Lillian was convinced he felt her wavering in her loyalty and switching allegiance to Steve Allen.

"I am *au gratin* with him," she said.

45

HOT TIMES,
OR,
THAT'S A NO-NO

Down we go through X-Rated Lane.

Warning: I am going to have to talk dirty. But not very.

I was brought up so properly in the Middle West by my conscientious parents that even today, at my advanced age, I feel I must apologize when repeating anything scatological, excremental, or lubricious.

Yet, paddling through life's gutters, we must stop up our nostrils in certain pockets of bad taste. We wouldn't have wanted to miss *Who's Afraid of Virginia Woolf?* or to have been buried in the classics when Elizabeth Taylor and co-stars talked of playing "Hump the Hostess."

Sexual subjects are often funny, asexual subjects even funnier. Allow me to say a couple of things I shouldn't.

In an early Broadway show I saw in the 1930s, George Jessel, pouring a drink for Sophie Tucker, said, "Say when."

"Right after this drink," said Sophie. I thought that was very suggestive.

Only a few years later Broadway's best minds thought it preposterous that any man would go on stage frontally nude. But five years after, bare-buttocked men and women were displaying themselves fully. We witnessed copulation itself, heard Lolitas discuss it, saw an Edith Piaf-type actress tinkle on stage.

"Skin" magazines published nice nude ladies' phone numbers beside their pictures. One could dial a love affair over the phone and charge it on the phone credit card. Well-known women were telling risque stories.

Sample: A married couple is at a bar. An intoxicated patron rather noisily passes wind. The enraged husband howls, "How dare you do that before my wife?" The drunk ever so meekly says, "S-s-s-so sorry. I didn't know it was her turn."

The much-bylined Martin Burden, entertainment expert of the *New York Post,* has notebooks bulging with off-color tales he can't get into the papers, though he has heard them being enjoyed by thousands in the clubs and at shows.

On the premise that you as a reader are entitled to know just what these vulgar people are saying, I pass along other samples.

Many came from the Friars Club "roasts." The Friars are constantly "honoring" a Show Business star with a stag luncheon where outstanding comedians make prepared speeches paying tribute to the honoree by picturing him as a hopeless degenerate and pervert. His shame at being an inadequate lover is emphasized, and it is not forgotten that he makes oral love to all sexes, human and animal.

The honoree, in his rebuttal, tries to out-dirty-mouth his peers. The word *penis* is rarely used. But all its synonyms are.

Former baseball manager Leo Durocher, who once supposedly said, "Nice guys finish last," found that Friars aren't to be trusted.

"It isn't true, is it?" a Friars official, Jesse Block, asked him. "You'd rather be a nice guy than a good manager, wouldn't you?"

"Right," Durocher replied.

"You're full of shit," snapped Block.

When Howard Cosell was a victim, a speaker roasting him

alleged that on his wedding night his sweet said, "Are you going to make love to me?"

"I can't," he said. "It's Lent."

"You schmuck, why didn't you borrow somebody else's?"

Don Rickles was saluted by Milton Berle: "What can you say about Don Rickles that hasn't already been said about hemorrhoids?"

Humphrey Bogart was lulled into a false sense of euphoria at a Friars tribute by that gifted actor Red Buttons. Seeming to change the mood of the occasion to a serious one, Buttons told Bogart that one of his movie performances had aroused him to patriotic fervor.

It was a war picture, and Red Buttons was stirred to his very soul by Bogart's bravery as he hit the beaches and captured the enemy island almost single-handedly. Bogart nodded as Red built up his courage to the apogee of suspense.

"What a movie!" Red said, almost on the edge of tears. Did Bogart share his sentiments now in retrospect? Bogart kept nodding; he himself was moved!

"You're a goddamned liar!" Red Buttons's voice crackled at him, with the suddenness of a gunshot. *"That wasn't you in that movie. It was John Wayne."*

Veteran Friars couldn't remember any performer receiving a bigger response than Buttons got that day, and Red was almost always the best-prepared speaker on the dais.

Maurice Chevalier was the first honoree at a roast in 1949. His large lovers' lips and his rumored greatness in continental-fashion lovemaking made the romantic French balladeer a perfect target for the Broadway comedians. The required foundation of every speech since that time has been sexiness—almost everybody attempting to be dirtier than Lenny Bruce.

Quite the most bizarre production was put on during 1983, when a well-known comedian was the honoree and found himself sitting on the dais two or three places removed from his son-in-law, also a comedian.

As the attacks on the honoree got heavy, the son-in-law turned on his father-in-law. "I never did like him, so I got even with him by f————-- his daughter," the son-in-law said. "I married her, and so I am still f————-- his daughter."

Instead of being angry at this frankness, the honoree said loudly, "I didn't mind. I had her when she was 14."

A world-famous comedian who was master of ceremonies that day called out, "I screwed her when she was four and still a virgin."

If anybody but me felt this was overdoing dirtiness, no one showed it. The applause for the son-in-law especially was uproarious; he had won his seat on the distinguished dais by telling of f————-- the honoree's daughter. I thought of the feelings of the girl when she would eventually be told that she was the *piece de résistance* at the Friars roast thanks to her father and husband, and don't forget the famous toastmaster.

Still, it is my belief that women enjoy telling these stories and keeping them alive more than men, who have lustier things to discuss. There is one that I have heard going around for a decade.

A nervous, self-conscious man went into a drugstore and, when approached by a woman clerk, asked if he might see "the pharmacist."

"My sister and I own this store," she replied. "We can take care of your needs."

"W-w-w-w-well," he stammered, "I wondered what you could give me for a permanent erection?"

"Just a moment," the lady clerk said. "I want to talk to my sister."

In minutes she returned, and, in a voice trembling with excitement, she said, "My sister and I talked it over. We will give you the store and $500."

And that is almost as old as Milton Berle's definition of a gentleman as "a man who gets out of a bathtub to urinate."

A woman storyteller also informed me of a man at a urinal expressing amazement to the man at the next urinal about the small dot at the end of his penis.

"Oh, that's a tattoo," the man said. "A tattoo with my girlfriend's name on it."

"Her name," said the inquisitive one. "But it's small, like a dot. What's her name? Dottie? Or Dot?"

"You'd be surprised," said the proud owner. "When that's

stretched out to its full length, that spells out Marguerite Cunningham.''

And that's it. They may not be funny, but they're physical.

The quest for laughs goes on forever, like the search for the Fountain of Youth. Remembrances of their success with past jokes drive comedians on and on. Now, in the '80s, it's notable that Tallulah Bankhead's wit has been resuscitated in a musical, *Tallulah*, by Tony Lang, off B'way, a hit starring Helen Gallagher.

Tallulah responds to the charge that she often drinks before the show. "I never take a drink until the show is well under way."

She bolted the movies because of something L. B. Mayer said. He heard of some incidents involving Tallulah and the stage-hands, the grips, men and women. He heard she was "hibernating" with them.

"I've heard it called everything but that," Tallulah said.

The Tony Lang recreation of Tallulah is probably going to be most memorable. This erotic lady wants to try everything once and be tried by everybody once.

"I was raped in our driveway when I was 11," she says. "It was terribly painful. We had all this gravel."

She had a Lesbian period and a song to go with it: "If Only He Were a Woman":

"That's when she knows
What curls her toes
Is a Miss, Not a Mister."

Tallulah encounters a famous husband and wife acting team in an elevator. They don't speak to her. She blasts both of them, "I know why you don't speak to me. I've had both of you."

"Tonight" star Johnny Carson, whose monologues have kept night-watchers amused for years, discovered a very lush fount of humor in his divorce battle with his wife Joanna. Most of his jokes for the monologue (a monologue is supposed to be a long speech delivered by one person) are prepared by a staff of six writers.

Carson's wife wanted $220,000 a month interim alimony and something like $17 million eventually. Carson shied from mentioning the case until Speaker Tip O'Neill said that, if Ronald Reagan retired as President, Nancy Reagan would become "the queen of Beverly Hills."

Speaking to his TV audience, Johnny said forcefully, "Nancy would *not* be the queen of Beverly Hills, and I have the royal tab to prove it."

His audience got his point immediately, that he thought Joanna Carson was going to be queen of Beverly Hills. The roar of laughter surprised Johnny, who, after a moment, said that joke might prove to be "costly." Was he fearing still another legal action from Joanna?

And that's how Johnny Carson found out that there are laughs in family fights. God help and save us all!

Forgive me for talking dirty. *X-rated* may become the handiest expression in our language, next to *bleep*. Pity our poor mothers, who were going to wash our mouths out with soap. In these years they could have used all their soap on soap operas alone.

46
ONE I
CAN'T FORGET

There was an Easter brunch fashion show at the Hotel Plaza but I wasn't staying. Few celebrities were present, and they weren't making news, so I told my wife Rosemary that I had better get to work. I had to check up around town at the other gathering places. But the B.W. wanted to stay for the rest of the fashion show.

"There's a phone booth in the hall," I said. "I'll tend to some business."

I went to the phone booth. Skitch Henderson, the master of ceremonies, decided he should introduce some of the guests. He chose Van Johnson to be the first. Then Skitch Henderson called on "Earl Wilson." Mrs. Earl Wilson shuddered.

Van Johnson, next to her, pushed her to her feet and told her to explain about me. Flustered, she arose.

I poked my head back in the room in time to hear her respond.

"Earl's not here," she told the full house. "He's out in the phone booth doing his business."

CURTAIN

One golden nugget of information about Show Business that I picked up along the way may be useful to others.

Show Business is, besides determination and industry, a lot of accidents, luck, and even mistaken identity.

Ingrid Bergman, waiting in New York for Hollywood to make her famous, read for a minor role in a play, *Liliom*. She was ecstatic when producers said she got the job, but quite alarmed when she discovered she was cast not in a minor part, but in the lead, Julie, opposite Burgess Meredith. Producer Vinton Freedley had made a mistake. He thought she was another Scandinavian beauty he had in mind, Signe Hasso. "It's too late to change now" he said. Ingrid was already doing the part beautifully.

It's a true version of an old Show Business tale about one of Hollywood's young ladies, who said:

"It's too late to learn to act now—I'm already a star."

THE END

INDEX